ASTROSHAMANISM

book 2

The Voyage
through
the Zodiac

Franco Santoro

FINDHORN
Press

© Franco Santoro 2003

First published in 2003

ISBN 1-84409-013-2

British Library Cataloguing-in-Publication Data.
A catalogue record for this book is available from the British Library.

Edited by Lynn Barton
Layout by Pam Bochel
Cover design by Thierry Bogliolo
Cover photograph © PhotoDisc
Illustrations © Franco Santoro

Printed and bound by WS Bookwell, Finland

Published by

Findhorn Press

305a The Park, Findhorn
Forres IV36 3TE
Scotland
Tel 01309 690582
Fax 01309 690036
e-mail: info@findhornpress.com
www.findhornpress.com

Contents

ACKNOWLEDGEMENTS

I wish to gratefully acknowledge the permission to use quotations and references from the following works:

Franco Santoro, *Iniziazione all'astrosciamanesimo: la via zodiacale alla Guida Interiore,* Edizioni Mediterranee, Roma, 2000.

Mattie Davis-Wolfe and David Thomson, *Walking the Sacred Wheel: A Year's Journey of Initiation around the Sacred Wheel,* Sacred Circles Institute, Mukilteo, WA, 1995.

Portions of *A Course in Miracles*® copyright 1975, 1992, 1996 reprinted by permission of the *Foundation for A Course in Miracles, Inc.*® (www.facim.org). All rights reserved.

Osho, *Meditation: The First and Last Freedom,* St. Martin's Press, New York, NY, 1996. Used by permission of the *Osho International Foundation* (http://www.osho.com).

Edwin C. Steinbrecher, *The Inner Guide Meditation: A Spiritual Technology for the 21st Century,* Samuel Weiser, York Beach, ME, 1988. Reprinted by permission of Samuel Weiser Inc.

ProvOrdo Etnai Pratinindhe Pradhikara's Southern Europe Archives for the Year 1984, Anaghaseva, 1985; *ProvOrdo Etnai Sagdhanatabe,* Anaghaseva, 1988. Used by dispensation of Anaghaseva.

Careful work was made to receive permission to reprint brief citations from previously published sources. In a few cases, permission was not granted in time for formal acknowledgment. Any omission will be corrected in future editions upon notification. However, all published quotations have been officially listed in the related notes and bibliography.

I would like to offer my deepest appreciation to all those who, in different ways and times, have supported and helped me in my work. In particular I am grateful to my parents Marisa Testoni and Nunzio Santoro, my sister Annamaria Santoro, Grazia Romano, all my relatives and ancestors, Cluny Hill College and its territory, the members, guests and all beings, seen and unseen, of the Findhorn Foundation and the New Findhorn Association in the north-east of Scotland, all the researchers attending astroshamanic events, workshops and individual sessions in Great Britain, Italy, Germany, Greece and other parts of the world. Abundant gratitude to my Guides and mentors, Ur Ichì, Ur Kraab, Ur Kuran, Ji N'kho, Ratusel, the Bhi Jinah, the Sacred Cone Circle, the Delegate Authority of the Provisional Order (ProvOrdo Etnai), A.F.S. Bogus, Osho, Kabir Jaffe, the Sacro Cerchio in Bologna. I wish to give special mention and appreciation to Judy Wyld who attentively went over the first draft. Loving thanks to Thierry and Karin Bogliolo at Findhorn Press for their decisive support, Lynn Barton for her precious editorial assistance and Pam Bochel for the final layout. Grateful and heartfelt acknowledgment also to Tina Agiorgiti, Leo Anfolsi, Lucia Bruno, Eileen Caddy, Gianni Canonico at Edizioni Mediterranee, Mattie Davis-Wolfe, Rita Inì, Katharina Kroeber, Fiona Mackenzie, Pumapahe, Penelope Perrin, Paola Pierpaoli, David Thomson, Sauro Tronconi, the Podere Valpisa, the authors mentioned in the bibliography and many other soul friends and companions, who I have not mentioned for lack of space or memory.

To all my relationships in all times and spaces I express my deepest consideration. Kahesha Opa!

The ideas expressed in this book, unless otherwise ascribed, are my own and do not necessarily agree with those of the persons, beings or institutions mentioned in these acknowledgements.

PREFACE

This is the second volume of a work aimed at providing a brief introduction to the principles and practices of astroshamanism. The term *astroshamanism* provisionally identifies a spiritual system of healing aimed at expanding human perception through the integration of the basic principles of shamanism with experiential astrology and the contemporary revival of archaic mystery traditions. Its present form is the result of researches developed since 1976, thanks to the contribution of shamans and teachers of various cultures and dimensions. The earliest original reference to astroshamanism is based upon a strategic initiatory lineage currently defined here as the *Sacred Cone Circle,* or *ProvOrdo Etnai.* The basic intent of this tradition is to foster the release of our illusory identity based on separation and to support the process of the reawakening of our authentic multidimensional nature. The principal trait of this and other similar traditions is that its teachings cannot be communicated by one human being to another. Although mentors or shamans can provide precious inspiration and tools to access basic information, the actual mysteries are revealed to the initiates only by direct experience and connection with shamanic realities.

Astroshamanism employs different tools that facilitate the exploration of non-ordinary dimensions and help create a bridge with conventional reality to provide healing, transformation, true perception and clarity of intent. In this context astrology is used as a *Sacred Circle* to access information on the geography of shamanic states of consciousness and to allow their safe exploration, knowing where to find Spirit Guides, Totem Spirits, allies, wisdom, power, grievances or blocks. Here the horoscope is not interpreted or analysed, but reveals itself through emotions, movements, dances, sounds, rituals, images and situations aimed at extending awareness and supporting strong transformational processes.

In astroshamanism the astrological wheel is employed in accordance with its original nature as a Sacred Circle. The chief trait of the Sacred Circle is that through its use it is possible to establish a direct connection with Spirit, the Divine, the Self, God, the Centre (or whatever name you use for That), instead of through an intermediary relationship with a human spiritual authority. Astroshamanism is based on the system of the Twelve Sectors. The advantage of this model is that besides being very old and widespread, it represents the easiest symbolic structure for the majority of human beings. Almost everybody has some familiarity with the twelve zodiacal signs, considers a year of twelve months or regularly looks at a watch with a circle of twelve numbers. In astroshamanism the Twelve Sectors represent the various ways and energies which lead to the Centre. In such a Centre, awareness is whole: there is no separation and there is only the experience of unity. The Twelve Sectors are emanations of the Centre. Their aim is to make the Centre understandable for minds conditioned by the illusion of separation. Here the Sacred Circle is the container of all possible situations and experiences. The most comprehensive spectrum of existence is described in this system. This means that, no matter where I am, my exact location can be spotted in the Sacred Circle and from there I can find my way to the Centre.

A major part of the work with astroshamanism has to do with the undoing of the illusion of separation through honestly acknowledging and releasing grievances and pent-up emotions or thoughts. In this context the image of a cone is often used. The *cone* describes a spiral circular movement that, starting from an emanation point, creatively develops ad infinitum. This represents the progressive demanifestation process of the universe, the ascensional movement of matter toward the reality of spirit, the abandonment of the separation created by the ego and the journey back to unity. This process does not occur by escaping or transcending the physical dimension, but through using it as a teaching device to fulfil our true Intent in this plane. Rather than ignoring grievances and hidden emotions, trying to dispel them by focusing only on the 'positive' or using the will to push them into the unconscious, I can instead learn to open up to their true nature. Then I can feel and accept them for what they are. Astroshamanism is about taking full responsibility for my presence in the material plane, giving up denials and patiently undoing separation. True forgiveness and release occur when I have fully seen and understood what I am letting go of. Those who honestly accept the exploration of their shadows, withdrawing their projections on others and integrating them into the wholeness to which they belong, are doing a major service on this planet.

Note on gender: To avoid the clumsiness and overemphasis of opposite polarities in the usage of double personal problems like *he/she, her/him*, etc., unless I specifically refer to a female creature or goddess, I use the generic terms *he, him, his* to indicate human or non-ordinary beings in general, both male and female. This is a makeshift option due to the fact that in the English language there is no appropriate singular personal pronoun that applies equally to men and women. Therefore I would like to make it clear that in the context of this book the forms *he, him, his* are meant to be inclusive and could as well have been replaced by *she, her*.

Caution: The practices provided in this book have been safely used in the course of many workshops and sessions. Yet, any application of the practices, ideas and suggestions in this book is at the reader's sole discretion and risk. Before doing the exercises in this book, consult your physician or therapist if you have relevant medical or psychological problems. The instructions presented are in no way intended as a substitute for proper medical or psychological treatment. The author and publisher disclaim any liability or loss in direct or indirect connection with the practices and topics described in this work.

The Circle of the Totem Spirits

INTRODUCTION

This second volume contains technical as well as experiential information about the Twelve Sectors of the Sacred Circle and details about each of the Four Directions. In the system employed in astroshamanism, every sector corresponds to an astrological sign and each direction aligns with a certain season of the year,[1] element, part of the body, colour, etc. There are many other systems of Sacred Circle and they all have their specific traits. According to the tradition involved the correspondences assigned to the directions can vary slightly or radically. In the context of astroshamanism no model is considered right or wrong. Each one has its reasons for experiencing the directions in the way it does. The model you are being introduced to in this book was born from spending a long time in attunement and discernment. Although I have reasons to support it, please consider this model as simply strategic. As you develop your own experiences, you may discover a total resonance with the correspondences of this system, or be drawn to other associations and come to a different understanding. Whatever happens, remember that a major aim of this book is to awaken and support your true inner guidance and not to require you to conform to a specific doctrine or model.

For each sector you will find a list of correspondences derived from various traditions and sources. Such indications do not constitute a complete survey and are only meant to provide some examples. The need to find correspondences between what is perceived by ordinary human beings and what is unseen and belongs to non-ordinary dimensions is very ancient. Its basic motivation comes from the awareness of the underlying unity of all existence. This unity is an obvious fact that can be observed at all levels of life. Yet human beings seem to reside in a split reality based on the identification with an autonomous entity (ego) that supports the belief in separation. In the course of its evolution, the ego has shaped a complex collective hallucination. Its form is spread into a myriad of fragmented pieces, each one purporting to stand on its own and refusing to acknowledge the whole to which it belongs. As the ego's reality is based on separation, a tactical way to explain to human beings the nature of unity is that of starting from separation itself. This is the essential strategy of the work with correspondences. During human history this work has been adapted by various cultures and undergone several modifications, though its inner motivation has always been the same: to connect the illusive reality of separation (that causes me to perceive something as separate from myself) with the true dimension of unity (where I experientially acknowledge everything as part of me). In astroshamanism the sectors and their Totem Spirits encompass the key archetypal representations of all that exists according to human perception.

The associations given in the text are gathered from many sources. You will notice that some correspondences apply to more than one sector. This means that they have characteristics related with various sectors. It can also mean that they are ascribed to different sectors according to different sources and traditions. There are many divergent views on the topic. The correspondences given in this text do not purport in any way to be better or more significant than others. Please also be aware that the ideas and practices featured for each of the sectors reflect the nature of the sector itself and could seem extreme or contradictory when compared with those of other sectors.

For each sector the icon of the related Totem Spirit and a first list of basic correspondences: i.e. *Sign, House, Planets,*[2] *Rays,*[3] *Element, Quality, Direction, Season* are given. Indications of the *Totem Spirit* and *Epic States*, according to the *Epic of the Sacred Cone* are also supplied.[4] Please be aware that the astrological and general information provided merely reflects my current understanding as I can briefly and provisionally describe it at an introductory level. This does not purport, in any way, to be absolute.

A second list of correspondences covers a wider spectrum and includes the following categories:

Animals: These associations are significant, as for many traditions the sectors were designated by the name of an animal. The word *zodiac* itself comes from the Greek *zodiakon* ('pertaining to animals'). Some correspondences derive from ancient myths and indicate the emblems or the animals used as a sacrifice to the planetary gods.

Plants: The vegetable kingdom was the major field of research for traditional astrological correspondences. To trace the original vibration and find the planetary correspondence, medieval people considered colour, form, smell and other characteristics of the plant. In Europe this practice was called *signatura rerum* ('signature of things') and became the basis for identifying healing remedies. The plants that had affinities with a planet or a part of the body were used to treat the ailments related with that specific planet or part of the body. The shamanic approach may differ in that it tends to disregard the physical form of the plant and focus instead on its inner vibration. The purpose is that of connecting and establishing a relationship with the spirit, or *Deva,* of the plant. Plants can be used in different ways to evoke or connect with the qualities of a sector. They can be employed as smudging herbs, ornaments, food, beverages and for building ritual tools or shamanically relating to their energies. Please be careful when using plants and make sure that what you do is appropriate and respectful both of the plant and yourself. Also, as some plants could be poisonous or dangerous for your health, it is essential to consult a competent herbalist before attempting to use them.

Minerals: Associations here differ considerably according to tradition.

Spirits: Included in this category are just a few examples of gods, demigods, heroes, immortals, apostles, angels, saints, nature spirits and other mythical entities who are traditionally associated with the sectors. They are given with the indication of their culture or tradition of reference written in parentheses.

Anatomy/Physiology: The anatomical parts and physiological functions of the body are given according to traditional astrological correspondences.

Associations: A general list of sundry associations is provided.

Colours: The colours of the spectrum associated with specific planets and signs are listed. There are many models according to traditions. The given correspondences represent a general consensus of opinion.

Detectors: These further detailed correspondences are based upon the astrological system of the *derived houses,*[5] which disclose information about the state of each sector and all its related associations. These detectors, as they are met both in dreams, thoughts or in the outer reality, operate as links to specific sectors and astrological houses. They comprise virtually anyone or anything: from my closest relations up to a distant third cousin or even the dog of my neighbour and the car of my sister's employer. The detectors are a useful device to bring awareness as regards projections and to help the mind to get acquainted with the web of life and the sectors of the Sacred Circle. The way in which I perceive the detectors of a sector also shows me the quality of my relationship with the related Totem Spirit and all the corresponding associations. Examples of detectors are listed for each sector, together with combinations of numbers identifying the derived houses. For example, Sector 12 includes the combination 10-3. This means that any correspondence to Sector 10 or detector of the tenth house combined with any of Sector 3 can be a detector for Sector 12, i.e. the career (10) of my first brother (3), the knee (10) of the partner of my third son (3), etc. Please be aware that these details are provided only for the astrology-minded reader and are not considered essential in order to work with astroshamanism. For further information on detectors see Book One, Chapter 7, 'Sector Detectors and Shamanic Forms'.

Grievances: These are the lower expressions of the sector and include any physical, emotional, mental or spiritual attitude, situation or behaviour, even of apparent well-being, that supports the ego and the illusion of separation. A term which is often employed in the text to indicate grievances is *Graha* which, according to the *Epic of the Sacred Cone*, represent the key material of multidimensional exchange that, when consciously acknowledged, experienced and released for this purpose, contribute to the undoing of the illusion of separation and the perception of unity. If this is not the case, *Graha* operate as antagonistic forces bolstering up the hallucination of separation, blocking the portals to the territories of the sectors and preventing the connection with the Spirit Guide. *Graha* can also be considered as inner aspects connected with shadow sides in ourselves that prevent the access to key strategic operative areas. Here *Graha* hamper the development of our powers until we find clarity about the purity of our Intent and are willing to connect it with our Function. In the context of the Epic, there are various categories and expressions of *Graha*. Basically they articulate according to the traditional scheme of

Totem Spirits. The list of grievances briefly mention *excesses,* *deficits* and *physical* manifestations for each sector. (For more information on *Graha* see Book One, Chapter 7, 'Demons and *Graha'*.)

An *excess* occurs when the energy of a sector is overemphasised and becomes the major form of identification. This condition is bound to support the generation of *Graha*. Astrologically it may be identified by the prevalence of a certain sector in the natal chart (for example, many planets or factors in a sign or house, strong aspects or transits on the ruler of a sector or its proximity to an angle or mid-point). These excesses can often be balanced by employing healing tools related to the polar opposite sector (for example, excesses in Aries can be healed by employing the healing tools of Libra). A *deficit* exists when the energy of a sector is lacking or denied, repressed and projected. Astrologically this may be represented by a lack, inhibition or disturbance of a sector (for example, no planets or relevant factors in a sign or house, detrimental aspects or transits of Saturn on the ruler of a sector, the sign and house of Saturn, and even an excess of planets and factors in a sign or house). Deficits are often healed through the use of tools related to the energy of the sector which is lacking. *Physical grievances* manifest through physical illness and ailments which correspond to the specific physical pathology of the sector involved. Emotional, mental and spiritual grievances are not treated in detail in the text, though some of them are mentioned in the *excesses* and *deficit* lists.

Qualities: These include the higher expressions of the sector.

The text for each sector continues with a description of the general characteristics of the sector, its *sign, house* and *planets*. This section also contains reflections, visions, teachings, personal experiences, *basic practices, healing tools* and *astroshamanic reports*.

Basic Practices: These practices are described in Book One and constitute a preliminary aspect of the astroshamanic initiatory programme. You are welcome to follow them if you choose to introduce yourself to the experiential nature of this work. Please be aware that you do not need to adhere strictly to this model if you develop or already have one that works better for you. In the initiatory context of astroshamanism what counts is to employ the same basic principles. You can also adapt your practice in accordance with the technique of journeying that you find most effective (lying on the back or face down, sitting or standing, trance dance, chanting, astroshamanic postures, etc.).

Healing Tools: A wide range of practices are given in this section. If you decide to employ this book as an experiential guide, the invitation is to use two or three of these practices at least once, then choose one and do it preferably daily, every other day or three times per week minimum (achieving a total of at least twelve practices), either for 21 days or for a cycle of the Moon (28 days). Astroshamanism gives essential priority to the spiritual dimension of grievances. In this context it does not involve any medical diagnosis or psychotherapeutic analysis. All healing tools are used for the health of the soul and the expansion of human awareness. There is no one particular healing tool which works for everybody and you are encouraged to explore your own path in this field within the structure provided by this book or further teachings and your own guidance. Please also keep in mind that the ideas and practices of each of the sectors reflect the nature of the sector they deal with and could seem contradictory when compared with those of other sectors.

Astroshamanic Reports: These include the partial description of journeys, practices and other shamanic experiences related to the sector involved. They constitute a short anthology of my early voyages and reflect initial traits of my apprenticeship, which do not necessarily coincide with my current experience and understanding.

Basic Practices

In the first volume I have introduced the general aspects of astroshamanism and provided details about the Sacred Circle, the concepts of Intent and Function, a series of astroshamanic basic practices and rituals, the astroshamanic voyage, the Spirit Guide, the Totem Spirits, the Spirit Medicines and Sacred Tools. I have also given a brief description of the astrological language and an appendix featuring a compendium of the basic myth to which the astroshamanic tradition refers. I am not going to duplicate the same information here. I will summarise, however, some basic general indications (Intent and Function, Sacred Circle Pieces, journal, opening and closing of shamanic voyages, meeting the Spirit Guide, exploration of sectors and relationship with Totem Spirits) as they are relevant for those who use the basic practices given for each sector. Please be aware that in order to effectively employ this second volume as a self-study experiential guide it is necessary to be familiar with the information and practices of the first volume. It is therefore preferable that before exploring the sectors and using the related techniques, you review and assimilate the first volume. I would also suggest periodically reconsidering both volumes. Another option, which does not necessarily require understanding or awareness of the first volume, is that of simply reading the second volume without doing the basic practices.

It is my belief that anyone can safely employ shamanic work as long as instructions are carefully followed and there are not any serious physical or psychological problems. If you wish to further expand your shamanic experience and do not feel safe to proceed alone, you can ask for assistance from a competent mentor or take part in specific workshops. If you intend to receive first-hand training in astroshamanism or individual sessions and tuition, information is available from the author (please see 'About the Author' on page 245 for contact details). Although this work is based on experience and does not require adherence to a particular belief system, it is important to be aware that it entails dealing with unknown spaces and most powerful and denied forces. Shamanic journeys, as I regard them, are not fantasies or exercises of creative visualisation. The situations and the beings met in these experiences are as real as those of ordinary life. Everyone can work with shamanism and treat it in a playful way, giving to this work the meaning that he finds appropriate. At the same time, I believe that in order to play with integrity, in this as in other cases, it is necessary to understand and respect the agreements of the game.

Intent and Function: The terms *Intent* and *Function* are featured prominently in this text. The *Intent* represents the expression of my purpose in life, or in a specific situation in space or time, as it is perceived within the separate reality of the ego. The clarification of the Intent generates a field of energy that allows me to be in a position of power and draw the forces that are needed to implement my purpose. According to my tradition the Intent is a basic tool for inner transformation when it aligns with the Function, that is, when I cease to use my will to nourish the ego's perception of separation and employ it to retrieve my original unity. The term *Function* identifies itself with *forgiveness*, meant as release, undoing or healing of the illusion of separation. In this context the Function represents the ultimate aim of human beings.

The Intent is a basic requirement for shamanic journeys and spiritual practices, as it allows definition of my true motivation. The fact that the Intent needs to be connected with the Function does not mean that their content is the same. In astroshamanism, the Intent is simply what, according to my current awareness, I honestly want. It does not matter what it is, or whether it can seem selfish or silly. The Intent does not necessarily have to take the form of an achievement which is totally clear. It may also be that of getting to know what my major goal or potential is either in this current time of my life or in general. In this case it can be expressed as a question which can simply be: 'What is my Intent?' What counts is to be clear and truthful regarding the Intent, and committed to realising it. Any shamanic work is based on this premise. The ego never truly commits because it is not ultimately convinced about what it wants. The ego only knows what it does not want: this is the only thing on which it is very clear. And this is the reason why most human beings, thinking of what they do not want, lose their purpose in life and support what they fear.

The Sacred Circle Pieces: They constitute the basic equipment for building the Sacred Circle and also a significant astroshamanic tool of power. To create them you start by getting twelve pieces of stiff card or wood (or twelve stones, gems or any material that attracts you) to be used for each sector. Five other pieces of different dimensions are employed for the Four Directions and the Centre. The type of material you use or where it comes from is not important. What matters is that you like it and that it *speaks* to your heart or draws your inner attention. If you decide to collect stones or other objects from nature, it is customary and advisable to state your Intent and explain to the Totem Spirit, or shamanic form of the place, what you plan to do with the stones. Then, you can ask permission and wait silently for a sign of confirmation. If you sense that it is all right to take the stone or object as a piece for your Sacred Circle, it is good practice to leave an offering in its place as a sign of respect. This can be seeds, nuts, herbs, a hair from your head, or anything that is fitting and can be recycled in nature. It is also important that you are aware of the local human laws, abstaining from collecting items protected by special regulations.

When you have collected all the material you need, you can activate the five pieces for the Directions and the Centre. With these you can already create the structure of the Sacred Circle and start your first practices. Then, every time that you work with each astrological sign, you are going to activate one of the other twelve pieces. The activation consists of drawing or painting on the card, wood or stone what is related with your intuitions or visions about that sector. You can also simply write down the name, number or astrological symbol of the sign given in the correspondence section of each sector or you can create collages. If you use stones, they can be painted, carved, left as they are or chosen according to their natural colour. Another possibility is that of using a sheet or carpet on which to draw a circle with twelve spaces for the twelve signs and five for the Directions and the Centre. You can either use it to array the Sacred Circle Pieces or draw them on the sheet itself.

Once you have activated the piece, sit in front of it, be aware of your breath and open up to what comes to you. Do what is spontaneous for you and notice what happens. At any moment, whenever you need to explore a particular sector, you can always position yourself in front of it. Once you have completed all the pieces and experienced a direct connection with each sector, which generally takes one full year, you will possess a powerful tool and will have realised the basic circumference of the Sacred Circle.

The Astroshamanic Journal: Keeping a journal allows you to create a bridge between shamanic and ordinary states of consciousness. This is in itself a powerful shamanic practice, as it supports the acknowledgement of non-ordinary realities and the development of a field of resonance aimed at amplifying the essence of your spiritual journey. In the journal you collect reports or drawings of your voyages, dreams, insights, visions, life experiences, images, symbols, quotations, notes, and whatever can be useful for your spiritual work. In this way you preserve information that can easily be lost or forgotten. The spaces of the spiritual world do not usually receive the same attention as those of the physical world. A lot of records are available as regards the geography of the ordinary reality. On the contrary, for your shamanic territories, you are the one who has to do the exploration and the mapping.

Opening and Closing for Shamanic Voyages: There are different ways to open or close a shamanic voyage. They change according to individuals and traditions. As such none of them is wrong or right. What matters is whether they work and serve the purpose. These sequences are fundamental at the beginning, as they demarcate your entry into and out of your shamanic world. By becoming familiar with such practices, you train your mind so that you can easily shift your state of consciousness.

The following is one of the traditional astroshamanic beginner's procedures for opening and closing a shamanic journey. I offer it as a suggestion and you are welcome to employ it during the first stages of your work. Please be aware that although the model that follows is mainly of a visual nature, shamanic voyages do not necessarily have to be visual. Sight is just one of our senses. The experience can also develop through other senses.

1. Before you start, make sure that you have read and understood the information found in Book One, Chapter 5, 'Basic Indications for Shamanic Voyages and Explorations of the Sacred Circle'. If you wish, you can call the directions and open the Sacred Circle (see Book One, Chapter 4, 'Calling in the Directions and Opening the Sacred Circle').

2. Lie down or sit comfortably on the floor or on a chair. Make sure that your spine is straight. Take off tight clothes and shoes. If it is cold, use a blanket. It is highly recommended to journey in a dark environment or, if that is not feasible, to use something to cover your eyes (your arm or a blindfold). Whatever the case, keep your eyes closed during the journey. Connect with your breath and allow it to move in all parts of your body, relaxing and grounding yourself. Allow your Intent to gently emerge as you breathe. Focus on your Intent. Be honest about your motivations and do not judge them according to the conventional standards of what is right or wrong, spiritual or non-spiritual. (For further information on the Intent see Book One, Chapter 3 and points 5 and 6 in Chapter 5, 'Basic Indications for Shamanic Voyages and Explorations of the Sacred Circle'.)

3. Once the Intent has been established and expressed, you can allow your vision to unfold. Be open and let go of any prejudice or expectation. Relax for some time, focusing on your breath and body. When you are ready, start a drumming tape or CD,[6] if you have one, and feel or imagine a real place on Earth where you can see an entrance. It can be a place where you have been once in your life, a familiar spot or even a place that you have seen in a movie or photograph. As shamanic journeys start from ordinary reality, it is preferable that the departing point be a place existing on this planet. This can be a door, the entrance to a cave, a bridge, a hole in the ground, a lake, a pool of water, a passage between two trees, an opening in your body, etc. What counts is that you feel comfortable with it. Once you have found it, focus on the entrance and take your time to see and sense it clearly in all its details. Then step inside.

4. When you are inside, bring your attention to what you perceive of the place: temperature, colours, smell, sounds, etc. Employ all your senses to discover the environment you are in. Try and understand whether the place is warm, cold, damp, dry, etc. Feel your feet and the weight of your body. Bring your attention to the type of floor and be aware of the air, colours, sounds and any other impressions that you can gather from the place.

5. Continue to move until you find a point of light or opening at the end that will take you outside into another environment or landscape. If you meet obstacles or blocks, move around or pass through them. Finding this entrance is easy and will not require much time. Once you have found it, in the next journeys you do not need to look for it any more. You simply go the same way as before.

6. Go through this entrance and be aware of the landscape around you using all your senses. Listen attentively to the sounds that are there; feel the ground underneath your feet; sense the air and the smells; watch whatever you can perceive and be as present as possible. Then after some time, somewhere near you, see a short path leading to a circular area with twelve stones placed around a *Great Tree*. Beyond the circle of the twelve stones there is a border area indicated by four bigger stones representing the Four Directions. This whole area is your Spirit Circle.[7] It is a place where you can

go whenever you need energy or protection. Its importance is tantamount to that of your home or room in ordinary life. In your Spirit Circle, you can take rest, feel safe, do spiritual work, balance your energies, meet your Spirit Guide, connect with Totem Spirits and other beings, etc. This place is also the strategic starting point of all your explorations of non-ordinary reality. It operates as an area for rebalancing or decompression aimed at facilitating the movement from one dimension to another. The twelve stones that are arrayed around the Great Tree represent the access to each of the Twelve Sectors of the Spirit Circle. From there, once you connect with the Guide, you can move to explore specific areas of the inner world.

7. Once you are fully aware of your Spirit Circle, approach the Great Tree at the centre and look around acknowledging all the stones and whatever you can see. Be aware of what you feel and allow yourself to be totally at ease. Give permission to the Great Tree to balance your energy and release grievances or anything that prevents you from experiencing a sense of peace or power. Receive energy, love, support and all you need from the Tree. Open yourself to its nourishment and experience a total connection with the sacred environment that you are in.

The closing sequence is briefer than the opening one. Leave the Circle by following the same route, in reverse order, until you come back to the first entrance. In the drumming tape, the closing sequence is often indicated by a change of beats (for example, three groups of seven slow beats, a very fast drumming, and three groups of seven slow beats again).

After the journey, adjust and stretch your body, breathe deeply and gradually come back to ordinary reality. Always jot down what you experienced in your astroshamanic journal. Do that as soon as you finish and avoid leaving it in the belief that you are going to remember everything later.

Meeting the Spirit Guide: Astroshamanic work is based on the connection with the Spirit Guide and Circle. The terms *Spirit Guide* and *Spirit Circle* are synonyms that can be used interchangeably to depict qualities such as unity, unconditional love, ecstasy, light, joy, or whatever is related to the Divine, or

Prime Creator. Although their essential meaning is the same, their different expressions serve to cover two prevalent models common in the imagery of most human spiritual cultures. In this context, the Spirit Circle refers to a collective and territorial unit (*Spirit People, Heaven, Ecstatic Dimension,* etc.) whereas the Spirit Guide may be described as the main representative, or prime emanation, of the Spirit Circle (*Spirit Teacher, Inner Guide, Holy Spirit, Higher Self, Guardian Angel,* etc.).

The experience of Guides is one of the most typical features of shamanism. Their presence is essential, for they provide a sense of security and protection which is a basic necessity in order to move beyond the borders of ordinary reality. The Spirit Guide operates as bridge between dimensions and is a constant source of balance in all shamanic enterprises. In situations of weakness he is able to stimulate and generate the required power. Yet, whenever you are decoyed by the illusion of separation, he can also be the cause of frustration, pain and despair. For your true nature, the Guide is the deepest companion, just as for the ego he is the fiercest enemy.

The nature of the relationship that takes place with the Guide is an exchange between equals. On one hand I let go of my excess energies, which are welcomed and transformed by the Guide, while on the other I receive the resources I lack and that are abundant in the Guide. The act of releasing my grievances in the presence of the Guide creates the vacuum that allows me to receive. A basic indication for your first meeting is to let go of all your preconceptions, stick to your Intent of contacting your Guide and employ a technique for this purpose.

The Guide can be approached through a large variety of practices: meditation, shamanic journeys, chant, dance, dreams, etc. In the beginning, to avoid confusion, it is preferable to utilise a specific procedure. The example that follows is aimed at providing a model for those who contact the Guide for the first time. This procedure is based on the astroshamanic work of exploration of the sectors and is simply one possibility among several options. In order for the meeting with your Guide to occur, you need only follow the steps and be willing to experience what happens. Again, be aware that the process need not necessarily be of a visual nature. What counts is that you experience the connection with the Guide, no matter which sense is involved.

1. Start by using the sequence described in the Introduction, 'Basic Practices, Opening and Closing for Shamanic Voyages', and in Book One, Chapter 5, 'Sequence of Opening and Closing for Shamanic Voyages'.

2. Once you are in the Spirit Circle, go to the Great Tree and call your Guide. Focus on the Intent to meet him and allow the connection to take place. The Guide can appear in different forms (as a person, animal, light, plant, sphere of energy, voice, sound, and also as body sensations). Receive the first image or feeling that comes to you. If you meet difficulties and do not see or feel anything, state again your Intent of connecting with the Guide and open up without making judgements. If you are not comfortable with what you see or feel, ask the Guide to come in another form. You can also meet a spirit animal that will lead you to the point where you can find your Guide.

3. When you meet your Guide, watch him and receive impressions about his appearance or energy. If you cannot see his face or other details, do not strain yourself. Often, in the beginning, the face of the Guide is hardly visible. Ask him if he is your Guide and if he has the power to protect and support you in your shamanic journeys and spiritual path. Usually, after such a direct request, a true Guide will reply positively either with words and gestures or through any other signal of loving consent. The Guide is also identifiable because he causes strong feelings of unconditional love, protection and support. If you do not feel total acceptance and love, you are probably with a false guide (see Book One, Chapter 6, 'False Guides'). If you do not receive a confirmation that you are in the presence of your Guide, focus again on your Intent and give direct permission to your Guide to be perceived by you. Make a clear invitation and open up to receiving your Guide. According to certain traditions, a Guide is also acknowledged as authentic when he is seen at least three times during the same journey.

4. Once you have received the confirmation that you are with your Guide, establish a connection and give him permission to express the love he feels for you. Stay open to a direct energetic connection and use all your senses to experience it.

5. When you hear the call back (if you are not employing a tape for shamanic journeys, use a gentle alarm clock or let your intuition signal when to return) conclude your meeting. Find your way to thank the Guide, say goodbye to him and use the sequence of closing given in the Introduction, 'Basic Practices, Opening and Closing for Shamanic Voyages', and in Book One, Chapter 5, 'Sequence of Opening and Closing for Shamanic Voyages'.

6. Take three deep breaths, then gradually return to the full awareness of your body and your environment. Jot down the major details of your experience.

During the following days continue to relate with your Guide. Once you have established the first connection it is a question of keeping it alive and deepening the relationship. It is useful to practise this meeting with the Guide regularly (daily or every other day) for a minimum of 28 days. This is the approximate time the Moon takes to move throughout all the signs of the Zodiac and allows a balanced distribution or activation of energy. During the first two or three meetings it is preferable to have simply a silent, loving and energetic contact with your Guide. For example, you can place your right hand in his left hand and allow him to receive your excess energies. Then you can put your left hand in his right and open up to receive from your Guide. Once you have acquired an intimate familiarity with him, and this usually needs at least three meetings, you can ask questions which are relevant for you and your life. Yet, every time you meet the Guide, before addressing questions and receiving the answers, still continue to devote some minutes to establish an energetic connection. Finally, be aware that this relationship needs time to be grounded and grow in your awareness. The ordinary reality and its major belief systems tend to ignore, ridicule or oppose such a connection. For this purpose it is preferable to keep the information about your Guide to yourself.

Exploration of Sectors: Once the connection with the Guide has been established, the second phase of the work usually consists of exploring the Twelve Sectors. In practice, this means to have a direct experience of the energy of each sector and to retrieve missing parts. This can take place in many ways and is sometimes similar to the traditional shamanic practice of *soul retrieval*. The choice regarding which sector to visit is often determined by the position of the Sun or Moon in the sky.[8] This means that, unless there are specific needs or the Guide suggests otherwise, the right time for exploring a sector is generally when the Sun or the Moon is transiting the corresponding sign. You can do as many or few of the astroshamanic explorations as you want, using the order you prefer. Yet, in the teaching context of this volume and according to my tradition, the best approach is to start the exploration and practices of each sector close to the time when the Sun enters the related astrological sign. For example, with Sector 6 (Virgo) you begin around 24 August (which usually marks the ingress of the Sun in Virgo). In this way you have an entire month to go through the text, do your voyages and use the basic practices. Then around 23 September you can move to Sector 7 (Libra) and so on until you have covered all the Twelve Sectors. This means that you can start this volume from any sector that corresponds to your time of departure in this one-year journey.

The experiences and the characteristics of the sectors vary enormously from person to person. According to lineage, ancestors, planetary positions and other data, each individual meets different situations and beings. Various methods of exploration are employed. The ideal type, which I recommend as part of the initiatory structure of this volume, involves establishing a connection with the Totem Spirit of each sector. This is associated with the traditional astrological ruling planet of the sign: for example, the Moon for Cancer (Sector 4), Saturn for Capricorn (Sector 10), etc. In this instance, it is not necessary to have an individual astrological chart as the Totem Spirits are in the same position for everybody. Another kind of exploration entails meeting the Totem Spirits corresponding to the planets as they are positioned in the natal chart. This means that if I want to meet the Moon, which in my chart is in Scorpio, I need to go to Sector 8 (i.e. the sector of Scorpio), whereas with the previous method I would go to Sector 4 (the ruling sector of the Moon). A further and more advanced possibility is connecting with two or more Totem Spirits at a time as represented by the position of the Sun and the Moon in the sky or by planets in aspects. Such meetings are used to heal conflicts among Totem Spirits and concern one of the major features of astroshamanic advanced work: the undoing of the *Paheka Rubhe*.[9]

What follows is merely a model aimed at describing one of the basic practices of initiation to astroshamanism. If you decide to have a complete experiential introduction to this work, you are welcome to consider these essential instructions and use them during your explorations of each sector. Please be aware that you do not need to adhere strictly to this model if you develop or already have one that works better for you. In the initiatory context of astroshamanism what counts is to employ the same basic principles. Also you can adapt your practice in accordance with the technique of journeying which you find most effective (lying on the back or face down, sitting or standing, trance dance, chanting, astroshamanic postures, etc.). I invite you to treasure your insights, honouring the validity of your experiences and keeping in mind that in shamanism no one has the authority to challenge them.

1. If you have your Sacred Circle Pieces, position yourself in front of the piece corresponding to the sector you are exploring. When you connect with your Intent, remember to focus on the purpose of your journey. This could be stated for example as follows: 'I intend to visit Sector... to meet the related Totem Spirit and receive information on my Intent and Function so that I can express my potential of light for the benefit of myself and the whole. I will use the information I get with integrity.'

2. Once you reach the area of the Spirit Circle, go toward the Great Tree at the centre and call upon your Spirit Guide or do what it is your custom to do at this stage.

3. Greet your Guide and establish an energetic connection.

4. Tell your Guide which sector you intend to visit and invite him to accompany you during the journey. Ask if there is something that you need to know before going. Invite the Guide to offer you protection and direct your way.

5. Follow your Guide as he moves from the Great Tree towards one of the twelve stones of the Spirit Circle. The Guide will point it out in some way. That stone represents the access to the territory of the sector that you have chosen to visit. Be aware of it in all its details. When you are ready to go, place both your hands on the stone. At this stage the stone is going to move and show the access to a corridor. This corridor leads to a pathway that allows you to reach the territory of the sector.

6. Let the Guide lead you through this pathway. The characteristics of the way change according to sector and means of transportation. For example, the way can be a narrow corridor, a river, a lake, a road, a railroad, etc. and you can walk, ride, drive, sail, fly, etc.

7. The pathway comes to an end when you reach the territory of the sector. Sometimes you can notice a specific sign that indicates the entrance or border. Whatever you perceive, always keep the connection with the Guide and, before doing anything, ask for advice.

8. Then you may find a representative of the sector, or *Auxiliary Guide*, which can have the form of an animal, man, woman or whatever. The Auxiliary Guide's purpose is that of escorting you within the territory and taking you to the Totem Spirit. As you move with your Spirit Guide and, if you met him, the Auxiliary Guide, be aware of your perceptions: landscape, weather, temperature, colours, animals, plants, sounds, inhabitants and their activities.

9. When you reach the area where the Totem Spirit abides, ask your Spirit Guide what to do. For example, you can wait for the Totem Spirit to come and meet you, or you can call him, go directly to see him, offer a sacrifice or pass a test.

10. When you are in front of the Totem Spirit, make sure that your Guide is close to you and, if you do not know what to do, ask him. Generally you are supposed to greet the Spirit and express your Intent. If you feel safe, you can also establish an energetic connection with the Spirit. Then you can communicate with him in the way you prefer. The purpose of the first meeting is that of receiving information on the way in which you can express your highest Intent in the sector concerned and on how you can apply your Function (i.e. releasing the grievances related to that sector). These objectives may develop in accordance with the nature of the three stages of the *Basic Ritual* (described in Book One, Chapter 4, 'The Astroshamanic Basic Ritual of the Sacred Cone') and are summed up by three questions that you can ask the Spirit:

a) *What is my highest Intent in this sector?*

b) *What is my Function and what do I need to release or do to honour my highest Intent here?*

c) *What do I need to retrieve from this sector?*

The answer may come verbally or in the form of images, sounds, codes, movements, actions, drawings, etc. Whatever happens, accept the first answer or sequence that comes to you, even if it seems not to make any sense. Sometimes the way Totem Spirits communicate appears weird or absurd. This is often a strategy to get through the censorship of the ego system. Let go of your usual ways of thinking and be open to the first answer as it develops. If its meaning does not make sense to you, instead of rejecting it or, on the contrary, pretending that you have understood, ask your Guide or the Totem Spirit for further explanation. If you question directly and honestly, you can be sure that sooner or later you will receive an answer. This generally contains information that identifies your specific potential and the way to develop it. If you are willing to get down to work and practical understanding, it is essential *to ask*. The Guide does not usually provide information if you fail to ask. When you do ask and keep on asking until the answers are clear, you are bound to receive specific suggestions, practices, courses of action. It is good practice to consult your Guide before agreeing to accept whatever the Totem Spirit may invite you to do. If the Spirit corresponds to a planetary energy that is blocked or operates disharmoniously in your system, he could sometimes draw you to do conflicting and dangerous things, or to act in a way which is contrary to your true Intent. In this phase of communication with the Spirit, your aim is to get clear information, which is acceptable both to you and your Guide, about something that you can do practically in your life to express your potential.

11. When you have received the answer, you can invite the Totem Spirit to offer you a gift in the form of a *Spirit Medicine*. It can also be the Spirit himself who gives it to you or you and your Guide that decide to get it with the consent of the Spirit. This can be, for example, a stone, sword, wand, sphere, ring, fruit, plant, body-part. It may also be received or retrieved as a fragmented piece of your soul and

appear as a younger version of yourself or in the form of an animal or human being. Consider the first object or being that is shown to you and avoid changing it in accordance with your expectations of what you think a Spirit Medicine should be. Before accepting it, ask your Guide if that is appropriate or check within to see whether you feel all right in receiving the Spirit Medicine. If the answer is negative, thank the Spirit and go to step 12. If the answer is positive, take the object. The Spirit Medicine is usually an essence which has been adapted to your own nature in order to manifest your potential and release grievances. It allows you to act out the qualities of that sector and to connect with your Intent and Function. When you receive it, watch its shape with care and ask for explanations on its usage or properties. Continue until you have a basic understanding of its functions. Also ask what the name of the medicine is. Here you can get a name in your mother tongue or in some other language. Always accept the first name you receive whether it makes sense or not. Often this name is a sort of access code that enables the Spirit Medicine to work. Then you can ask the Totem Spirit to store the medicine in a place of your body. Be aware of the connection of the medicine with that specific part of your physical body.

12. In the end, after thanking the Spirit, take leave of him. You can also ask for permission from the Totem Spirit to visit the sector again. He will automatically agree, as this is just a strategic formality that enables you to be clear that you are always welcomed. If you have decided not to accept the Spirit Medicine or your Guide has suggested that, you can return at other times and try again.

13. On conclusion of each exploration, it is good practice to ask your Guide if your energies and the exchanges you had with the Totem Spirit are balanced. When you receive something from other dimensions it is advisable to know clearly the terms of negotiation and what is to be given as a form of exchange. The Guide will tell you if you remember to ask him. For example, he can invite you to perform a certain action or to offer an object, say a prayer, burn some incense, have a walk in the wood. For further information on Spirit Medicine, see Book One, Chapter 8, 'Spirit Medicines'.

14. Then go back following the same path you used before. If the Auxiliary Guide was with you, take leave when you reach the point where you originally met him. Thank him for his help and then move through the corridor up to the stone of the Spirit Circle. Thank the stone of the sector, place your hands on it and then close the access. At this stage, if you wish, you can still stay with your Guide for a while and ask questions about your journey. Then come back to your ordinary state of consciousness.

---

[1] The seasonal time for each sector and its description in the text is designed for the northern terrestial latitudes.

[2] The *planets* are grouped into the following categories: 1) the *exoteric rulers*. They include: the contemporary rulerships employed by most astrologers after the discovery of Uranus (1781), Neptune (1846) and Pluto (1930); the rulerships used in Ptolemaic astrology and based upon the Sun, Moon and the five traditional planets (Mercury, Venus, Mars, Jupiter, Saturn); an additional rulership, used by some astrologers in the past twenty years, which considers the four major asteroids (Ceres, Vesta, Pallas, Juno) and the planetoid Chiron. The exoteric rulers represent the major focus of this text. 2) the *esoteric rulers*. They consist of the rulerships which, according to esoteric astrology and the teachings received by Alice Bailey, apply to advanced individuals and initiates. Please be aware that these rulerships are given merely for astrological reference and do not necessarily imply that astroshamanism is connected with the ideas of esoteric astrology.

[3] According to the esoteric astrology of Alice Bailey, the Seven Rays are the particular forces, or types of energy, that underlie the entire functioning of the universe.

[4] The *Epic States* refer to the correspondent denomination, according to the *Epic of the Sacred Cone,* of the sectors in *Handor* and *Rodnah* respectively.

[5] The technique of *derived houses* consists of examining each of the 12 astrological houses as the ascendant of a further cycle of 12 houses, making a total of 144 houses. This traditional method was introduced by Eudes Picard (see: Eudes Picard, *Astrologie Judiciare,* Leymarié, Paris, 1936). It has also been used by Edwin C. Steinbrecher (see: Edwin C. Steinbrecher, *The Inner Meditation Guide: A Spiritual Technology for the 21st Century,* Samuel Weiser, 1988.) though with some differences in the allocation of houses.

[6] Drumming or rattling musical aids created for shamanic journeys can be purchased in specialised record shops. The author also has available compact discs and cassettes specifically produced to provide support for astroshamanic voyages. For information: Franco Santoro, Cluny Hill College, Forres IV36 2RD, Scotland. www.astroshamanism.org

[7] As mentioned in Book One, the Spirit Circle pertains to the shamanic state of consciousness and is different in nature from a Sacred Circle which is

visible to the body's eyes (that is, a circle that you arrange with your Sacred Circle Pieces or any stone circle, medicine wheel, etc. that belongs to the physical or ordinary environment). Please also be aware that the Great Tree mentioned in this text is a *Spirit Tree*.

8 To find out the exact position of these two celestial bodies you can employ an astrological calendar or the astronomical ephemeris.

9 According to a specific reading of the *Epic of the Sacred Cone*, the current ordinary human DNA is limited to two helices, or sectors, due to the block caused by the *Paheka Rubhe*. This term, which can be translated as the *Binary Net of Totem Spirits*, indicates the 144 combinations of the twelve *Paheka* (as they are *epically* called), or Totem Spirits' double polarities that prevent the expansion of human perception. Undoing these combinations and re-establishing the twelve-helix system is one of the major strategic tasks of advanced astroshamanic work.

DIRECTION EAST

~ ELEMENT: Fire ~ SEASON: Spring ~ BODY: Spiritual ~
~ KINGDOM: Human ~ PART OF DAY: Dawn ~
~ SIGNS: Aries, Taurus, Gemini ~ SECTORS: 1, 2, 3 ~
~ HUMAN AGE: Birth and childhood ~
~ TOTEM SPIRIT KEEPER: Ruha Sadoh ~
~ COLOURS: Red, gold, yellow ~ CELESTIAL BODIES: Sun ~
~ JOURNEY: Way of the Visionary ~
~ SPIRIT PATHWAYS: Clarity, wisdom, illumination. ~

ANIMALS:	Predatory (badger, coyote, eagle, hawk, tiger, wolf)
QUALITIES:	Authenticity, clarity, courage, creativity, honesty, power
GRIEVANCES:	Anger, anxiety, deception, hysteria, inertia, projection
HEALING TOOLS:	Athletic activities, dance, drama, jogging, mantras, movement, shamanic chants, singing, telling the truth, vision quest, walking
INSTRUMENTS:	Bell, knife, pipe
MINERALS:	Amber, carnelian, citrine, fire opal, iron, moss agate, pipestone, sulphur
PLANTS:	Dandelion, tobacco, yarrow
SPIRITS:	Xipe Totec (Aztec); Brigit (Celtic); Archangel Raphael (Christian); Ares (Greek); Mars, Vulcan (Roman); Salamanders (Nature Spirits).
FESTIVALS:	Spring Equinox (21/23 March), Beltane (1 May).

The path of the East represents the emergence or birth into a new dimension or cycle sparkling with opportunities to access alternative visions lying beyond the limited perception of the body's eyes. In this area of experience I learn to keep the connection with the Spirit Guide and Circle in the midst of chaotic situations, confusing stimuli and forceful energies. It is like dwelling in the centre of a cyclone. Massive numbers of objects and patterns move at high speed, causing tremendous noise and upheaval, while at the Centre, where my true nature abides, everything is still, peaceful and undisturbed. From that position life ceases to appear as a mass of disconnected experiences of joy, pain, frustration, action, challenge, struggle, passion, turmoil or whatever, and is acknowledged as a sacred return to the original Source.

The East is the place where I meet my authentic essence through the vigorous release of the ego's insane expectations as they are apparently reflected in other people or in false guides. Here I face and accept my Intent and bravely take up my Function. This direction marks the start of new enterprises and heroic deeds which provide major teachings on how to direct my energies.

My adherence to the Intent is at its peak as I move my first steps into the glorious eastern path of the Sacred Circle, and this is bound to activate the confrontation with the Function. It is at this crucial stage that I meet the greatest challenges. Here I run the risk of forgetting about my original task and being absorbed into the madness and oblivion of the ordinary reality. Here I have the opportunity of accepting and embracing my true Function, and take a quantum leap into the vertical axis for the benefit of all that exists within and without. This powerful moment of choice is activated by the presence of edges in the ideal course of action or state of being, as I perceive it according to my Intent. (For example I may get thoughts such as 'This is too much' or sense feelings of fear and limitation and move into my right to freedom or autonomy.) Edges and shadow areas are walls created by egoes to preserve their consensus reality and keep out whatever is unknown or causes problems. The most common edges are found at the boundaries of Level 1^1, or at the limits of my ordinary awareness. When I deny something and consider it as not being part of myself, this is an edge. Opening up to an edge is a transformational experience, as it challenges, confuses or erases my conventional identity. For example, I may be single because I need freedom to devote energy to great creative projects without being conditioned by the involvement in a relationship. If it happens that I fall in love and enter into a relationship with somebody, well, this is an edge. Another consistent and widespread edge is that most human beings consider as real and significant only that which is filled with physical matter (bodies, houses, plants, earth, etc.) whereas all the spaces that appear as *empty* are regarded as irrelevant, meaningless and usually defined as *nothing*. As a matter of fact the filled spaces constitute only a microscopic part of what I can potentially see. The border area between ordinary visible matter and what seem to be empty spaces, or gaps, is one of the major edges of mankind. 'This space you see as setting off all things from one another is the means by which the world's perception is achieved. You see something where nothing is, and see as well nothing where there is unity; a space between all things, between all things and you. Thus do you think that you have given life in separation. By this split you think you are established as a unity which functions with an independent will.'[2] As long as I am in this dimension I am asked to deal with this split reality and need to use its symbols. This does not mean that I have to be deceived by them. 'Thus what you need are intervals each day in which the learning of the world becomes a transitory phase; a prison house from which you go into the sunlight and forget the darkness. Here you understand the Word, the Name Which God has given you; the one Identity Which all things share; the one acknowledgement of what is true. And then step back to darkness, not because you think it real, but only to proclaim its unreality in terms which still have meaning in the world that darkness rules.'[3]

The value of edges and all situations which threaten the illusory perception of the world is that they warn about danger and keep me away from situations I am not yet strong enough to handle. Their disadvantage is that the fear of the edge, and not the true issue, can keep me away from a significant opportunity of transformation. Beware not to get into the trap of dwelling on the conflict of whether to go beyond the edge or not. This is usually one of the best games of the ego: to challenge with conflicts and create a virtual reality where there is always something to lose or gain. During your shamanic work, you will have the chance to come up against some edges and take decisions about what you are going to face or release. Go into your shamanic world and meet the power of the edge. Call upon your Guide and any force able to confidently face the edge that challenges you. You can also recall people that you met in your life who showed you examples of how to get over that edge. Maybe there were also situations in your past when you managed to face that specific issue. Whatever the case, amplify that energy which easily moves through the edge and allow yourself to fully experience it.

[1]   *Level 1* is related to the physical realm and the identification with three-dimensional forms. It represents the *personality* level and conventional reality as it is experienced by most human beings. For further information see Book One, Chapter 2, 'The Three Levels'.

[2]   *A Course in Miracles, Workbook,* p. 345.

[3]   ibid., p. 346.

SECTOR ONE

~ **Sign:** Aries ~ **House:** First ~ **Planets:** 1) Mars, 2) Mercury ~
~ **Ray:** 1st (Will/Power), 7th (Ceremonial Magic/Law) ~
~ **Element:** Fire ~ **Quality:** Cardinal ~
~ **Direction:** East ~ **Season:** Spring ~
~ **Totem Spirit:** Kahe Pah Sadoh ~
~ **Epic States:** Kirway, Yawrik ~

ANIMALS: All predatory and aggressive animals, badger, crow, eagle, fox, hawk, panther, raven, robin, shark, spider, tiger, vulture, wild boar, wolf, woodpecker.

PLANTS: Often thorny, with red flowers or fruits, and conic roots. Aloe, anemone, arnica, basil, broom, cactus, caper, coriander, damiana, dandelion, fern, garlic, gentian, ginger, holly, hemp, leek, mustard, nettle, onion, pennyroyal, pepper, pine, poppy, radish, rhubarb, tea, thistle, tobacco, violet.

MINERALS: All reddish stones, bloodstone, brimstone, carnelian, diamond, fire agate, flint, garnet, iron, magnetite, malachite, pink tourmaline, red coral, red jasper, red opal, ruby, steel, topaz.

SPIRITS: Khamael, Samuel (*Angels*); Huitzilpochtli (*Aztec*); Nergal (*Babylonian*); Belatucadros, Brigantia, Cernunnus, Cocideus, Morrigan, Teutates (*Celtic*); St. Barbara, St. Peter (*Christian*); Amun, Khnum, Neith (*Egyptian*); Laran (*Etruscan*); Ares, Achilles, Amazons, Athena, Dione, Jason, Hercules, Nike, Phrixus and Helle (*Greek*); Indra, Agni, Durga (*Hindu*); Odin, Tyr,

	Wodan (*Nordic*); Mars, Pallas, Minerva, Bellona (*Roman*); Emperor, Tower (*Tarot*).
ANATOMY/ PHYSIOLOGY:	Adrenal functions, brain, eyes, head, muscular tissues.
ASSOCIATIONS:	Energy, fire, activity, masculinity, passion, desire, attraction, fevers, burns, cuts, scalds, strife, heat, violence, murder, war, army, munitions, knives, slaughter-houses, surgery, competitive sports, engineering, mechanical industries.
COLOURS:	Red, black.
DETECTORS:	Paternal grandmother, maternal grandfather, 5th son/daughter, ex-partner of partner, partner's paternal grandfather, friends of 1st brother/sister, 6th brother/sister, employer of mother, home of father. 12-2, 11-3, 10-4, 9-5, 8-6, 7-7, 6-8, 5-9, 4-10, 3-11, 2-12.
GRIEVANCES:	*Excess:* aggressiveness, anger, antagonism, coarseness, competition, contempt, hostility, impatience, impulsiveness, irritability, lust, recklessness, stress, violence, wilfulness. *Deficit:* chronic fatigue, fear of action and competition, lack of initiative, lack of self-assertion and spontaneous action, limited physical expression, passivity, repression of anger, weakness. *Physical:* burns, colds, conjunctivitis, cuts, eczema, head injuries, headaches, high fevers, infections, inflammations, insomnia, sinusitis.
QUALITIES:	Alertness, assertiveness, clarity, courage, daring, decisiveness, desire, eagerness, emergence, enthusiasm, excitement, identity, satisfaction, spontaneity.

Sector 1 embodies a plain and direct expression of energy. Its immediate aim is survival and defence at personal or family, tribe, national, planetary and universal levels. This attitude manifests itself through a forthright, spontaneous, unpremeditated, instinctive and unilateral action focused on satisfying primary desires and objectives. The energy of Sector 1 is neutral. It is like a petrol station, which provides fuel but does not specify how this fuel is to be used. I can employ this energy to support my highest objectives or to attack, destroy or compete, contributing to the preservation of grievances and pain. What matters is how I choose to employ the energy: that is my Intent. If I am not aware of my Intent, anyone who is actually aware of their own can manoeuvre my energy and use it to support what they want. The energy needs Intent in order to be moved. I can either be aware of it or not. In the latter case, I am bound to be directed by *someone else,* who can be perceived either as a specific visible being (Level 1) or as a specific unseen being (Level 2).[1] If this being has a loving Intent, the effects that I experience may be positive. When that is not the case, the outcome is bound to be unpleasant. However, in both circumstances, no matter whether I am manipulated by *someone* with a positive or negative Intent, I am still disconnected from my own Intent. And this is not at all a situation of power, as it exposes me to the constant risk of invasion and prevents me from consciously directing my energy.

The exploration of Sector 1 is usually related to acting and moving toward what I want or desire by employing the vital or aggressive energy traditionally associated with the male polarity. The social life that has prevailed in the course of human history seems to have denied and repressed the genuine use of Sector 1. Its expression is the first that is barred in children, as its development hinders the acceptance of the virtual reality of adult human beings. This block causes a deep wound that creates the separation from the original Intent, the Guide and the experience of my true multidimensional identity. Each time that the energy of Sector 1 is stimulated and begins to flow, sooner or later it meets with a *no*. In that *no*, the memories of the primeval wound of separation are concentrated. From there stem the mysteries and the understanding of my presence in a physical body. The energy was freely circulating and, at a certain point, it was blocked and frozen, identifying itself with an illusive and apparently definite form: the ego. Many explanations could be given about such an occurrence. In the context of this sector, complex elucidation is not going to help. Here what matters is to use methods that allow energy to flow and operate in conditions of emergency requiring prompt action. In this process I first establish the connection with the energy in its purest form and give it the chance to express itself in a sacred and protected environment. Then I become aware of the moment in which it meets the wound. At this stage, the task is that of using tools to transform the wound into a *sacred wound*. This can happen if I am ready to let go of my little personal story and become the channel of a greater history. When I fail in this, the events of the little story keep being endlessly repeated while the illusive solutions that I find will only sustain, prolong or postpone the agony of my script.

Sector 1 entails connecting with a mythic reality by sacrificing ordinary personal history. The work here consists of acknowledging my dominant wound, the one that is most visible at the present moment, and then allowing it to extend towards a wider perspective. This means to support the transition from the personal identification with the little story (that is, the history of the ego) to the awareness of a greater story, allowing the first to pave the way for the process. In this way, my little story, with all its petty limits, becomes the golden gate of access to that greater story which will then provide the true perception of who I am.

Sector 1 carries the vibration of my original energy. It is like a primal wind that blows all the time and in every direction. It covers whatever exists and all that can be conceived. Its whispers and silences form the universal language of all dimensions. This language is not made up of symbols and its meaning cannot be translated into any current language. As a matter of fact the expressions of this energy do not have a meaning. They are indeed the meaning itself. Here there are no words, for what is said is direct and cannot be reduced to symbols. It is a language of energy, not of symbols. Symbols serve the purpose of keeping me away from the energy. This is hard for the conventional mind to understand. I cut off from the energy and created a dream out of the belief in separation. This dream is a *separate reality* made up of a long concatenation of symbols that are reflected in every thing I do and in the way I communicate with ordinary languages. These languages contribute to the preservation of separation. They are dualistic in nature and based on symbols of symbols. This makes the aim of getting to the pure energy very hard indeed. A symbol is something that represents something. A symbol of a symbol is something that represents something that represents something and so on. The language of energy, which I call *sacred idiom*, doesn't represent anything but itself. It has no need to hide from the energy. It is the energy itself. Let's take the word *light* for example. The first symbolic level I encounter here is the spelling of that word: *l-i-g-h-t*. These alphabetical letters are all symbolic signs which, when put together, give form to another symbolic level: that of the word *light*. At a third symbolic level I find what that word represents in terms of sound. Here *light* is the symbol of the phonetic sound [*lait*]. Then I come to a fourth symbolic level that has to do with what that sound corresponds to. This can be given through the use of other symbolic combinations of letters and words, such as 'the medium of illumination that makes sight possible', to quote the *Collins English Dictionary*, or through an image which represents a supply of light (the sun, a torch, a fire). To sum it up, first I get my mind to process the spelling of the word, secondly

I receive the written word, thirdly its sound and finally I get an explanation of what that sound means through a definition or an image which is still symbolic in nature. After all these passages, I am still unable to get to the energy or experience of what *light* is. Of course, I can have an idea of it. But if I am in the darkness and need to have some light to find my way, the idea of *light* is not going to be of much help. *Sacred idiom*, the primal language of energy, is alien to such abstract concatenations, as its sole concern is the experience. Its expressions are the experience itself and if there were an equivalent of *light* in that language, the result of its use would be the immediate manifestation of light. It is a powerful creative communication. It is very strong and I use symbols to disconnect from it. I do that because I am afraid to face the energy. I am afraid to face the energy for there is a big wound there. This wound is the *Mahagraha*, the Grey Demon (see Book One, Chapter 7, 'Demons and *Graha*'), and has to do with the accumulation of all that has been going on after the separation occurred. The impact of that wound is tremendous for it sheds light on my true Intent and Function here. Behind it lies the original energy. When I manage to get there and have a brief experience of it. Then a feeling of bliss pervades me and the dream of separation dissolves to give space to the reality of unity. All the symbols I have been building for ages suddenly collapse and I am left with the energy that was behind them. It can be a sort of enlightenment, but it can also cause panic. All my identifications, habits, safety and ego trips break up and this can cause great pain, even though they were anything but true. That is why the tendency to escape from the direct connection with energy is so strong. And I do it by creating and proliferating symbols, chaotically inflating this universe with new manifestations and plans of expansion. These are like narcotic painkillers. In certain circumstances they can be useful. What is probably wrong is that I have employed them to such an extent that I have become addicted to them. And in order to cure the pain of that addiction I have adopted other painkillers and so on until I come to the point where I am strangled by a gigantic mess and do not have any idea of how to get out of it.

The original energy circulates everywhere and connects everyone and everything there is. On the contrary the ego perception is that of living in symbolic insulated boxes which keep us separate from our environment and all its beings, be they human or non-human. This process is very evident in relationships. I build up special relationships whose purpose is that of concatenating symbols one after the other. First, I separate myself from God, the Guide, the Spirit Circle, the Higher World, the Lower World, etc. That causes a tremendous wound. Then I find myself alone on this boulder spinning in a remote corner of the universe. And the pain of my wound is so unbearable that I need to do something to forget about it. I then locate somebody to act as a symbol for God, the Guide, the Spirit Circle. I fall in love with him or her and this gives me a lot of relief, as it helps me forget about the pain. When I am with him or her I feel united with God, the Guide, the Spirit Circle again. Then something goes wrong and I separate from that special partner. The pain is again unbearable and I have to do something. I then find another symbol (somebody else) to act as the symbol of the previous symbol (the other somebody from whom I have separated myself).The cycle continues as I persist in finding more symbols for symbols of symbols and so on. The more I go on with this story, the more symbols are produced and discarded. They are created by myself and by the fear of facing *Mahagraha*, the primal wound. They cause further pain and complication and keep me apart from the original energy. Its final recovery has to do with going back to square one. It means finding my way through the long concatenation of symbols back to the ultimate experience. This process seems painful to the perception of the ego mind, but no real progress can be made until I am ready to face this return journey.

Aries: This sign begins with the spring, or vernal, equinox, the day when the Sun apparently moves from the southern to the northern hemisphere and day and night have the same duration. It is the moment that marks the lengthening of the time of light. The seasonal period of Aries is that of the explosion of spring: the time when the force of nature, after being hidden for months, comes forth with assertiveness and courage. According to some ancient astrologers the process of separation developed when all the planets were joined in conjunction in Aries. This renders it a cyclical blooming moment for the ego's plan of fragmentation, as well as a major chance to release its insane intention and set off a course of action based on the retrieval of the original unity.

The first sign of the zodiac represents the sudden emergence of a clear and individual conscience out of collective confusion and indefinite darkness. Its energy has a specific pioneering aim within the cycle of the Sacred Circle. At a certain stage, once it has achieved its purpose, it is meant to be given away and dissolved. The aim of the ego is to block and freeze this energy to give form to a separate identity which can only survive in an environment that is also separate. This according to astroshamanism, is the world that most human beings consider as real.

Aries constitutes the purest expression of the ego: the most powerful, but also that which is easiest to identify and heal. The recognition of this kind of ego is generally more direct and devoid of the complications and subtleties which proliferate as the separation develops into other signs. At the stage of Aries, the work consists of giving away the energy which transits through my system and consciously directing it in accordance with my Intent. It is an act of donation and sacrifice which has nothing to do with mortification or pain. It sometimes requires disregarding the ego's desires and giving out energy so that the world may reach its highest goal. At other times it means embracing the *ego's desires* and overtly manifesting them, so that I may reach *my* 'selfish' goal, together with the highest goal. In this process the energy that was frozen and blocked is bound to melt and move to its original source. Aries, like the Lamb of God, is a being that resurrects from death and therefore cannot fear it. And this is indeed the feature of Easter (which always falls under this sign): the resurrection of the Son of God.

First House: The cusp of the first house is the *ascendant*, that is the point that was rising on the eastern horizon at the moment and place of your birth. During a whole day each zodiacal sign moves through this point, taking an average of about two hours. Each of the 360° of the circle rises approximately every four minutes. As a result, to determine the ascendant it is necessary to have a fairly accurate time of birth.

The ascendant indicates an essential position in the journey around the Sacred Circle. The planets close to the ascendant have a powerful influence, as they show – together with the rising sign and the position and aspects of its ruler – the potential qualities and the outer tools that the individual can employ to realise his Intent. The risk of using such qualities to support the ego is very strong here. In contrast to the *immum coeli*, or the cusp of the fourth house (see Sector 4), which may show the ancient identity of the soul, the ascendant relates to where the individual comes into the world and physical life. It is directly connected to the basic horizontal Intent or initiatory path of the soul in the third-dimensional reality. In an ideal context this Intent can be in harmony with the vertical or multidimensional nature of the immum coeli (see Sector 4) and medium coeli (see Sector 10), and align with the Function. If this is not the case, the ascendant easily becomes the source of major conflicts and grievances. When, as it is often the case, the inner nature and expanded perception is not acknowledged or supported by the family and the social environment, the individual gives form to another identity. In order to be accepted and integrated in the ordinary reality, he chooses to give up his multidimensional identity and connections. The latter, although they are authentic and alive, confront him with the fear that comes from not being accepted by the conventional world. And to run from that fear, the ego gives form to a separate identity that begins to move like a puppet around the Sacred Circle. This identity needs to be gradually undone or aligned with the awareness of our multi-dimensional nature before any effective spiritual work can develop.

The ascendant and the first house, besides describing the chief trait of the individual's purpose and characteristics, also give clues about the type of birth one had and the physical appearance or health. This point outlines the distinct individual nature of the subject, his specific orientation and the way he moves his body on the horizontal plane. It is the gateway both to the outer and the inner realm. In astroshamanism it often constitutes the starting and returning point in the exploration of non-ordinary realities. As such it is usually identified by a curtain, gate, cavern, bridge or opening in a tree, through which the person is invited to move at the beginning of a journey and then come back through when the voyage is over.

Mars: The position of Mars in the natal chart provides indications about my natural way to direct energy, the potential for action, what causes me to become angry, what triggers my desires and what I am ready to compete or fight for. Mars constitutes the first step in the process of individuation, how I emerge and separate myself from the collective, and the way of bringing about this process. It shows how I operate to accomplish things and the way sexual energy can be used to experience deep fulfilment or connection with my Intent, as well as the type of partners that I draw and all areas of potential conflicts in relationships. It is the primeval and biological urge which can either preserve the perception of the ego's hallucination or be directed into a process of undoing aimed at disclosing the original reality of unity.

In a man the position of Mars generally depicts the particular masculine archetype he identifies with or aspires to, whereas in a woman it may be similar to Jung's concept of *animus* or to the features of demons described in Book One, Chapter 7. The position of Mars in a woman's chart tends to show what aspects of the masculine archetype cause most attraction or are projected onto external partners. Astroshamanic work in this area has to do with the retrieval of these qualities and the development of the *holy relationship*, that is a state in which the inner partner is fully integrated and acknowledged, no matter with whom I am in an external relationship or whether I am in such a relationship at all.

The warrior is related to the energy of Mars in its diurnal and nocturnal representations (Aries and Scorpio respectively). As such it finds a place both in the Direction East and the Direction West, with the former being connected to the visionary, *yang*, outer or enterprising expression and the latter manifesting the transformational, inner, *yin* features. The warrior is overtly promoted through the books of Carlos Castaneda where he is defined as a man of knowledge that moves wide-awake, with unbending intent, clarity of mind, strenuous labour, fear, respect and self-confidence. Obviously, he has nothing to do with conventional human wars. The concept of the warrior is not related to violence or to the aim of killing or destroying somebody or something. The war is against my limits and weaknesses, a fight with the forces that oppose transformation, a battle aimed at retrieving the choice to elect how to be and live. The most typical trait of a warrior is that of striving for impeccability in every moment. Impeccability is the optimum use of power. It is a determination in choosing that which is most aligned with my Intent and giving my best in whatever I do. The warrior is constantly on alert and never surrenders. Even the apparently most insignificant act of his life is seen as a major challenge, the opportunity to go beyond his limits, to express power, to let go of the ego. A warrior has various armaments at his disposal. His fundamental weapon is the unbending *willingness* to hold and manifest his Intent and vision, no matter what. This allows him not to be dragged by the stream of fearful or idle thoughts, and to keep moving on his path. There are no possibilities of compromise here. The warrior makes of every act an ultimate battle in which the awareness of possible death is constantly present. Death is indeed one of his greatest allies, as it permits him to keep a noble sense of detachment toward everything and everyone. Using willingness, strategy, impeccability, control, and the ceaseless awareness of his imminent death, he learns to reduce his needs to a minimum. In this way life becomes very simple, as it is built upon continuous decisions and choices aimed at aligning him with his Intent. This creates joy and love in every moment. As he is not burdened and manipulated by his illusory needs and goals, he can access the dimensions of unlimited abundance which exist beyond the hallucination of scarcity prevalent in conventional reality.

Basic Practices

a. Using the guidelines (given in Book One, Chapter 7, 'Connection with the Totem Spirit' or Book Two, 'Introduction, Basic Practices, Exploration of Sectors') meet the Totem Spirit of Sector 1.

b. Activate the piece for Sector 1 of your Sacred Circle Pieces (see Book One, Chapter 4, 'The Sacred Circle Pieces' or Book Two, 'Introduction, Basic Practices, The Sacred Circle Pieces').

c. Choose one of the following practices ('Healing Tools') and do it daily, every other day or three times per week, for at least 21 days.

Healing Tools

1. **Movements:** Those of Sector 1 involve giving and receiving a lot of energy which can be used to summon physical strength when doing heavy work or feeling weak. A typical dance rhythm consists of a series of sharp, angular, fast, powerful movements, with a clear beginning and end, accompanied by rapid and deep exhalations. All movements which evoke a sense of emergency, combat, assertiveness, competition, hunting, etc. are ideal for dances in this sector. A typical situation, which can be imagined, is that of pushing your way through a crowded railway station in order to catch a train which is about to leave. Put your mind in your third and second chakra, focus your attention there and draw energy from the legs and belly. You can try these movements regularly for at least seven minutes.

2. **Release:** The material to be released in Sector 1 relates to the process of assertion of the ego-dominated identity and to the huge proliferation of grievances which result from the obvious impossibility of truly asserting this identity, due to the fundamental illusion on which it is based. Well, this is a breathless statement! An example of release practice follows: after opening the Sacred Circle and calling your Guide, visualise a sphere of red light moving through all parts of your body. As it moves, invite each grievance to come out into the open. State with clarity your intention to let them go. Then allow them to gradually be released so that you can acknowledge what they are about. As grievances are released, let the red sphere move around them and your body. Be aware of the areas of your body which feel stronger or weaker. Allow energy to be released from those areas. To support this process, if you wish, you can move your body or send out sounds. If there is anger, relinquish it in a way which is safe for you and your environment. Give your consent so that all the energy you release can be used as fertiliser for your Intent and to bring love, peace and ecstasy into your life and that of the world. All forms of attack or anger are desperate attempts to project the guilt and the load of one's inner grievances on an external object. Anger has no reason to exist unless I perceive myself as separate and believe that I am attacked and therefore justified in defending myself by attacking as well. Anger is given form through attacks which then result in guilt and the consequent fear of a punishment. Such fear of an imminent punishment generates further anger and so this insane cycle proliferates until it manifests a whole universe based on anger, guilt and fear.

3. **Assertion:** Sector 1 can offer great opportunities to embarrass the ego and all its ideas about how things should be. A useful way is that of using some assertion exercises. This means doing whatever would make the ego uncomfortable or awkward. For example: buying a second class stamp with a £100 banknote without expressing any kind of excuse; getting a salesperson to give you a refund for something that you purchased and that you do not like any more; not respecting a long queue at the post office; being direct and saying what you feel disregarding what other people may think of you.

4. **Cathartic or Chaotic Techniques:** In the beginning, when you start to explore the inner world, after the first

images of enchantment and ecstasy, that often operate as baits, it is rare to have pleasant experiences. Many people give up meditation or shamanic work because they fear they are on the verge of mental breakdown and do not know how to deal with what is triggered by their practices. It is at this stage that cathartic or chaotic techniques can help. In this context, all practices that allow the release of anger, without causing damage to yourself or others, are particularly associated with Sector 1. 'When you feel angry, there is no need to be angry with someone; just be angry. Let it be a meditation. Close the room, sit by yourself, and let the anger come up as much as it can. If you feel like beating, beat a pillow. Do whatsoever you want to do; the pillow will never object... One can never imagine how helpful a pillow can be. Just beat it, bite it, throw it... You will feel ridiculous, foolish, but anger is ridiculous; you cannot do anything about it. So let it be and enjoy it like an energy phenomenon. It is an energy phenomenon. If you are not hurting anybody there is nothing wrong in it. When you try this you will see that the idea of hurting somebody by and by disappears. Make it a daily practice – just twenty minutes every morning. Then watch the whole day. You will be calmer, because the energy that becomes anger has been thrown out; the energy that becomes a poison is thrown out of the system. Do this for at least two weeks.'[2] Various of Osho's meditation techniques, such as *Dynamic Meditation* and *Mandala,* are useful to activate and heal Sector 1.[3] The majority of these meditations start with stages of intense release – through jumping, wild movements, chaotic breathing, shouting, etc. – and end with stillness and silence.

Another exercise to release anger and repressed energy consists in *panting like a dog.* Here you hang out your tongue, and move around panting like a dog. Do this daily for 15 minutes in the course of 21 days. Practice this in the intimacy of your room or in a place where nobody can hear or intrude. You can also use a mirror and watch yourself, barking and growling at your image. Be total in this exercise and allow your body to be completely involved.

5. **Physical Exercise:** Running, jogging or other physical exercise, when performed as a sacred act, can be powerful tools for balancing the energy of Sector 1 and the whole Circle. When I run with totality, the stream of conventional

thoughts ceases to obstruct my awareness, blocks are released and the energy can freely circulate. A technique consists of running at high speed on the spot for a minimum of twelve minutes, preferably naked, lifting the knees up to the level of the navel, stretching the arms upward (or moving them up and down), shouting aloud or inwardly, and using a drumming tape. Another possibility consists of running very fast in a natural environment, continuing until you feel so exhausted that you fall down on the ground.

6. **The Medicine Walk:** This is a journey taken in the ordinary reality, yet with the same attitude employed during a shamanic journey. A full day is suggested for this experience and you need to be alone. If possible, it is preferable to start the walk at dawn. Choose a place in nature that especially draws you. Take a water bottle, your journal and pen, drawing material and some of your sacred tools. Do not take any food or avoid eating anything until the sun sets. Please also be aware that this walk is not an ordeal or act of endurance. Its aim is to ground your highest Intent in the natural environment and achieve a state of balance between ordinary and non-ordinary reality. Begin and end the walk with a ceremony. Focus on your Intent, then start and walk. As you wander, be alert. Sense where you are drawn and move in that direction. Be aware of the beings (relatives, partners, friends, teachers, etc.) that come to your mind as you walk. Remember that thinking about other people is as shamanically effective as physically meeting them. Exercise forgiveness and express your true feelings towards whoever you meet. During the walk you are going to find an object that you can take as a significator of your walk. Make sure that you give something in return (seeds, hair, saliva, etc.), once you have picked up that object. Conclude the walk with a brief ceremony and report your experience in your journal.

7. **I Statements:** One major potential related to Sector 1 is its capacity to release the social conditioning of the plural or impersonal identity which reflects in patterns of speech based on *you* and all kinds of similar generalisations. Use *I statements*. Try replacing the pronoun *you* with *I* as much as you can. Notice how you feel in all those instances and be aware also of how others perceive you.

8. **The Paheka Sadohe Korah** (Chant of the Totem Spirits and Guides): For Sector 1 this chant is *Kahe Pahe Sadoh*. Please

use this practice only if you intend to establish or support a regular relationship with the Totem Spirit of Sector 1. If you intend to use this chant, you can either sing it from time to time to accompany a cycle of twelve shamanic journeys in Sector 1 or as a practice on its own to be done preferably once or twice a day for at least seven minutes during a period of 21 days.[4]

9. **The Chant and Scale of Mars:** When you are in situations of anger, irritability, strong sexual desire or have difficulties in relating to your energy; do not manage to express it openly; feel yourself impotent, debilitated, repressed, tense, destructive, furious, horrified, mad (and the hell knows what else), the Chant and Scale of Mars can be used. Its chant is:

Naizy Day Hoh Hi Mah, Naizy Day Hoh Hi Mah,

Naizy Day Hoh Hi Mah,

Naizy Day Hoh Hi Mah, Kah Kah

The simple pronunciation of the chant is sufficient to draw energy when you feel tired or need to make a special effort, like lifting weights or climbing a long set of stairs. This chant operates on the energetic body as a whole and uses the colour red. If you employ the Sacred Circle, sit or stand in Sector 1 or the sector where Mars is positioned in your natal chart. You can also stay in the sector where Mars is transiting at the moment. After calling the Guide, according to your habitual procedures, connect with your Intent. Then sing the Chant of Mars. Continue the practice, moving gradually from lower (anger, aggression, competition, etc.) to higher expressions of Mars (courage, clarity, enthusiasm, etc.).[5]

Astroshamanic Reports

On a day of new moon in Aries I received guidance to hold a medicine walk in the nature area near my birthplace so as to get a vision for the new annual cycle. Upon entering the park, I was about to go straight to the *Great Tree* (the name I used for the most prominent tree in the area), when I felt drawn to move in the opposite direction, towards a large hill full of trees and usually unattended by people. I chose to head that way. As I was climbing uphill I received an inner message to find other sacred places besides the Great Tree, as it was not suitable for the type of work required in the next cycle. I ascended along a narrow footpath and then reached a spot with a tree. It immediately looked familiar. It was the first sacred place that I activated in the park many years ago. I was amazed to find the medicine wheel which I placed there at that time. I smudged and cleaned the spot and then connected with my Guide. Through him I contacted the Spirit of Sector 1 and was given information for this new cycle. Among the instructions received was that of taking up a new practice for the whole annual cycle: activating and working with one tree for every sector according to the movement of the Sun in each sign of the zodiac. Every tree would then become a sacred site aimed at channelling the energy and releasing the grievances of that particular sector. I was also told to pay more regular visits to these places in nature. This idea gave me a lot of excitement. The tree where I received this vision became the tree of Sector 1, the first one of the series. After this connection I rearranged the stones of the medicine wheel and left some seeds of spelt-wheat as my give-away. As I did that a spider fell down on the precise spot where the seeds had been placed. That gave me great joy. After other ritual procedures I descended along another path so as to reach the original Great Tree. As I watched the Great Tree from the hill, I noticed how prominent and distinct from all other trees it was. I was aware that the routine of my medicine walks had to change. I would first go to the tree of the sector of the month, have a celebration and inner journey there, then move to the Great Tree and stay there for a little time. The Great Tree, I was told, was not a suitable place for rituals and journeys any more. As I approached the Great Tree I saw some material around it. When I went nearer I discovered that the municipality had just installed two large benches and wide tables, together with a dustbin, very close to the Tree. This material was still wrapped. Around the dustbin there was a note that somebody had put saying: 'Aren't you ashamed to put a dustbin next to the most beautiful and ancient tree in the park. We will take legal action about it!'. I was amazed and a bit irritated at first. I realised that soon the place would lose all its power and become a regular venue for people playing cards, eating and chatting. I was almost about to join the protest. Then I became aware that this was not my story. Everything was all right the way it was. I understood the reason for the messages and the detour, and was grateful to the Spirit of the park for that experience. After a few days I went again to the tree of Sector 1: there I had other beautiful experiences. Then I moved to the Great Tree. The benches were already operative and full of retired people playing cards. I sat on a nearby rock and communicated with the Tree. My first reaction last time had been one of irritation with the municipality for having *profaned* a sacred place in such a way. Now I had the confirmation that there was nothing wrong. On the contrary it was beautiful to see those people gathering and enjoying the energy of the Great Tree. And on noticing the dustbin so prominent by the Great Tree, I laughed at its implications. It was for me an official acknowledgement of all the release work I had done there for years.

These are some excerpts taken from my early journals:

I reach the area of access to Sector 1. It reveals itself as a long path cutting through a desert and leading to a pass made of two big horns. From there I can enter into Sector 1. Climatic conditions are very hard and in order to proceed further I need to focus strenuously on my Intent. As I approach the pass, I see a predatory bird hovering right at the entrance. I understand it is waiting for me. Once I arrive on the spot, it descends and glowers menacingly at me. I am aware that it wants to prevent me from entering. I also understand that here it is not a question of finding an agreement. If I want to enter, I have to fight and kill the bird. Although this sounds appalling, I am invited to put the bird to death, unless I decide that I want to be put to death myself. The sense of compassion and unity typical of Sector 12 does not make any sense here. How is it possible? I wonder. However unacceptable I may feel it to fight and kill, I notice here the connection with another form of melting. Although apparently cruel and ruthless, it is indeed unity. The other, once it has been seemingly annihilated, becomes part of me. It is a union based on a sacrifice. After a brief fight, I kill the bird and pour all its blood over me. I finally cross the pass and enter into the territory of Sector 1. There I meet a warrior with a thick sword, a shield and a horned helmet. I realise at once that he is also one with whom it is impossible to come to any agreement. Either he kills me or I kill him. In this case the enterprise seems more difficult than with the bird. After a fierce fight, I kill him. I then march towards a fortress. When I arrive, the gate is closed. I knock it down, surprising myself by the amount of strength that I have. Once inside the fortress, I find myself surrounded by the guardians of the place. They are ready to fight with me. I draw my sword and begin to cut them to pieces. Then I am assaulted by other types of guardians. They are invisible. Battling with them is quite exhausting. In the end I manage to decimate them all. Now I seem to be alone in the fortress. I shout and challenge anyone else who wants to fight to come forward. I realise that nobody is left. There is only me in the fortress. There is also the Totem Spirit of Sector 1. I cannot see him.

I do realise that he is indeed inside myself. I tell him (and myself) that I am fed up with all this fighting. Yet I feel that there is another challenge waiting for me. Bravely I provoke it to come forward. In that precise moment I hear the telephone ringing in the ordinary reality of my flat. It is like a penetrating knife. After a while I can hear the voice coming from the answering machine. It is a friend of mine. I am tempted to run and answer the phone. With a strenuous effort I try to remain in the non-ordinary reality. Yet the force which tries to take me out is unbearable. I understand that this is the challenge I had invited. Once this is clear to me, I immediately know what to do. After asking the Guide reassurance that my act is not going to affect the ego reality of my friend, I face her inner form in the fiercest fight so far. It is much longer than all the others and at certain stages I am almost about to succumb. My body is bleeding abundantly. Then I am reminded about my sword. I draw it and kill that inner form. I hear a voice within shouting, 'There is now nothing outside of me, everything is within me!' I begin to chant and then I rest. After a while I sense the energy of Mars approaching and I immediately put myself in position to fight. 'Calm down now!' he says. 'There's only you and nothing else but you with your Intent. You are alone here in Sector 1. You care only about you, exterminating whatever is not you, as nothing else exists.' His words are ruthless, yet they make a lot of sense. I ask the Guide to explain what has happened. I do realise how in this process I have almost forgotten about him. 'In Sector 1,' the Guide explains, 'you are alone and wipe away all there is. This allows you to start from square one and in accordance with a new Intent. In Sector 1 you mobilise the force of the warrior, that of clarity and initiation. It is a situation of emergency where vision has to be strategically lucid. This force is brute and instinctive. The warrior is the first bulwark. As such it is rarely acknowledged or is manipulated by so-called antagonistic forces. These forces play a major role in Sector 1. The warrior is often projected onto people or situations that stimulate open or hidden conflicts. It is a question of facing such figures in their inner form and suppressing them. The first step is to disregard the shadows of the outer projections and face the inner adversary in order to become the adversary itself. There is no possibility of compromise. In Sector 1 there are only two options: to suppress or be suppressed. Also those who do not find themselves in an apparent state of adversity are suppressed. It does not matter how loving your relationship with them is, in the work on Sector 1 you remain alone. Each external component is incorporated and aggressively drawn toward the Intent. The second step allows you to dwell in the devastated land of your war. Here you can perceive your power and the radical responsibility in taking a new course. With the third step your individual story joins the collective. The strategic aim of the preceding phases is now evident. The linking with the universal epic is imminent. In this context you retrieve your true sense of belonging and repeat the process of the first step, not alone, this time, but together with all your allies and others. The incorporation of the adversary takes place at a collective level until only in all and in the whole you find your total authentic identification. The individual story and fight connect with the myth that all beings of this universe share.'

[1] *Level 2* is associated with the mental realm and with the split mind which dominates or affects most seen and unseen beings currently living in this universe. It includes the ego thought system based on the illusion of separation and the residual memories or reflections of thought systems founded on unity. Level 2 constitutes the causative source of Level 1 and the agent of choice between either the preservation and expansion or retrieval and undoing of the fragmented universe produced by the ego. The theme of the levels is addressed in Book One, Chapter 2, 'The Three Levels'.

[2] Osho, *The Orange Book,* Rajneesh Foundation, 1983, pp. 41-42. (This book, which contains a wide range of meditation techniques, is out of print and is currently replaced by Osho, *Meditation: The First and Last Freedom,* St. Martin's Press, New York, 1996).

[3] For detailed information about these techniques, consult Osho, *Meditation: The First and Last Freedom,* St. Martin's Press, New York, 1996 or *Osho International Foundation,* (http://www.osho.com).

[4] *Paheka Sadohe Korah* (Chants of the Totem Spirits and Guides) are chants that activate the energy field of each sector and allow connection with their Totem Spirits and Auxiliary Guides. Their structure involves the repetition of the name of the Totem Spirit followed by the term *Sadoh* (which can generally be translated as 'Spirit Guide'). If you elect to employ these chants please read further information contained in Book One, Chapter 9, 'Chants of the Totem Spirits and Guides'.

[5] The planetary chants, channelled by Andrew Ramer and introduced by Donna Cunningham (see: Donna Cunningham, *Astrology and Spiritual Development,* Cassandra Press, 1989, pp. 105-116), consist of a series of sounds connected to the astrological planets. Their function is that of sending out vibrations that allow the activation of high levels of energy. If you choose to practise the chants please read the information contained in Book One, Chapter 9, 'The System of the Planetary Scales' and also refer to Donna Cunningham's above mentioned book.

SECTOR TWO

~ SIGN: Taurus ~ HOUSE: Second ~
~ PLANET: 1) Venus, Earth. 2) Vulcan ~
~ RAY: 5th (Concrete Knowledge/Science), 1st (Will/Power) ~
~ ELEMENT: Earth ~ QUALITY: Fixed ~ DIRECTION: East ~
~ SEASON: Spring ~ TOTEM SPIRIT: Rata Sahe Pah ~
~ EPIC STATES: Trent, Tnert. ~

ANIMALS:	They have a strong connection with the earth, robust bodies and often good voices. Buffalo, bull, cattle, elephant, lark, tortoise.
PLANTS:	Often with attractive and pleasant features, tasty fruits, green and smooth leave. Almond, apple, apricot, beet, cherry, daisy, dandelion, flax, ginger, larkspur, lily, moss, myrtle, peach, pear, plantain, plum, rhubarb, rose, spinach, strawberry, verbena.
MINERALS:	Agate, alabaster, aquamarine, chrysocolla, clay, emerald, jade, jasper, kunzite, lapis lazuli, magnetite, rose quartz, sapphire.
SPIRITS:	Anaele (*Angels*); Coatlicue (*Aztec*); Aine (*Celtic*); St. Simon (*Christian*); Bastet, Geb (*Egyptian*); Aphrodite, Ariadne, Astarte, Daedalus, Dyonisus, Europa, Hephaestus, Minotaur, Theseus (*Greek*); Brahma, Ganesh, Kubera, Lakshmi, Uma (*Hindu*); Freya (*Nordic*); Venus, Mithra, Vulcan (*Roman*); Ki (*Sumerian*). Hierophant, Empress (*Tarot*).
ANATOMY/ PHYSIOLOGY:	Mouth, neck, thyroid gland, throat, voice.

ASSOCIATIONS:	Food, earth, gardening, money, possessions, resources, land, property, prosperity, physical form, matter, sensuality, beauty, furniture, sculpture, art, architecture, music.
COLOURS:	Red-orange.
DETECTORS:	5th brother/sister of mother, partner of 2nd brother/sister of mother, friends of mother, employer of 1st son/daughter, 2nd brother/sister of father, 5th brother/sister of mother, mother of friends. 1-2, 12-3, 11-4, 10-5, 9-6, 8-7, 7-8, 6-9, 5-10, 4-11, 3-12.
GRIEVANCES:	*Excess:* avidity, fear and denial of non-material and unpleasant aspects of life (death, illness, spirit, etc.), greed, materialism, over-eating, over-indulgence, over-sensuality, possessiveness, stubbornness, resistance. *Deficit:* incapacity to experience pleasure and enjoyment of physical world, lack of practical sense, money problems. *Physical:* angina, diabetes, diphtheria, hyper-cholesterol, over-eating, over-weight, sore-throat, thyroid malfunction.
QUALITIES:	Calmness, comfort, contentment, delight, determination, ease, enjoyment, patience, pleasure, practicality, receptivity, relaxation, rest, security, serenity, simplicity, stability, steadfastness, well-being.

With Sector 2, I enter into the land of form, matter, prosperity and what is generally considered to be physical. This sector appears as the most evident trait of the perception that human beings have of planet Earth, and is exalted by the key identification of the ego: the physical body. The body is a basic element in human hallucinatory and separated perception. 'There is no dream without it, nor does it exist without the dream in which it acts as if it were a person to be seen and be believed. It takes the central place in every dream, which tells the story of how it was made by other bodies, born into the world outside the body, lives a little while and dies, to be united in the dust with other bodies dying like itself. In the brief time allotted it to live, it seeks for other bodies as its friends and enemies. Its safety is its main concern. Its comfort is its guiding rule.'[1] According to this understanding, the physical body is the manifestation of the thought of separation and the hiding place for nourishing guilt and resentment out of the illusive idea of having been abandoned by God. On the same basis, it is also a neutral device whose aim is defined by the mind, a symbolic tool for connecting the Intent to the Function and a major instrument for undoing the ego's separate reality.

The astonishing thing about the physical body is the fact that there is not a single instant in which it exists as it seems to be. There is indeed nothing solid or fixed in the body. It is an aggregation of infinite units moving and transforming themselves at a speed that the ordinary perception refuses to acknowledge. This gives the illusive impression of a static form. By journeying into Sector 2, I have the opportunity to probe the real consistency of the body and to honour it as a sacred symbolic learning device.

According to A Course in Miracles, gnosticism and various ancient mystery schools, the physical body and the Earth, as human beings perceive them, were not created by a loving God. This view is basically different from that of most traditional religions as they express themselves at Level 1. Here the world and the bodies moving on its surface simply represent the projection of my separate identity and, as a matter of fact, they do not exist. 'The body is a fence the Son of God imagines he has built, to separate parts of his Self from other parts. It is within this fence he thinks he lives, to die as it decays and crumbles.'[2] This awareness is also the fundamental understanding of many esoteric spiritual teachings at Level 2. Yet, the physical dimension is the basic expression of the ego system and, as such, it cannot be liquidated so easily. Religious traditions have often distorted and misunderstood the role of matter and the physical body, or have provided explanations suitable for the level of communication of their people. It follows that there are many misconceptions on this topic. Certain teachings appear to deny or discount the importance of the earthly aspects of life, to the point that total or partial abstinence from some physical functions and the denial of material pleasure are often considered essential for spiritual development. It is true that some forms of abstinence and austerity can serve as effective strategic devices and contribute to achieving results. This occurs when they are operated by balanced individuals or in a context that provides the necessary support. On the contrary, if such practices are not used with care, consequences can be painful and sustain the consolidation of the sense of separation that they purport to undo. Yet here it is not a question of inviting abstention from so-called material pleasures. The physical body is not negative, it is simply neutral and, as such, it solely assumes the role of an instrument of communication. In this regard it can only be employed in two possible ways: to express love and unity or to promote hate and separation. What counts is the Intent, not what the body does or does not do.

According to holistic vision humanity is a channel connecting Heaven and Earth. Its specific function is not that of closing the doors to material life and ascending to the peaks of Heaven. This latter attitude is expressed in the classical fracture between Spirit and Matter (or belly and head, Lower World and Higher World). Some esoteric traditions tell us that in living beings energy follows a natural flow of ascent and descent based on the principle of *polarity*. According to this principle, the presence of two opposite polarities determines a condition in which the energy is moved, and then supported through the reciprocal exchange of the two extremities themselves. Without this movement, there would not be any life. In brief, energy descends from the Higher World (or Heaven), and is drawn down into the Lower World (or Earth). At the same time, energy moves to its point of origin through the magnetism of the Higher World on the Lower, and so on. When a correct connection between Lower and Higher Worlds is lacking, energy does not flow freely and generates zones of stagnation and condensation, of energetic deficit or excess. Among people open to non-ordinary reality or with strong prevalence of Sectors 3, 7, 11 and 12 in the natal chart, there is often the tendency to lose connection with the Lower World and the Earth. When this happens, although their visions and experiences can be outstanding, they tend to be unable to manifest practical objectives in their lives or to be blocked constantly by material and physical difficulties of all kinds.

In Sector 2, all material goods and forms of all kinds can contribute to the realisation of my Intent. Here everything is considered according to its most immediate connection to the dense physical dimension. There is no space for theories, ideas or abstract thoughts. Everything is seen in a factual way as either black or white. What counts is only the tangible reality that is accepted by most human beings. This represents a test zone for mystics or very idealistic people, as it confronts them with their physical presence and data that can only be measured and touched at Level 1. When Sector 2 is mastered through a complete experience of the symbols of physical reality and, in particular, of basic symbols such as the material body and money, a deep grounding is established. This allows progress on a spiritual journey with more authenticity and power. The life of Siddharta Gautama (the Buddha) is a perfect example. The path that led him to enlightenment was not the result of sacrifice or repression of material life. On the contrary it was the outcome of a spontaneous dissatisfaction stemming from 29 years spent in a most wealthy and pleasant environment.

Taurus: The seasonal time of this sign corresponds to the fullest expression of spring, between the equinox and the solstice. It is a time of abundant vegetation, green fields, blooming flowers and newborn animals. The resources of the Earth are available in great quantity and physical beings are often pervaded by a strong feeling of pleasure and sensuality that favours romances and procreation.

At Level 1, Taurus is a builder that shapes ideas into concrete form, laying foundations, employing amazing reserves of energy and also appreciating all pleasant aspects of life and the gifts from the Earth. Whereas Aries is impulsive and direct, Taurus is slow, constant and patient. The first sign of the zodiac is a pioneer that, after a harsh fight, succeeds in conquering the land and planting the seed. The second sign takes possession of what is conquered and starts to build and grow. Its spiritual challenge is that of giving its resources to a higher Intent and of being willing to connect it to the Function.

Second House: Whereas in the first house the individual defines his identity and Intent, in the second house he begins to move horizontally to satisfy what he believes he is and to give form to his Intent. Here he advances in the world and establishes foundations for the development of his existence. This house is related with material and portable goods and with resources or values at any level. It indicates the attitude toward money and all that can be owned (cars, food, furniture, jewels, etc.). The physical body and the identification with the ego is the main possession of human beings and the basic dilemma of the second house regards the way this temporary form of existence can be used.

Venus and Earth: Venus is the planet traditionally associated with Taurus. According to classical astrology Venus rules both Taurus and Libra. As with Gemini and Virgo, both ruled by Mercury, this double rulership emphasises a missing planetary energy. Before the discovery of Uranus, Neptune and Pluto, other pairs of signs (Aquarius–Capricorn, Pisces–Sagittarius, Scorpio–Aries) shared the rulership of the same planet (i.e. Saturn, Jupiter and Mars respectively). Then, the new planets took over the rulership. As for Taurus there are contrasting opinions among astrologers. In astroshamanism what matters is to be experientially aware of the characteristic of the energy of a planet rather than of its denomination. Sector 2 is a very earthy energy that was attributed to Venus due to the confusion generated after the decay of female goddesses. Sector 2 relates with a planetary energy that at Level 1 can be identified with the Earth and at Level 2 with Vulcan, the esoteric ruler of Taurus. As the astrological chart has a geocentric nature, planet Earth is seldom considered, for it corresponds to the point of the observer. In order to spot the Earth on the chart, one has to take a heliocentric perspective and, in this instance, this planet is directly opposite the Sun. The position of the Earth can give information about the way in which the Intent can be expressed or grounded on this planet and can also provide indications on what the Earth is asking me to do or be. Vulcan is supposed to be situated between Mercury and the Sun. It is considered by some esoteric astrologers to be the most powerful planet of the solar system, which may explain why it has yet to be discovered. It is associated with the power at the core of the Sun that connects our central star with the centre of the universe.

Basic Practices

a. Using the guidelines (given in Book One, Chapter 7, 'Connection with the Totem Spirit' or Book Two, 'Introduction, Basic Practices, Exploring the Sectors') meet the Totem Spirit of Sector 2.

b. Activate the piece for Sector 2 of your Sacred Circle Pieces (see Book One, Chapter 4, 'The Sacred Circle Pieces' or Book Two, Basic Practices, 'The Sacred Circle Pieces').

c. Choose one of the following practices ('Healing Tools') and do it daily, every other day or three times per week, for at least 21 days.

Healing Tools

1. **Activity of Pleasure:** Opening up to the energy of Sector 2 can often produce strong involvement of the physical body and its senses. The more the body is contributing to the voyage, the stronger the effects usually are. In this sector it is important to allow the enjoyment of experiences that give pleasure. Go to your Spirit Circle, call your Guide and ask him to take you to a place where you can thoroughly enjoy something that you like. Engage totally, as if it were happening in that moment. Do it for at least five or ten minutes. Stay in touch with your feelings and responses. What gives you pleasure? Where do you feel good? Do you feel pleasure or strong sensations all over your body, or just in certain parts? Which of your physical senses are involved? Can you choose to involve any other senses? Can you stay with what you feel without judging or controlling? Are you at ease with just feeling good, or do you need to have a purpose?

2. **Sacred Sites and Ceremonial Lands:** The creation and the attendance of sacred sites and ceremonial lands is another feature of Sector 2. *Sacred sites* are points where the physical reality meets with the spiritual and non-ordinary reality. Some of them were created by ancient cultures; some are the result of recent human actions; while others are the manifestation of events caused by nature, unseen beings and Totem Spirits. *Ceremonial lands* are spaces used to perform rituals or sacred activities. All human traditions have sacred sites and ceremonial lands. Sometimes they are unknown, as they have not been attended for ages or are only visited by a few people. Some common phenomena that occur in such places are: feelings of unity with the environment, calmness and slowing down of time, expansion of the aura or a sense of embracement by some larger presence, altered states of perception, loss of the sense of identification with the ego. Also the feeling of being observed by somebody as you walk, for example, in a wood or by a river can often indicate that you are in a sacred site. When you visit such places, take something with you as a give-away (herbs, incense, seeds, etc.) and do a simple and brief ritual. Also take care of the place. For example, if there

is rubbish there, you can collect it and throw it away. Spend some time there and use it as a physical representation of your Spirit Circle.

3. **Communicating with Money:** Money represents a typical way in which the grounding energy of Sector 2 can become explicit. Four basic laws are generally described as regards money and the use of material resources: *earning, saving, spending, and investing.* Those who are capable of mastering these four laws in their material existence, once they approach spiritual life, can easily have stable and lasting experiences. Normally most people tend to have difficulties with one or more laws. These problems are related to grievances and conditioning existing in the subtle bodies. In order to be released they require inner deprogramming rather than outer economic operations. A most typical grievance related to money is to worry or complain about it. Whenever this occurs it is better to stop and think or do something else. To worry or complain about money has never helped anybody to improve his financial situation. The use of tools, such as affirmations, prosperity rituals, shamanic journeys or contracts with Totem Spirits and specialised Guides, can facilitate understanding about the true motivations of one's relationship with money. An interesting feature about money is that it constitutes the basic thought and intent for the majority of human beings at Level 1. Yet, only a small minority find the time to truly communicate with money. Establishing a direct relationship with money is the essential step for getting to know what such a substance really implies. A group of people lead by Roberto Assaggioli, the founder of Psychosynthesis, at the end of each day used a practice that consisted in placing all the money they had in their purses or pockets on an altar. Then these people would place their hands on that money, transmitting love and blessings. In this way, money, once spent, would continue to carry that beneficial energy. Such practices are useful for those who have problems with money or who wish to contribute to the general well-being of the planet. Money is the visible material that has the most circulation among human beings. It moves from hand to hand, purse to purse, unceasingly charging itself with the vibrations and intents of many beings. My individual responsibility consists of employing money according to my Intent connected with my Function. When I do that, money

becomes the carrier of my sacred motivations and allows them to be guided in all directions. This is an extremely powerful operation, whose implications constitute one of the essential parts of our work on Earth. Each evening or at least three evenings per week, take out all the money you have in your purse or with you. Place it on your altar or in the centre of your Sacred Circle. Then find your way to communicate with that money. State with clarity your Intent and your willingness to connect it with your Function. Place your hands over the money, sending out love and light, and releasing grievances. This is a sacred act that allows money to be used as a tool of power and transformation. In this way, money, once spent or put in a bank, will contribute to communicate your Intent. Money is in itself the major symbolic representation of energy that has been devised on this planet.

4. **Grounding:** This practice is typical of Sector 2. Grounding helps you prepare to let go of the conditioning of ordinary reality and enter a state of ecstatic consciousness. This is another way of activating the Intent and Function. It allows you also to return to a state of ordinary consciousness after you have done shamanic work. There are many grounding methods and after trying some of them you will easily find the one that suit you. Lying on the ground, taking a shower, placing your forehead on the floor, chanting, drumming, breathing deeply are some of the possible examples. The following practice is more elaborate: a) Relax and close your eyes, taking 13 deep breaths. b) Be fully aware of your physical body and of your environment. Bring your attention to the ground below you. If you are inside a building, shift your awareness down until you reach the ground. c) Spend some minutes being aware of the weight of your body and of all that is standing on the Earth around you. Feel the connection with the soil. Then stretch your attention downward, through the layers of rocks and soil, until you come to the core of the Earth. As you descend be aware of the different strata. Feel the Earth as a living being, delighted to receive your attention and willing to be of service to you. d) Once you reach the core of the Lower World below the Earth, open a channel of connection from the base of your spine to the centre of the Earth and anchor it solidly there. This channel is the trunk and root of the Great Tree, a column of light, the central artery of the Sacred Cone. e) Then employ

this connection to release all excess tensions and grievances that you have accumulated during the day. Let them be transmuted by the energy of the centre. After you feel complete, let the energy of the centre rise up through the channel into your body. If you meet with difficulties, ask the support of your Guide. f) Then open up another channel that moves to your head through the stars to reach the centre of the Higher World. Create a connection between the Lower and Higher Worlds through your spine. Be grateful for this connection and enjoy your function as channel. g) Stand up and raise your arms toward the sky, stretching yourself and breathing deeply. State your Intent and face your day with love and energy, reminding yourself of this sacred connection.

5. **Possessions:** To the extent of the degree of my attachment to a possession, a part of my energy is tied up in that possession and is not available for expanding my perception and awareness. Some spiritual paths or tribes require that their members renounce all their belongings or give them to the community. This act represents a way to express the willingness to release any attachment that would affect the power needed to attain major spiritual goals. The simple intention or availability to do this is enough, as it allows looking at or managing one's possessions with an attitude that does not create dependence. It is good practice to get rid of what no longer serves in a productive way. It is also very important to complete any unfinished work or plan. The mind keeps the data of all our decisions and promises. If I tell myself that I want to learn German, buy a course with tapes and books, and yet never manage to finish it, a portion of my energy is hooked to what I said I wanted to do. To the extent that my energy is tied elsewhere, I have less energy for other tasks and for spiritual work. Examine your possessions and consider those things that you are not using any more or that you have never used. Reflect on whether you intend to carry on the projects or ideas related to those objects. If this is the case, commit yourself to manifesting them and set a date or time of work. If you realise that you are not truly willing to use those materials, let go of them. Find somebody who wants to purchase them or swap them for something that you want now. You can also give them as a present to somebody that needs them, offer them to a charity or throw them away.

6. **Relationship with Trees and Nature:** This is an important aspect of astroshamanism and constitutes one of the best ways to activate the energy of Sector 2. During this time of the year you can decide, as part of your practice, to spend regular time outside in nature. It would be ideal to be in nature every day or every other day for at least half an hour. If it is not possible for you to leave town, you can go regularly even to a small public park and then visit a natural place out of town at least three times this month. I invite you to find a specific spot that you can acknowledge as your place of power. Look for a place where you can feel comfortable, secure and well. First work with your imagination and find the spot there. Make sure that it is your ideal place and enjoy it for a while. Be aware of your body and scan its feelings. Then search for this spot in the outer environment and notice what is happening to your body according to where it goes or stops. Monitor the changes in your body and see which parts are involved. When you have found a suitable area, spend at least 15 minutes there. Visit it regularly and be aware of your body feelings.

7. **The Paheka Sadohe Korah** (Chant of the Totem Spirits and Guides): For Sector 2 the chant is *Rata Sahe Pah Sadoh.* Please use this practice only if you intend to establish or support a regular relationship with the Totem Spirit of Sector 2. If you intend to use this chant, you can either sing it from time to time to accompany a cycle of twelve shamanic journeys in Sector 2 or as a practice on its own to be done preferably once or twice a day for at least seven minutes during a period of 21 days.[3]

8. **The Planetary Chant and Scale:** For Sector 2 the planetary chant is both that of Venus:

   Nah Ti Nah, Nah Ti Nah, Nah Ti Nah, Nah Ti Nah, Oh.
   And Earth and Moon:

   Si Idriah, Si Idriah, Si Idriah, Si Idriah, Neh Hah Mah Set

   The Scale of Venus (see Sector 7) applied to Sector 2 emphasises the earthy aspects of this planet (sensuality, pleasure, patience, etc.). The Scale of Earth and Moon (see Sector 4) is here related to form, matter, grounding, manifestation, and possessions.[4]

Astroshamanic Reports

Here follows the report of two of my first visits to Sector 2:

As soon as I activate my Intent and bring it to a peak I am transported into a place from where I contemplate an immense and familiar crystal sphere. As the sphere slowly rotates, it sends out the invitation to join it, leaving behind whatever is grieving. As I choose to approach the crystal sphere, I am soon overwhelmed by an ecstatic silence of joy and awareness, by a reassuring sense of void: a void that I can fill with whatever lies in my heart, be it love, passion, bliss, songs, dance. I stay there for a while, and then I operate according to the specific instructions I received on my previous journey. As I connect with the Guide, I revise the events of my preceding journey. [...] Then I enter Sector 2. I am asked to state my local Intent, i.e. the reason for my visit in that specific sector. 'My Local Intent,' I declare, 'is that of grounding my sacred dream and taking full responsibility for being on this planet and in this body.' My admission to Sector 2 is accepted. I am invited to use a specific drumbeat and I do so. I hear the voice of the Totem Spirit of Sector 2: 'In Sector 2 you honour the form, whatever is material and you can touch with your hands, everything which is solid. You connect with the Spirit of Form and let it become your ally. That's the basic condition here. You touch whatever you encounter and feel the form, entering into a supportive connection. All physical forms can give support to you. Any of them can carry your Intent if only you are willing that this be so. You ground your Intent here and are responsible for implementing your dream. With the help of the Totem Spirit you allow your dream to become a physical manifestation. You are alert and vigilant. Whatever you see, connect with that form and ask support, make an alliance, for you share the same Intent. The alliance can spread all over. You go into the other through touching, and by doing that you overcome all types of grievances. That is the gift of Sector 2. Take this gift. [...] Through it you can connect with everything in the world. You proclaim your Intent and then feel the support and comfort of all that surrounds you. You can either give it or receive it: it's just the same. Are you determined to create a cosmic family, to connect the outer with the inner, to let your dream become a reality, to go about and see all the ecstatic shapes that elude ordinary sight? This is a great Intent and we are ready to support it! You have our power by touching. Touch the gift and what you see in the inner is going to be given form in the outer. That's our power and yours: to create the dream and give it concrete form. The Spirit of this sector is in all forms and by touching the gift you can feel Him/Her.'

I ask the Spirit how I can give form to my astroshamanic work [at that time I was about to start it]. The Spirit replies: 'You pay regular daily visits. You don't get stuck with theories. Visiting means having experiences with us. It also means to attend to all practices, exercises and rituals. Of course it can be useful to write and store this information. But remember the basic work is first about experiencing and practising, then secondly about writing. You have the support of whatever has form and it is your responsibility to ask for that support. At the same time you are not urging it, as you are confident that by keeping the agreements, support will come on its own.' [...]

With the Guide I reach an area in nature with an estate made up of wonderful rural houses. This place is the perfect representation of one of my Intents: a spiritual retreat and community centre. I sense a strong obstacle to the realisation of such Intent. I ask what this is all about. I see a stone in a well. I ask the Guide what to do with it. He says that if I wish I could retrieve the stone out of the well. Before I do that, he invites me to look around and check whether I really want to give form to my Intent. I meet the Spirit of Sector 2 and ask her how I can give form to my Intent. 'What is your Intent?' she replies. I explain that my Intent is that of creating a bridge between my inner world and outer reality. The Spirit says: 'The first condition is expanding your inner world. Look around you. Is what you see here the kind of outer world you desire?' The place is majestic. It is indeed the community centre of my dreams. There is glowing accommodation for residents and guests, sanctuaries, group rooms, store sheds, working and social areas, sacred and ritual spaces, shamanic pathways and also a publishing house [...] (This is actually the precise description of the Findhorn Foundation environment, but at the time of this journey I did not know anything about it.) *'In order to accomplish this, it is required that you go totally into this dream. And this is not dependent on others: if they join, it's all right, and if they don't, it's also all right. Follow the right procedures and connect with the universal cycles. Are you willing to do it?' I say yes and then move to the well and begin to retrieve the stone. The Spirit points out that once I recover the stone, things are going to change for me. 'On a material level you will have a focus point. This means that all your resources will move toward your Intent.' I enquire about the conditions of my agreement. I'm told to devote my resources to the work of the Sacred Cone Circle. [...] Finally I get the stone back and lift it out of the well. I place it on the grass as a representation of my agreement. The stone gets bigger and this prevents its falling again into the well. It is now in the garden of the community centre standing as a powerful symbol of this retrieval. A part of my soul was retrieved today. I hold the gift.*

1 *A Course in Miracles, Text,* p. 585.

2 *A Course in Miracles, Workbook,* p. 425.

3 See Sector One, note 4.

4 See Sector One, note 5.

SECTOR THREE

~ SIGN: Gemini ~ HOUSE: 3rd ~ PLANET: 1) Mercury; 2) Venus ~
~ RAY: 4th (Harmony/Beauty/Art), 5th (Knowledge)~
~ ELEMENT: Air ~ QUALITY: Mutable ~
~ DIRECTION: East ~ SEASON: Spring ~
~ TOTEM SPIRIT: Mahe Rahe Tahe ~ EPIC STATES: Tudor, Rodut. ~

ANIMALS: Bee, blackbird, butterfly, coyote, deer, fox, greyhound, hare, hawk, jackdaw, jay, lark, magpie, monkey, mullet, parrot, spider, squirrel, swallow, weasel, small birds in general.

PLANTS: Anise, ash, azalea, celery, clover, cumin, dill, elecampane, endive, fern, fennel, flax, ginger, hazel, horehound, lavender, lemongrass, lily of the valley, liquorice, marjoram, medlar, mint, mushroom, myrtle, nux vomica, parsley, pomegranate, tangerine, thyme, verbena, yarrow, all plants that remove obstructions, seeds in general.

MINERALS: Chrysocolla, chrysoprase, marble, mercury, moss agate, pyrites, tiger's eye.

SPIRITS: Raphael, Ongkanon (*Angels*); Nabu (*Babylonian*); St. Christopher, St. Nicholas, St. Anthony of Padua (*Christian*); Anubis, Thoth (*Egyptian*); Turms (*Etruscan*); Hermes, Castor and Pollux, Meti (*Greek*); Sarasvati, Hanuman (*Hindu*); Mercury, Apollo, Romulus and Remus (*Roman*); Magician, Lovers (*Tarot*).

ANATOMY/ PHYSIOLOGY: Arms, hands, lungs, shoulders, nerves, breathing, organs of speech and hearing, nervous system, mental faculties.

ASSOCIATIONS:	Communication, language, writing, publishing, printing, correspondence, translations, radio, television, advertising, mail, internet, telephones, messengers, teaching, stations, short journeys, transport, trade, markets, fairs, shops, humour, frauds, thieves, divination, brothers and sisters, neighbours.
COLOURS:	Orange, yellow, amber, saffron, plaids, metallic shades.
DETECTORS:	1st brother/sister, 1st brother/sister of maternal grandfather or of paternal grandmother, 6th son/daughter, partner of 3rd son/daughter, friends of 1st son/daughter, 1st son/daughter of friends. 2-2, 1-3, 12-4, 11-5, 10-6, 9-7, 8-8, 7-9, 6-10, 5-11, 4-12.
GRIEVANCES:	*Excess:* ambiguity, amorality, cheating, criticalness, cunning, carelessness, deception, dissimulation, excitableness, flattery, forgetfulness, gossip, inconstancy, indecisiveness, lack of intimacy and depth, lies, nervousness, over-talkativeness, restlessness, shiftiness, teasing, thieving, trickery, unreliability. *Deficit:* aloofness, clumsiness, communication problems, confused or unrealistic thinking, heaviness, inflexibility, lack of lightness and detachment, language and learning difficulties, rigidity, seriousness, shyness, soberness, stupidity. *Physical:* allergies, asthma, bronchitis, lung difficulties, nervous diseases, insomnia, stammer, thyroid disorders.
QUALITIES:	Adaptability, communication, cleverness, curiosity, eloquence, flexibility, fluency, humour, insights, intelligence, lightness, lucidity, playfulness, understanding, versatility, wittiness, young outlook.

With Sector 3, I enter into the realm of communication and information. Here the role of the mind is essential as it is constantly stimulated by large amounts of data. My way of thinking determines what I am, the quality of my life and how I perceive the world. This means that if my experiences are painful and unpleasant, the thoughts, inner dialogue, communication, concepts and beliefs that prevail in my mind inevitably have a similar nature. My habitual thought forms are based on a series of key events of the past, which can be located in specific areas of the Sacred Circle or natal chart. Such experiences are linked to specific episodes that, although they apparently belong to my personal story, find their true causes in the primeval origin of this universe as it has developed in the process of separation and consolidation of the ego. The human mind can be likened to a sophisticated multimedia computer whose data (thought forms) are projected onto a virtual external screen (our experience and perception of the world). All I see, feel and experience, the people, the things and the situations are, in this context, the projection of my thoughts. When certain thought forms are dominant or duplicate, their data can clog and block the access of other information. In this way, the services of the mind are extremely reduced and life becomes the continuous repetition of the same routine. The mind that we human beings currently use is a split mind: one part operates in accordance to an Intent connected with the Function, while the other is asleep and dreams of a fragmented reality. The latter is the ego: the belief that I am a separate identity with a personal history, private thoughts and changing emotions. The ego projects programmes of separation, grievances and conflicts on the screen of the computer, although it does its best to disguise them as the representation of high ideals and love. The part of the mind which is connected with the Function – that is, forgiveness or the acceptance of unity and the undoing of separation – transmits programmes of healing and joy, although the ego tends to portray them as unpleasant and painful occurrences. The ego and its programmes operate as viruses spreading a plague of terror and guilt. They protect and nourish only those kinds of experiences that can sustain the belief in the ego itself, whereas they censor, suffocate or disregard all situations that can engender doubts or alternative visions. This is part of a process which often develops at high speed and automatically. It is the consequence of an ancient conspiracy filtered through a series of apparently recent conditionings (childhood, education, society, etc.). Here I do not mean to judge this conditioning and support the idea of a mind split into a 'good' and a 'bad' side. This is usually one of the tricks of the ego employed to support its ideology of separation. Astroshamanism aims at bringing light on the actual effects of one's processes so as to favour choices and decisions based on a global awareness rather than on a limited or unconscious vision. My life begins to change when I am available to take responsibility for my thoughts and perception of the world. Meditation techniques and shamanic journeys have been used since ancient times to support this awareness. In particular it is a question of cleansing our archives of all thought forms and data that are not connected with the Intent and Function, at once receiving information and thought forms of support. It is a regular process that reflects on the mental plane what happens at a physical level through the assimilation of nutritional substances and the release of excrement.

Everything I see is the result of my thoughts. And these thoughts are not significant or trivial, big or little. They are simply either connected with unity or separation, the Spirit Guide or the ego. Every thought that I have contributes either to the reality of unity or the illusion of separation. The ego maintains the trick of its existence by setting up a virtual reality of mirrors and tapes that reflect back its illusory face and voice. This environment we often fight to preserve and, although the depression, sadness, anxiety and guilt that follows is unbearable, it is our decision to save its sophisticated wall of glass. Yet we can choose otherwise. We can be as vigilant against the ego's face as for it. I can decide to watch my mind for the illusions of the ego, and not be deceived by them. I can elect to engage with the Spirit Guide, systematically undoing the environment of mirrors that has been built since the advent of separation.

Sector 3 is vital for the exchange of information and the connection of the Twelve Sectors of the Sacred Circle. Its mastery allows tuning in to the vibrational frequencies and tools of your Intent. When this quality is acquired, each expression, whether physical or verbal, becomes the representation of the Intent itself, which can then expand and manifest without limits. Sector 3 can lead to the original language: a *sacred idiom* which lets you express your deepest nature and communicate with all types of living beings in a way that clearly acknowledges them as part of you and you as part of them.

Ⅱ **Gemini:** The seasonal time of this sign is that of the transition between spring and summer. Trees are full of leaves and branches lift up to the sky, while flowers thrive. This moment of great expansion for nature is represented by the abundant distribution of pollen, the continuous exchange of data and the last busy wave of human activities before the pause of summer. Gemini is animated by an insatiable thirst for information and a ceaseless curiosity. This sign hops from one place to another, extracting what it can and moving to the next. As it sees from all perspectives, it can find it hard to come down to a decision or be direct. It is a genius in circumventing obstacles and improvising when in critical situations. This sign brings the gift of lightness in life and the ability to be detached from, or fly through, the emotional dramas which block access to other levels of perception. An urge to support the communication system and the movement of the energy to its spontaneous destination is a basic motivation here. This allows a rapid connection with whatever exists, though it may not leave much energy for deep understanding.

Third House: It is connected with the integration structure of the whole chart, the ordinary perception of the mind and its use in everyday communication. It also concerns the familiar environment (in particular the appearance and personality of brothers and sisters), short trips and routine travels. Here one learns to use and adapt energy in relation to the general human context. This house can also provide information as regards the routine conditioning of the mind and attitude or appearance of *false guides* (see Book One, Chapter 6, 'False Guides').

☿ *Mercury:* The position of Mercury in the astrological chart gives indications about the kind of mentality or intellect of the individual and the way he thinks, expresses himself and learns. Its placement may also provide clues of easy and informal ways of communicating with Totem Spirits, non-ordinary beings, Guides or whoever we meet in life. Aspects and transits of this planet may help pinpoint areas or times where difficulties in communication, mental disorders and grievances in the realm of Sector 3 can occur.

Like its metal *mercurius* (quicksilver), Mercury is neutral and adapts itself to the quality of the environment. This allows planetary archetypes to relate to each other and establish connections. Mercury also operates as major junction between the Higher and Lower Worlds and serves the function of gatekeeper and warden of communication. In this respect, its main purpose is to facilitate the traffic or exchange of information at all levels and to prevent the formation of blocks.

Basic Practices

a. Using the guidelines (given in Book One, Chapter 7, 'Connection with the Totem Spirit' or Book Two, 'Introduction, Basic Practices, Exploring the Sectors') meet the Totem Spirit of Sector 3.

b. Activate the piece for Sector 3 of your Sacred Circle Pieces (see

Book One, Chapter 4, 'The Sacred Circle Pieces' or Book Two, 'Introduction, Basic Practices, The Sacred Circle Pieces').

c. Choose one of the following practices ('Healing Tools') and do it daily, every other day or three times per week, for at least 21 days.

Healing Tools

1. **Gibberish:** A highly cathartic practice for Sector 3 is *gibberish*. This technique consists in using nonsense sounds and words accompanied by expressive movements of the body. This allows free communication without the limitation of conventional languages. Gibberish interrupts the automatic flow of thought forms and supports a deep release of blocks. Osho describes it as follows: 'For fifteen minutes move totally in the gibberish. Allow yourself to express whatever needs to be expressed within you. Throw everything out. The mind thinks always in terms of words. Gibberish helps to break this pattern of continual verbalisation. Without suppressing your thoughts, you can throw them out – in gibberish. Let your body likewise be expressive. Then, for fifteen minutes, lie down on your stomach and feel as if you are merging with mother earth. With each exhalation, feel yourself merging into the ground beneath you.'[1]

2. **Sacred Idiom:** A major achievement which can naturally stem from gibberish is that of retrieving some rudiments of your sacred idiom. This means to connect with a deeper mother tongue veiled by the layers of ordinary language. This idiom is a shamanic language employed in prayers, invocations and communication with Totem Spirits, non-ordinary beings, plants, animals, minerals and also among human beings who are willing to be transparent in their expression. This practice allows access to ancient languages which strongly resonate with the speaker and allow him to retrieve precious memories or convey what he feels at a level that his current ordinary language is unable to achieve. This phenomenon is also called *glossolalia*, from the Greek *glossa* ('tongue') and *lalein* ('to babble'), that is 'to speak in tongues'.[2] According to Felicitas Goodman, a scholar in this field, these tongues do not follow the rules of formal languages and are rather expressions accompanying the

physiological changes which take place during the religious trance or shamanic state of consciousness.[3] I perceive words and sounds as living entities coming from other dimensions and channelled in this reality by human beings. Here my function as a speaker, writer or singer is that of broadcasting a programme and working as receiver as well as transmitter. In the universe there are infinite programmes and radio stations. It is my Intent that determines to which frequency I tune in and the kind of entities I channel into this dimension. If this Intent is connected with the Function, my words and sounds are inevitably going to support the release of the illusion of separation and the reawakening of the reality of unity. A powerful exercise is that of establishing a deep connection with my Intent and then allowing myself to communicate it through words and sounds as freely as I can. All kinds of words, and in any language, can be used for the purpose. As I send out these sounds, I follow them in the air, gently touching and seizing them with my hands. I also direct them to specific areas of the Sacred Circle or of the world. This method is indeed a multidimensional internet system. If I regularly practice it, I can easily retrieve those dormant faculties of communication which have currently been replaced by computers and the like.

3. **Releasing Sounds and Words:** An alternative procedure is that of expressing negative thoughts through sounds and words. Instead of sinking into depression, anger or other grievances, I allow those energies to be released and sent out to a dimension where they can be transformed. In this case I am not broadcasting grievances on this planet, I am transmitting them to a recycling constellation. According to my tradition this is called *Handorian States System*. In the spirit of Sector 3 it can be described as a business agreement and export-import operation where I trade grievances in exchange for blessings. Grievances are precious resources in some parts of the universe. Their usage is beyond my understanding. Perhaps they are likely to be used as a sort of compost. Considering the resistance of human beings to releasing them, grievances seem to be precious even on Earth. The fact is that here they are so abundant, that it does not make any sense to trade them. It is like living in a country full of gold. Surely in that place gold is not going to be of any value. It has value only as long as it can be used as material of exchange with countries where gold is rare or absent. These other places can

provide what is lacking in the country full of gold. In a nutshell, this is the situation of human beings. They have enormous quantities of precious resources, yet because they have lost their connection with other dimensions, they do not know what to do with them and risk suffocation out of their abundance. The role of a shaman in Sector 3 is that of reopening the channels of communication and the trading routes so that all goods can freely circulate. Let your breath reach and embrace your grieving thoughts. Allow them to become sounds, any sound that can set them free, a moan, a sigh, a low hum, a howl, a melody. Give form to your destructive thoughts, let them go and stop being possessive about them. Invest as much energy as you can in this process, then sink to the ground and relax. Lie flat with palms open on the ground. Relax and let the energy flow through you. Let it flow deep into the Earth, where it will be cleansed and renewed. Then begin to receive and send out thoughts of peace, harmony and love as if you were a radio network, breathing and using all your energy field to support this broadcast. Breathe deeply and surrender your lungs. The lungs are the temple of Sector 3. At least twice per week for 21 days, release grievances through sounds for seven minutes. Then be silent and connect with your Spirit Guide or Circle. For twelve minutes allow words in an unknown language to come from that holy place. Connect with your highest Intent and allow it to be expressed through these words. Repeat them and let their vibration resonate all over your body. At the end of this practice, note down the words which were most relevant.

4. **The Art of Lying:** This practice is typical of Sector 3 and can benefit those who have low self-esteem or tend to be disturbed by negative thoughts. The technique of *telling lies to yourself* consists in writing an inventory of the main negative thoughts which transit in your mind, and then compiling a list of their exact opposites, i.e. the lies. For example, 'I cannot help it' becomes 'I can help it', 'I am always very nervous and anxious when I meet other people' becomes 'I am always very relaxed and peaceful when I meet other people' or 'I can't convey my feelings in words' becomes 'I can clearly express my feelings when I speak', etc. These *lies* are then regularly repeated for a whole cycle of the Moon (28 days) and preferably in front of a mirror, before going to bed and when getting up, and every time the negative thoughts try to take over. During the process, try expanding your lies and tell

them as if you were a myth-maker. Turn your lies into a complete story and then consider it to be true. Act exactly like the protagonist of the story.

5. **Planting Seeds:** A practice connected with this season is that of planting seeds. For this purpose it is recommended to use seeds of local plants, preferably endangered indigenous plant species. Choose a place in your garden or a seed tray and prepare the earth or compost with care. Chant a song, pray or speak in sacred idiom as you do this. Rattle over the earth and the seeds or do whatever you feel appropriate to send love and express respect. Close your eyes and connect with the seeds. Open up to their voice and listen with your heart. Then plant the seeds and tend them as they grow and flower. When they are ripe, you can harvest some of the seeds and offer them to friends or use them as a give-away.

6. **The Paheka Sadohe Korah** (Chant of the Totem Spirits and Guides): For Sector 3 the chant is *Mahe Rahe Tahe Sadoh*. Please use this practice only if you intend to establish or support a regular relationship with the Totem Spirit of Sector 3. If you intend to use this chant, you can either sing it from time to time to accompany a cycle of twelve shamanic journeys in Sector 3 or as a practice on its own to be done preferably once or twice a day for at least seven minutes during a period of 21 days.[4]

7. **The Planetary Chants and Scales:** Use the complete set of Planetary Chants as described in Book One (Chapter 9, 'The System of the Planetary Scales'). Practice at least four complete sets during the month and use the chant of the Sun and Mercury as much as possible, particularly at the start and end of the day. Take note of your experiences with the chants.

8. **The Chant and Scale of Mercury:** This is the second after the Sun in the sequence of Planetary Chants. Its words are:

Oh Hi Ti Nah, Oh Hi Ti Nah, Oh Hi Ti Nah,
Oh Hi Ti Nah, Ti Oh.

As you sing it you can visualise the image of the small sphere of Mercury rotating around the Sun at high speed. The Scale of Mercury can be employed to cleanse the language and any tool of communication. If you use the Sacred Circle, sit or stand in Sector 3 or the sector where Mercury is positioned in your natal chart. You can also stay in the sector where Mercury is transiting at the moment. After calling the Guide, according to your habitual procedures, connect with your Intent and Function. Then sing the Chant of Mercury. Ask your Guide to draw the energy of Mercury and the Spirit of Sector 3. Continue the practice, moving gradually from lower (restlessness, deception, ambiguity, thieving, etc.) to higher expressions of Mercury (right communication, intelligence, lightness, etc.).[5]

Astroshamanic Reports

The relationship with the Spirit of Sector 3 has played an important part in my astroshamanic experience. His form changes according to circumstances and at times he is formless or invisible. I sense him in the air as the linking agent among all visible things. His presence is very supportive and provides lightness, adaptability and divine humour. When I connect with him, it is as if he spoke through my own voice. When this occurs I usually say powerful words which heal and nourish me. In ordinary reality there are different tools that I associate with this Spirit: i.e. telephones, mail, stamps, dictionaries and trains. The latter are major allies of mine. From Bologna, where I once lived, I used to go by train to Rome every other week for three years to hold my courses. The Spirit of Sector 3 would take the form of the train itself and offer me such pleasant and inspiring journeys. I travelled on the primary national railway connecting the North to the South of Italy. On those occasions I did my best to employ the train as a sacred vehicle. As part of my regular practice, I left spelt-wheat seeds as a give-away to signify the planting of thoughts of unity and love in the carriage. I also applied my Function as I released thoughts of separation through the activation of the Sacred Cone. In this way I trusted that the application of my Intent and Function in the train would generate subtle waves spreading their effects all over Italy. In the train I could also prepare my workshops, study natal charts, meditate, journey and easily reach trance states thanks to the monotonous rhythm of the rails. When I felt that my energy was too high or unbalanced, I would shut myself in the WC and perform a short wild dance, or make some ritual gestures and grimaces in front of the mirror. The train gave me protection and shelter. I always managed to find a seat even on the most crowded days. I would ask for support from the Spirit before getting on the train and surrender. Only once the journey was a sheer nightmare. I stood for the whole time packed like a sardine in the corridor and, moreover, the engine broke down and there was a delay of almost two hours which affected all my schedules. I was so furious with the universe that day. Then I realised that I had totally forgotten to ask for protection. Instead of going into my usual practice, I had been taken away by strong and obsessive emotions about a passionate drama I was living at that time. The railway stations are also great places for gaining awareness, as they operate as projectors of the major junctions of the conscious collective mind. The *Metropolitana* (underground) of Rome was another outstanding area due to its relationship with the Lower World. By carefully watching the people and whatever happened in that environment, I could get significant clues about the characteristics of the unconscious energy which I was likely to deal with during the workshops.

Here follow the reports of two of my first visits to Sector 3:

As soon as I get out of the tunnel, I feel blocked and confused. I cry out the name of my Guide. He suddenly comes and takes me away at great speed. It is a swift journey, which conveys the need to operate with dexterity and agility. I feel safe as I move like a dart in the sky. I surrender to the speed, comforted by the smile of my Guide. We approach Mercury. It spins around the Sun's headquarters and spreads its message in the universe. It is the voice of the Sun, whose overwhelming presence is felt in the background. We land on Mercury and I am soon aware of a lot of activities going on. There are many beings, all involved in plenty of things, though they do them with playfulness and lightness. I feel at ease in this environment. After a while somebody, who introduces himself as the Communication System Manager for Earth, greets me. He is very slim and holds a luminous sphere in his hands, which whirls at high speed. 'Here,' he says, 'all possible languages, together with their keys of decoding, are contained.' The sphere suddenly stops, begins to send out some glyphs and then continues to rotate and stops again showing other glyphs. I introduce myself too. 'I would like to have information regarding my potential in Sector 3.' The sphere spins anticlockwise and then stops showing a circle of people holding hands. The circle opens and the persons involved begin to perform movements, which I follow with much attention. At the end I ask what is the significance of it all. 'This is a sacred movement connected with ...... [a long series of words in sacred idiom follows],' I am told. 'It is a ceremony aimed at purifying the language so that it becomes crystal clear and communication works effectively. This practice is most essential, as the translation apparatus needs maximum cleaning to allow effective communication from the higher spheres. Now a phrase related with cleaning and achieving effective communication will follow.' I then receive a long sentence in sacred idiom. 'Place your hands over the heart and trust that effective communication is taking place. You keep this sphere. Soon you will find a material object connected with it. Use the sphere. It allows you to translate whatever you receive into the right language. An energetic vibration connected to the Centre supports your expression through the ordinary language. A practice is to pay attention to the vibration. What matters here is not the meaning of what you say. What counts is having the vibration of your words connected with the Centre. Whenever you use words, you get in tune with Mercury through the subtle vibration of the sounds. Thus, your language becomes a dance, an expression of love, and releases the structure belonging to the world of separation. Learn to decontaminate your language and bring your attention to the vibration within the sound. It does not matter what you say. What counts is your focus on the vibration which is constantly linked with the ecstatic love and peace of the Centre.'

Some days ago I had my first visit to Sector 3. Today I decide to go there again to receive further information. I call the Guide and together we leave for Mercury. We land on the planet and then are directed towards a huge station full of galactic high-tech equipment. At the gate I am asked to exhibit a tool of identification. I am rather confused by this request and I ask the Guide to tell me what I am supposed to do. 'Show them the sphere you received the last time you came,' he answers smiling at me. With renewed confidence I take out the sphere and the gate opens. I move on a sliding corridor made of air until I reach another gate. There they ask me something that I do not manage to understand. The gatekeepers look at me as if they were saying something very obvious that everybody is supposed to know. I cannot make up my mind what it is about. I understand something is missing, but my mind is blank. I try to explain that it is only my second visit in Sector 3 and that I am not used to the local customs. The more I attempt to justify myself, the more the gatekeepers look at me with suspicion. My anxiety grows and all kinds of fears are drawn to me. My nervousness changes into panic when I notice that this situation is calling the attention of the beings in the back office. In particular I see somebody very tall and slim who looks at me from the window of his office. I notice that he is using a sort of mobile phone. I am sure that he is talking about me. He has the air of being a big fish in Sector 3. Then I see a group of people that look like wardens. They come towards the gate. I gather they have been called by the big fish. One of them says a few things to the gatekeepers and then calls a team of beings of dubious appearance. This situation draws a lot of onlookers and I am so embarrassed that I would rather blow up than face what is going to happen. Everybody is glaring at me and I am paralysed by sheer terror. Finally a fellow with a cloak comes close to me and says something in an unknown language which clearly sounds like: 'I know how to get you out of this trouble. Come and follow me...' At first he appears as a saviour and I am almost tempted to sell my soul to him. Then I realise that his energy is so cold that my body begins to freeze. I feel totally lost and do not know what to do. I need help, but there is nobody I can trust there. Who shall I ask for support? As I ask myself this, I suddenly remember that I have completely forgotten about my Guide. I look around but I don't see him. Then I realise that the agreement we have is that, in order for him to come, I have to call him. As soon as I do that, the Guide is there. The whole station with all its people suddenly freezes and goes into a deep and long silence. It is as if a pause key has been pressed. All is still. I seem the only one who can move, but I do not know what to do. 'Oh yes, I do indeed!' I say to myself as, out of a swift inner impulse, I grasp the hand of my Guide and move through the gate. As soon as I complete this action, the whole station, including the gatekeepers, the wardens, the tainted beings, the big fish and all the onlookers, begin to split their sides with laughter. The guffaw is so strong that all the alarms of the station are activated and this contributes to create even more laughter. I am stunned and I ask my Guide what is going on. As I do this I observe to my surprise that it seems as if he is making a tremendous effort to restrain his laughter. He is doing it in such a dignified way that I cannot help bursting into a noisy laughter. The moment I do that, the Guide joins me. Our mutual laughter moves throughout my body like a flood and opens gates within and without. I spend at least ten minutes of my journey laughing together with all the beings in Sector 3 and my Guide. Then I decide it is enough. I go with my Guide to the office of the Totem Spirit of Sector 3. One of his secretaries asks me to recapitulate the information I received on my previous journey. 'This procedure,' explains the Guide, 'is employed for security reasons and also to allow you to memorise the teachings.' After summing up my past experience, I am introduced into the Spirit's bureau. Around him there are twelve assistants. The Spirit seems very easygoing and invites me to explain the purpose of my visit. I ask his guidance on how to communicate to other people the type of work I do. This is the Spirit's reply as I manage to translate it: 'What matters is to bring the attention on the vibration of your words, allow them to be sent out emphasising their energetic charge rather than their significance. Bring your attention to the vibration of your voice. What counts here is your connection with the vertical axis. When you do that, what is truly essential is going to spread into the horizontal axis. As you speak allow the vertical axis to operate.

Avoid giving attention to those who are around you. You are not speaking to anybody. It is insane to adapt what you say according to a public that does not exist where you see it. You are not communicating with the horizontal. There is only one communication and this has to do with the vertical axis. This communication is unilateral and does not involve an exchange with horizontal listeners unless they also manage to connect with the vertical. If this is the case, the exchange will proceed directly from the vertical. If this is not the case, it is not your responsibility. Your work has to do with keeping the connection with the vertical. This is your sole responsibility. Be careful, as in this process there is the risk of cutting off from the vertical and remaining isolated. There are two possible risks. One is being conditioned by the horizontal listeners. The other is being conditioned by your centre as separate from the Centre. Use words as steps of an ecstatic dance. Be light and move in all directions. Sector 3 gives you total access and allows you to carry your Intent in all possible directions.'

---

[1]   Osho, *The Orange Book*, Rajneesh Foundation, 1983, p. 192. (This book, which contains a wide range of meditation techniques, is out of print and is currently replaced by *Osho, Meditation: The First and Last Freedom*, St. Martin's Press, New York, 1996).

[2]   This is also a common liturgic practice in some Christian congregations and refers to the miracle of Pentecost when the Apostles 'were all filled with the Holy Ghost, and began to speak with other tongues, as the Spirit gave them utterance' (Acts 2:4).

[3]   Felicitas D. Goodman, *Speaking in Tongues: A Cross-Cultural Study of Glossolalia*, University of Chicago Press, 1972.

[4]   See Sector One, note 4.

[5]   See Sector One, note 5.

DIRECTION SOUTH

~ ELEMENT: Earth ~ SEASON: Summer ~ BODY: Physical ~
~ KINGDOM: Mineral ~ PART OF DAY: Noon ~
~ SIGNS: Cancer, Leo, Virgo ~ SECTORS: 4, 5, 6 ~
~ HUMAN AGE: Adolescence and young adulthood ~
~ TOTEM SPIRIT KEEPER: Ratah Sadoh ~
~ COLOURS: Green; dark red, brown ~
~ CELESTIAL BODIES: Earth ~ JOURNEY: Way of the Healer ~
~ SPIRIT PATHWAYS: Growth, trust, love. ~

ANIMALS:	Peaceful animals of the earth, coyote, dormouse, fox, mouse, rabbit, turtle.
QUALITIES:	Creativity, growth, healing, innocence, love, patience, purification, stability, strength.
GRIEVANCES:	Addictions, boredom, depression, fear, perfectionism, self-inflation.
HEALING TOOLS:	Building and honouring sacred sites or tools, dancing, diets, drumming, fasting, laughter, lying meditations, massage, nature retreats or walks, physical movement, play, shamanic journeys, shield making, singing, story-telling.
INSTRUMENTS:	Drums and shields.
MINERALS:	Adventurine, jade, jasper, marble, rose quartz, serpentine, turquoise.
PLANTS:	Birch, sage, wildflowers.
SPIRITS:	Huitzilopochtli (*Aztec*); Ceres (*Roman*); Demeter, Pan (*Greek*); Archangel Michael (*Christian*); Ratahri, Gnomes, Brownies, Pixies, Pygmies, Sylvestres, Satyrs, Elves, Dryads (*Nature Spirits*).
FESTIVALS:	Summer Solstice (20 or 21 June), *Lammas,* or *Lughnasadh* (1 August).

The path of the South explores the physical realm and the understanding of material life on this planet. Here I learn to be grounded and to accept the implications of being in this physical reality. By acknowledging the body as a teaching and learning device, I can use it to give form to my Intent in connection with my Function.

The South is the period of summertime, of rapid growth, abundance, and also of healing and repair of the material plane. Here I face the task of using the dense material of the body as a way to represent and demonstrate my Intent and Function. The energy available in this season is plentiful and, when purposefully directed, can allow major healing at all levels.

A significant concept in the South is *embodiment*. This can be described as a process in which the spiritual energies of subtle dimensions expand in the ordinary reality. Here a shamanic voyage or vision represents the preliminary stage of manifesting those energies into the material level. Once I have connected with my Spirit Guide or other subtle forces, it is up to me to integrate the shamanic experience by implementing the related vision in the world. A first step in this direction is that of leaving a visible and material mark in the form of a drawing, dance, song, sculpture, etc. Also the act of writing down the experience in a journal serves this purpose and helps create a bridge between spiritual and ordinary reality.

The South is also the place of the inner child and of playful shamanic work. Innocence, enjoyment, spontaneity, dance, story-telling, divine jokes and games are major tools, as they allow the lightening-up of the discipline, dedication, endurance and seriousness that shamanic work often entails. The path of the South can be a way of laughter and play, where the heat of the season warms up the mind as well as the body. Here the teachings of my tradition are based on the strategic premise that the whole of life, as it is perceived, is part of a game (i.e. the *Game of the Sacred Cone*). The essential achievement is either to fully enjoy the game or to bring it to a conclusion (i.e. the *Game Resolution*).

Traditional roles of the South are those of Trickster, Coyote, *Heyoka*, Contrary, Divine Fool, etc. The *Heyoka*, or Contrary, is someone who does everything backwards. For example, instead of saying 'Hello!' he says 'Good-bye!'. He chants songs in a reverse order and before eating makes his hands dirty. These people upturn ordinary reality and break down the barriers of conventional life. Their presence in a community serves to remind us to stay in the present and not to take anything for granted. Their unpredictable behaviour causes surprises and shifts in awareness that disclose gaps in the ordinary mind, thus making it possible to open up to new lessons. According to the Lakota tradition, the Heyoka are extraordinary people who have received a special initiation involving great powers and commitment. This often involves hiding their major spiritual powers under a false appearance of humbleness or foolishness. Similar sacred obligations, which were once common in many traditions, are now carried out by some wise teachers in disguise who can seldom be acknowledged in the ordinary reality. These people do not display their talents and are not concerned with outer achievements. They operate behind the scenes and are often the true uncredited teachers or inspirational sources of many popular spiritual authorities.

The Coyote is a typical animal of the South and is very dear to the tradition of the *Sacred Cone Circle*. He teaches me to laugh at myself when I am carried away by a sense of being special or when I am taking myself or others too seriously. When Coyote is at work all attempts to do things properly or in a programmed way fail. Things get lost or don't work, strange or confusing situations happen. In such contexts it is essential to be straightforward, facing directly Coyote energy and forcing it to disclose its authentic and empowering motivation. This is inevitably related with testing or revising our Intent and further aligning it to our Function.

The Story of Kurandah: Kurandah, a celebrated hero of the *Epic of the Sacred Cone*, is often found in the South, where he belongs to the clan of Sector 6. His mythic gestures are narrated in many *Trudeh Etnaie Korah* (popular ballads) and he is an ideal representative of the Way of the Healer. This is how I once tried to translate his story:

Kurandah used to live in a village dominated by a ferocious monster. That demonic beast was a major source of suffering, illness and terror for all villagers. Only Kurandah was not affected by the monster. As a matter of fact, while all the other people could see the monster, Kurandah could not see or feel it at all. Although he did his best to be like all the other villagers and share their dreadful fears, the idea of the monster was totally beyond his mind. At times he pretended to suffer from some of the grieving symptoms that the monster caused the villagers, but as he was not a good actor, all his attempts would miserably fail. This situation was an immense source of sadness for Kurandah. He could not see the monster. He could not share anything with the villagers. He felt like a complete alien. Alone and neglected, he took refuge in the forest, which was considered to be the monster's usual dwelling place. From there the villagers could hear its horrendous shrieks. That was one of the reasons why Kurandah decided to move into the forest. He wanted to face the monster. Kurandah walked through every corner of the forest and could not find any trace of the monster, nor of anything like it. On the other hand something unexpected happened to him. He was reminded about the games he used to play when he was a child.

In those days Kurandah used to spend endless hours in the company of the Bhi Jinah.[1] As he retrieved the memories of the delightful games and the kindred spirits with whom he played then, he realised he was able to see his old friends again. He was again able to have fun with the Bhi Jinah and play with the Spirits, dancing and chanting, and getting to know their ever-changing faces in the human, animal, vegetable and mineral kingdoms. As of old, he became at one with the ways of the animals and also relearned how to play games with plants and stones.

Then, one day Kurandah met the Spirit of the Centre, otherwise known as the 13th. It was unusual for this Spirit to go about and talk, but that day he did. 'Now that you have relearned your old games,' said the Spirit, 'it is time for you to return to the village, be with your people and apply your true Function. Things are going to be different now and you will be able to share your songs and games with them.' Such news brought a lot of joy to the heart of Kurandah. For the first time he felt that he could be like an ordinary villager. At last he would be able to see the monster as everybody there did. This was not the case though. Upon arriving at the village, he found his people more frightened and ill than when he had left them. They came to him describing their symptoms and explaining in full details the features of the monster. Kurandah still could not see anything and was even more unaffected by the monster than before. He was full of compassion for his people, but did not know what to do. This made him very sad and frustrated. He decided to withdraw to a hut on the border between the forest and the village. There he could honour the indications of the Spirit to stay at the village and still be with his friends in the forest. Out of his sadness, Kurandah composed a song. There he cried his sorrow at being unable to see the monster and connect with his people. What a deep and loving song! As he was chanting that song, a woman passed by. The monster was causing so much pain to her body that she had decided to go directly into the forest and offer herself as a sacrifice to the heinous beast. Due to the pain, she was moving very slowly. This was a brave woman indeed! Her name is Dhirah. I won't go into the details of her story. Like Kurandah, she also belongs to the clan of Sector 6 and in that realm details can at times be overwhelming.

Upon moving into the border between the forest and the village, Dhirah could not help hearing the song of Kurandah. Enchanted by that melody, she paused and listened. 'What a magnificent song!' she sighed. The sound of that chant entered into her body. She could feel all her cells gleefully dancing together and witness her pain gradually dissolving. After a while she was totally healed. Full of amazement and gentle excitement, she ran to the village and explained what had happened. Other villagers came to listen to the song and they too were healed. Then the whole population of the village gathered in a circle around Kurandah. They were all listening to him in deep contemplation. Kurandah continued to sing undisturbed by the crowd. As a matter of fact, he was so involved with his song that he could not notice anyone around him. After some time everybody was singing and dancing as well as being healed. So many loving tears of felicity and gratitude were shed that a lake took shape. It was called the Lake of Kurandah. From other villages and places people also came and listened to the song. Kurandah continued to sing unaware of all that was going on around him. He was at one with his song and could not perceive anything else, as his song was everything there could be. The fear of the monster vanished and Kurandah became the Hero of the Clan. His song became the Song of Kurandah. It can still be heard in the forest. The Song of Kurandah is *still there. If only I am willing to pause and listen, I cannot help hearing it. His words lead me to the land where I belong. Truly I do not know if Kurandah is aware of the healing that his song has generated. Sometimes I wonder whether he is still singing out of sadness. Maybe his voice is just the sacred echo that eternally remains out of blissful events. Who knows? What I do know is that I love him so much. His ways are so gentle and sweet. He is a master of compassion and healing. He is a Hero of the Sacred Cone.*

The *Song of Kurandah* has been tended as a central and sacred fire in the Epic. By listening and singing it, I can get into a deep relationship with my Function. There are different ways of being with the song. Its tune changes according to the chanter and the space–time dimension he is located in. The healing power of the song is always sure. Many have tried to study the meaning of its words. Some sages have said that they are based on a specific amount of complex calculations which give form to a synergy of words and tune variations aimed at creating a cosmic structure of the same exact proportion as our universe and then releasing it so as to reveal the ecstatic realms that exist beyond. Well, that's a breath-taking phrase! Let me pause for a while... This explains why the song leads to such an ecstatic state and generates vibrations which bring healing. Others have said that the song belongs to a reality that can only be comprehended through direct experience. This reality abides in the core of the Three Worlds... Now, I'd better stop as it is not my intent to write an essay on the topic. I do not need to have full understanding of the significance of the song and all its complex implications. I am concerned with its essence. Whatever its variations, the meaning remains the same. My desire is to connect my Intent with my Function. My wish is that of spending endless nights and days with my Beloved. My Intent is that of experiencing the patterns, processes and cycles of the continual loving unfolding of this present moment. It is the only thing I am willing to give life to. And when I am asked about death, as the elders say, I can't but reply: 'I have already died'.

---

[1] *Bhi Jinah* are *epical* beings whose function is to fill the gaps that exist in the physical reality as it is perceived by ordinary human beings. The *Bhi Jinah* draw attention to the linking space that exists between all forms and which the conditioning system of ordinary mankind refuses to accept. Their work is meant to gradually reveal what lies beyond the limitations of ordinary perception.

SECTOR FOUR

~ **SIGN:** Cancer ~ **HOUSE:** 4th ~ **PLANET:** 1) Moon 2) Neptune ~
~ **RAY:** 3rd (Active Intelligence), 7th (Ceremonial Magic/Law) ~
~ **ELEMENT:** Water ~ **QUALITY:** Cardinal ~ **DIRECTION:** South ~
~ **SEASON:** Summer ~ **TOTEM SPIRIT:** Quiusadeh ~
~ **EPIC STATES:** Kallex, Xellak. ~

ANIMALS: Bat, bull, carp, cat, cattle, cockle, crab, crocodile, dog, duck, frog, goose, hen, jellyfish, mouse, octopus, otter, owl, oyster, pig, rabbit, scarab, seagull, shrimp, slug, snail, spider, swan, tortoise, woodpecker, all amphibious creatures.

PLANTS: The Moon is connected with sap and its plants are usually sap-bearing, with soft and fleshy leaves, white or yellow flowers, and watery and tasteless fruits. Cabbage, camphor, cauliflower, chickweed, cleavers, cress, cucumber, daffodil, daisy, endive, grape, iris, lemon, lentil, lettuce, lotus, lunaria, maple, melon, moonflower, mushroom, olive, palm, papaya, potato, pumpkin, rosemary, sage, seaweed, soy, turnip, watermelon, white lily, willow, all plants growing in water and grasses.

MINERALS: Aquamarine, carnelian, emerald, moonstone, opal, pearl, rhodochrosite, selenite, silver, all soft stones.

SPIRITS: Gabriel (*Angels*); Sin (*Babylonian*); Arianrhod, Ceridwen (*Celtic*); Mary, St. Andrew (*Christian*); Kwan Yin, Shing-Moo (*China*); Isis, Khonsu, Thoth (*Egyptian*). Losna (*Etruscan*); Artemis, Atlante, Astarte,

Hecate, Selene (*Greek*); Parvati, Soma, Subhadra, Tara, Kali (*Hindu*); Susa-No-O (*Japan*); Itzamna (*Maya*); Freyr, Hurakan, Mani, Nanna (*Nordic*); Lebhana-Leukothea (*Persian*); Diana, Lucina, Ops (*Roman*); Nanna (*Sumerian*); High Priestess, Chariot (*Tarot*).

ANATOMY/
PHYSIOLOGY:
Breasts, stomach, digestive system, pancreas, pituitary gland, hypothalamus, body fluids, menstrual cycle, ovaries, uterus during pregnancy, fertility, sympathetic nervous system, right eye (female), left eye (male).

ASSOCIATIONS:
Liquids, water, milk, sea life, rain, humidity, moisture, floods, shipping, fishing, mother, family, home, place of residence, marriage, menstruation, gestation, maternal instincts, midwives, nursing, fertilisation, fruitfulness, fermentation, vessels, brewing, baking, food, catering, hotels, laundry, public, popularity.

COLOURS:
Yellow-orange, blue.

DETECTORS:
Mother, partner of father, 3rd brother/sister of father, mother of paternal grandmother or of maternal grandfather, father of paternal grandfather or of maternal grandmother. 3-2, 2-3, 1-4, 12-5, 11-6, 10-7, 9-8, 8-9, 7-10, 6-11, 5-12.

GRIEVANCES:
Excess: attachment to past, mother, family and tribe; clannishness; co-dependency; emotional instability; fear of abandonment; food addiction; insecurity; manic depression; moodiness; neediness; obsessive romanticism; possessiveness; sex-addiction; shyness; spell-binding effects. *Deficit:* avoidance of commitments; disconnection from emotions and needs; fear of intimacy and closeness; incapacity to nurture oneself and others; lack of empathy and warmth; separation from past, mother, family and tribe. *Physical:* abortion, adenomas, alcoholism, anorexia, breast disorders, cysts, diabetes, digestive and gastric troubles, flaccidity, hypoglycaemia, menstrual problems, obesity, excessive pregnancies, ulcers.

QUALITIES:
Birth, caring, closeness, dependability, expectancy, family, innocence, kindness, nourishment, nurturing, receptivity, security, sensitivity, tenderness, vulnerability.

In Sector 4, I open myself to the urge to mother and be mothered, to receive nourishment, protection and shelter, and to give it in return by taking care of others. Here I can allow myself to be vulnerable, dependent and sensitive, and experience a sense of belonging to something greater (family, tribe, community, tradition, Earth, galaxy, universe, God). As the two sides of the glyph for Cancer (♋), two basic principles are at work in this sector: the pure expression of the maternal energy (nurturing, warm, empathic, sensitive, tenacious) and the capacity to receive such energy and unconditional love.

At its core level the exploration of Sector 4 concerns the search and finding of the primary roots and the original Intent of my being in a physical body. Here I have the chance of voyaging into time and space, experiencing and healing most ancient mythic recollection, retrieving the relationship with the inner child, revisiting ancestral lineages and gaining understanding about the collective Intent that truly motivates my life. Through the Totem Spirit of Sector 4, I can activate authentic and vivid memories that allow me to pinpoint true needs and release others based on grievances and oblivion. In advanced astroshamanism a specific initiatory process (*Quiure Saike*, or *Original Search*) is devoted to this enterprise. It involves scanning and releasing the blocks to those ecstatic spaces of unconditional love and protection which human beings desperately tend to seek in the ordinary reality. Just as in the ordinary life there are places and people that give temporary shelter and nourishment, also in the shamanic dimensions there exist similar areas. Yet their protection is not based on time and space. It is eternal, abundant and unlimited. There I can receive free and unconditional love, gradually releasing my co-dependence on the perception that has produced the ordinary world where I believe I live. When I manage to connect with the true source of security and nourishment, as it is represented by the Guide and the Totem Spirit of Sector 4, then I can really express my true maternal instinct and the sincere capacity to nourish and protect others. This Totem Spirit, identified with the Moon archetype, blocks the development of my genuine potential until I decide to halt the reproduction of the *seed* of separation. According to astroshamanic strategy, this course of action becomes operative, through the relationship with the Spirit Guide, once I am willing to face each Totem Spirit and come to terms with him. In this way I retrieve my connection with the parts that I separated from and allow *Pahai*, i.e. the *seed of light,* or *Sacred Cone* of the *Epic,* to spread abundantly. Until this time occurs, grievances continue to seek expression in a physical body. Here Sector 4 is also associated with what the Tibetans define as the *Sidpa Bardo*, the area where the dead man, unable to work through his grievances with his Guide, is drawn by the vision of his future parents copulating and, depending on the sex of his future reincarnation, he is attracted to the opposite sex parent until eventually he finds himself in the womb ready to be born again on this planet.

The dominant law of human societies is that of *scarcity*, the assumption that there is only a limited quantity of energy. Strife and competition are a direct consequence of this belief. Indeed, scarcity is one of the foundations on which the structure of the ego is based. The capacity to receive energy and nourishment is actually unlimited. This is the experience of those who have dared to journey beyond the threshold of ordinary perception, and it is also the actual existential reality of all beings regardless of whether they insist on believing the opposite. Such awareness is available to everybody. It begins to take root once I choose to release my identification with grievances and take full responsibility for the illusions I have created. In Sector 4, I can release automatic habits or reactions that affect and block my transformation. This is a process which requires a patient, caring and nurturing attitude. It cannot be rushed or undertaken alone. It needs the presence of the Guide and of whoever can truly support me unconditionally. This availability depends only on me. Immense forces of love and light are ready to help me. To the eyes of the ego they often appear as scary and dark. And their luminosity can only be sensed if courage to move through what is hidden and unconscious is present. These forces do not ask for anything in exchange. They are part of me, as I am part of them. They are all waiting for me to wake up from the old dream of separation. They stand around my bedside in tender nurture and care, expecting permission to enter into my current dreaming world. In this process I am the one who holds the control panel. All I need to do is just to switch it on at the convenient time and the rightful course of action will inevitably proceed on its own. Again, it takes care and time.

♋ *Cancer:* This sign starts with the summer solstice, the point of the year when the Sun reaches its most southerly position on the horizon of the northern hemisphere. This time marks the longest period of daylight north of the equator, while south of the equator it is the longest period of darkness. In ancient times the summer solstice was the time in which the Sun god or his representative was ritually sacrificed to the Great Mother, so as to begin his journey in the underworld. The summer solstice constitutes the turning point of the light half of the year. In the natural cycle it is a time of ripening and stabilisation after the intense growth of spring. It is a period of care and precaution inspired by the apex of the Sun's light and the awareness of its forthcoming descent into darkness. After the strenuous labour of the past months, now I can begin to harvest the fruits of the seeds that were planted in spring. In the midst of a busy schedule, Cancer says: 'That's enough! I need to take a break and nourish, and be nourished by, all that I have created so far.' The cycle of the year turns the corner and uncovers the inner work that awaits me. According to the Orphic tradition, Cancer is the threshold through which the soul enters into its present life. The Egyptians, who began their year in this sign, regarded Cancer as the soul's gate into incarnation. Many other ancient teachings also referred to Cancer as the *Gate of Men*, the portal through which all souls descend from the heavens and assume human bodies. It is an area where I can deeply connect with the true motivation that brought me on Earth, and learn to distinguish it from all other objectives that do not pertain to my original awareness.

Fourth House: The cusp of the fourth house corresponds to the *nadir,* or *immum coeli,* that is, the point of intersection between the lower meridian and the ecliptic or the position of the Sun at midnight. The immum coeli, opposed to the *medium coeli,* is located at the bottom of the natal chart and plays one of the major roles in astroshamanic work. It represents the essence of the soul, its innate qualities, the multidimensional foundations of my being and what I am or where I originally belong from this perspective. The sign of this house and its planets provide information on the lessons that have been learned in the past or in a most intimate parallel non-ordinary reality and that are brought into the present or ordinary reality as acquired potentials. According to my experience, this position is crucial in the understanding of one's shamanic path and it portrays the seed which in the medium coeli, the cusp of the tenth house (see Sector 10), reaches its flowering. Medium coeli and immum coeli constitute the two polarities of the vertical axis and refer to the Higher and the Lower World respectively. When I align to the energy of this axis I uncover my multidimensional nature and allow it to operate in accordance with its authentic Intent.

The fourth house is traditionally related to the natal home and family, the mother, the home town and country, past and old memories, the original race and roots, the collective unconscious and astroshamanically describes the most significant lineage or traditions of our multidimensional being.

☽ *Moon:* According to many astrologers the position of the Moon in the chart indicates the unconscious instinctive reactions, the inherited traits, habits, conditioning or behavioural patterns in everyday life, and the *id* according to the Freudian model of the psyche. The nature of the Moon is familiar and intimate, no matter whether it finds a harmonious or grieving expression. It is usually a safe return point in stressful and difficult situations or when nothing specific is happening and there is simply the need of relaxing or of being in a familiar territory. Sometimes the Moon is an indicator of the areas where energy can be blocked out of the fear to experience pain. Its placement in the chart can pinpoint such situations of suffering with all the defensive and unconscious strategies that the individual has developed to protect himself.

The Moon often describes the mother or those who have played that role during childhood. As for all other roles that can be spotted in the chart, it is indeed the projection of the mother and not the actual mother. Here the Moon describes the way in which the mother archetype has been experienced and the first interaction with the outer world which made an emotional imprint in the system of the person.

In astroshamanic work the position of the Moon plays a significant role as it provides significant clues regarding the lineage and the ancestral initiatory path or mystery school the person has already experienced. This area, which the individual is likely to have mastered in previous times or parallel realities, represents an essential foundation for the realisation of the basic Intent in this current life or dimension. At the same time, it can easily cause addiction, attachment or misuse if its acquired potential is not focused within the present path of initiation, which may differ considerably from the previous one.

The Moon carries the most ancient and significant memories of our life on this planet. It is often related to places and times which appear either as the most attractive or repulsive. The presence of planets in the angles or midpoints, the last planet that the Moon has met before birth, the position of the Moon, its ruling planet and that of the immum coeli, can generally pinpoint the tradition, place, lineage that most resonate in one's person life and that relates to significant past experiences or lives.

Basic Practices

a. Using the guidelines (given in Book One, Chapter 7, 'Connection with the Totem Spirit' or Book Two, 'Introduction, Basic Practices, Exploring the Sectors') meet the Totem Spirit of Sector 4.

b. Activate the piece for Sector 4 of your Sacred Circle Pieces (see Book One, Chapter 4, 'The Sacred Circle Pieces' or Book Two, 'Introduction, Basic Practices, The Sacred Circle Pieces').

c. Choose one of the following practices ('Healing Tools') and do it daily, every other day or three times per week, for at least 21 days.

Healing Tools

1. **Song to the Inner Child:** Another way of deeply connecting with your lunar nature is by singing a song to your inner child. You can either use a traditional chant or invent one in the moment using gibberish or sacred idiom. The inner child is not a music critic, nor is it familiar with ordinary languages, but it can easily understand the voice that comes from the heart. On many occasions when I have experienced sadness, a sense of loss, an unfulfilled need for tenderness and intimacy, or any other kind of emotional grievance, my Guide has invited me to act as a parent toward my child. Instead of fixing those emotions with whoever and whatever was around, finding some analytical interpretation of their cause or going into endless manipulation of other human beings, I now realise that it is often only a question of bringing attention and care to my inner child. Chanting a sweet song or lullaby can suffice. The emotions I perceive are not part of me. They come to me to receive tenderness and healing. I am a channeler of emotions and my function is that of making the journey of whoever passes by as easy and nurturing as possible. When I decide to tune into this awareness, the transit of emotions becomes effortless, joyous and graceful. Then I feel connected with my Function and truly united with everyone and everything. Compose a song for your inner child, as explained here, and sing it daily. Any moment can be appropriate for that song: for example, before sleeping, upon waking up, or whenever you feel that your child needs nurture, love, security and support.

2. **Dependence List:** Make a list of all the people on whom you feel any kind of dependence (physical, emotional, financial, intellectual, spiritual, etc.). Beside each name, write briefly what it is you are dependent upon that person for. Also make a list of all those you consider to be dependent upon you, specifying what needs you provide for them. Then, look at your lists. Be aware of their length and see whether you have left anything out. Which of the two lists is longer? How do you feel about that? Is there anyone you would like to be on one list or the other who is not? Did you become aware of any need that you had not considered? You can also look at the list of *detectors* for each Sector and see to which one the persons included in your list correspond. The associated sectors can identify the areas where either you are abundant or lacking in energy.

3. **Blessing What We Eat and Drink:** This is a beneficial practice to support Sector 4 and the whole body in general. In this way the subtle and spiritual energies of nourishment are amplified while poisoning elements can be easily released. Blessing also enhances the best conditions for digestion. Any prayer, gesture or formula which conveys an intense sense of blessing is suitable. Try and use your creativity in devising ways to bless whatever you take in as food or drink. As you have your meals also be as aware as possible of your relationship with what you eat.

4. **Sleeping Like a Child:** Before you go to sleep just sit in your bed – sit in a relaxed way – and close your eyes. Feel the body relaxing... If the body starts leaning forwards, allow it; it may lean forward. It may like to take a womb posture – just as when a child is in the mother's womb. If you feel like that, just move into the womb posture; become a small child in the mother's womb. Then just listen to your breathing, nothing else. Just listen to it – breathing going in and going out. I am not saying to say it – just feel it going in; when it is going out, feel it going out. Just feel it, and in that feeling you will feel tremendous silence and clarity arising. This is just for 10 to 20 minutes – minimum 10, maximum 20 – then go to sleep.[1]

5. **The Time Map:** This practice consists of tracing a spiral, starting from the moment of birth up to the present time. Then you can indicate along the line words or drawings of the most significant events and memories that come to your mind in chronological order. There is no need for pondering

over what to include in the map. The conventional nature of the events does not count. You can retrieve apparently meaningless episodes (for example, riding a bicycle during a cloudy day or eating an ice-cream at a beach), and completely forget about prominent ones (like your first day of school or your wedding). What matters is allowing all that comes to your memory to be recorded. Once the map is completed, allow it to rest for some days and then return to it for a shamanic time voyage. Move along the time map and revisit each episode together with your Spirit Guide. With the acquired awareness that the Guide brings, you may discover new unexpected details connected to those episodes. Upon voyaging along my time spiral, I was amazed at discovering how each of the episodes that I indicated could operate as a gap, or *stargate,* to other dimensions or levels of awareness. In particular, I was touched to see how the loving presence of my Spirit Guide had always been with me even at times in which I couldn't care less or didn't have any clue about him. *Quiure Saike,* an astroshamanic initiatory practice, deals with a similar exploration of the past. The time line moves here from the Big Bang up to the present time and is aimed at retrieving the basic Intent of my existence as it is connected to this planet and the whole universe. During this work specific episodes are monitored and amended so as to give space to my original purpose of light. If I simply watch myself and pay attention to the things, people and situations that I am attached to, I will be able to understand what I need to release. Every day I take time to scan my mind for those illusive dreams that have been trapped within me. I am learning to become aware of what they are, and I claim my natural power to choose whether to continue to nurture or let them go.

6. **Loving Your Body:** Sit or stand in front of a full-length mirror and look at the image of your body. Say to yourself as reflected in the mirror: 'I love you'. As you do that be aware of the resistances you have in doing this. Look at them and write down in your journal what they are about. Also consider all the feelings that you experience in doing this exercise. Do this for at least five minutes and open up to whatever comes to your attention.

7. **Retrieving Your Early History:** Take time to interview and talk with people who were present during your birth or

the first two years of your life. Ask them as much information as you can about what they witnessed in you, your family, their role and the general environment where you lived. Write this down in your journal. If some of these people are not available any more, then take a shamanic journey and ask your Spirit Guide to meet them as shamanic forms. Invite them to respond to your questions.

8. **The Paheka Sadohe Korah** (Chant of the Totem Spirits and Guides): For Sector 4 the chant is *Quiusadeh Sadoh*. Please use this practice only if you intend to establish or support a regular relationship with the Totem Spirit of Sector 4. If you intend to use this chant, you can either sing it from time to time to accompany a cycle of twelve shamanic journeys in Sector 4 or as a practice on its own to be done preferably once or twice a day for at least seven minutes during a period of 21 days.[2]

9. **The Planetary Chant and Scale:** For Sector 4 the chant is that of the Earth and Moon. In the system of the Planetary Scales, Earth and Moon are regarded as twin planets and share the same chant. This chant is ideal for retrieving ancient memories about our presence on this planet and grounding the experience acquired here or elsewhere. The chant is also useful to release and transform parasitic habits and dependencies, pent-up emotions, birth traumas, and all grievances related to Sectors 4 and 2. The words of the chant are as follows:

    Si Idriah, Si Idriah, Si Idriah, Si Idriah, Neh Hah Mah Set

    If you use the Sacred Circle, sit or stand in Sector 4 or the sector where the Moon is positioned in your natal chart. You can also stay in the sector where the Moon is transiting at the moment. After calling your Guide, according to your habitual procedures, connect with your Intent and Function. Sing the chant of the Sun (*Oh Hay Yah*, four times, followed by *Oh*) to focus on your Intent and then move to that of Earth/Moon (*Si Idriah*, four times, followed by *Neh Ah Mah Set*). Ask your Guide to draw the energy of the Moon and the Totem Spirit of Sector 4. Visualise the Moon orbiting planet Earth. Continue the scale, moving gradually from lower to higher expressions of the Moon.[3]

Astroshamanic Reports

In Sector 4, I trace back my ancestral roots and move beyond the limited perspective of what life has been according to my conventional memories. I journey into my historical biography and search for the gaps which disclose the reality of the myths that brought me where I am now. The access to this information is freely available when I am determined to open up to the hidden wisdom of the Totem Spirit of Sector 4. The conventional mind has laid aside all experiences contrasting with its own fragile structure. One of the major tools that can be employed to retrieve this information are space–time voyages. Sectors 4 and 10 are closely related with the structure of time. Journeys into their territories allow movement beyond my small illusive personal history and connection with the huge spiral chronicles of my true lineage.

I reach a mountain full of snow. The snow becomes liquid and changes into a lake of warm milk. I blissfully swim in this soft and powerful lake. I lose myself in its immense protection, allowing my body to be rocked by its gentle waves of cream. On my previous voyage I received an egg *from Quiusadeh Sadoh [Totem Spirit of Sector 4]. That egg begins to dig into my belly in search of something. I see a table covered with light blue formica and a child. On the table there is a white dish full of food and a metal fork. The child has been told to pierce the food with the fork and bring it to his mouth. The child is paralysed with fear. The aspect of the fork and of the food appals him. He is forced to stay there until he has eaten all the food. What I see is a typical drama of my early childhood. The most unpleasant moment of those times was when I was forced to eat. I realise that I have now the chance of healing that and I ask support to the Guide. He says: 'This is the apparent reality of separation. It is real as long as you consider it real. There are two possible choices: that of the mountain with its lake of infinite nourishment, and that of the child forced to eat. You have now the possibility of claiming your true choice and of asking the child to come with you.' I try it but the child says that he is not allowed to. 'My parents will never give me permission to move from here until I have eaten everything,' he utters. I allow my Guide to speak through me as follows: 'This was the past. Now circumstances have changed and you are free to make your choice.' Then I move in front of the child and I look deeply into his frightened eyes. My mouth opens into a gentle smile as the child gives me his hand. He asks me to take him to the mountain and together we go there. 'Sector 4,' says its Auxiliary Guide, 'takes you back to your original past and to the first sequences of nourishment. It is sheer joy! It is easy to reach it. When you do that, you amplify, spread and support it. This nourishment needs to be taken and given every day. Learn to nourish and be nourished, outwardly and inwardly. Allow yourself to melt into this white lake of cream and move your lips toward the breasts of eternal food. Do that before sleeping and on waking up, so that the whole night is going to be a ceaseless nourishment. You deserve this! Release the past! You have total permission to be fed from the source.'*

In this journey I meet my lineage ally, a major representative of my ancestral spiritual heritage. As I reach the Spirit Circle, I find him there already waiting for me. He tells me that his village is located not very far from the centre of the Earth. He asks me whether I wish to see that place and I say yes. We move downward through a hole by the roots of the Great Tree and reach a location in the Lower World. There my lineage ally acts as king or master shaman. He declares that his teachings are now officially at my disposal. I ask him questions about that and he replies that the function of his teachings is to connect the Roots with the Trunk and then with the Top of the Great Tree. 'Our village,' he says, 'is one of the centres where Graha are gathered and then released in the Middle World, so as to proceed to the Higher World.' I reply that I am available to receive his teachings. Then I experience some moments of confusion with my mind wandering somewhere else. I realise that this is a decoy. I go back to what I had seen before I was distracted. I notice that my mind went astray when it saw the shaman handing me a large bowl. I go back to that scene and take the bowl. I see that the liquid in the bowl is transparent as water. I am invited to take it as part of my first teaching. I drink it and then go into a state of lucid trance. I see a group of deer pulling a gig with a laughing man aboard. He sings songs of joy and rides in a region similar to Siberia. Then he stops for he sees something luminous on the ground. It is a crystal cone, very bright and beautiful. As he wonders what to do with it, he hears a voice saying: 'Place it on the Heart'. He does so and then hears the following words: 'Pahai Attha, Pahai Idriahe, Pahai Pahai Pahai'. An Angel descends and says: 'Oh dear brother, you have been chosen to spread the energy of this Sacred Cone everywhere. You plant its apex into the ground of the Middle World. That way you allow the release of what is in the belly of the Earth and the liberation of your companions there. Once they get out, they will pass through the Middle World, from where they move again towards the Sky. The Middle World is like a station, a point of passage between the Earth and the Sky and vice versa. Your function is that of endorsing this exchange.' At my question regarding his identity, the Angel turns out to be the Guide of the Higher World. He then asks *me to concentrate only on the use of the Sacred Cone and to bring everything back to it. 'I deal with the Higher World,' he says, 'while the companions who gave you the bowl deal with the Lower World. They provide information about what is to be released in the Middle World where you abide.' The effect of the liquid ends and I wake up. I find myself again with my ally and some members of his tribe. I ask the ally what to do with the vision I have received. He tells me to nurture it regularly. I ask him what the name of his tribe is and he says Quiumakai. I then ask what kind of work I can do. The shaman gives me a black substance and pronounces a word in sacred idiom. He instructs me to take that substance to the Middle World and then release it in the Higher World. I also see a black crystal. Then the drumming ends and I say goodbye to the ally who invites me, at my request, to come again and receive other teachings. During the following twelve months I receive daily teachings from this ally in what becomes a long training of formation. The procedure is always the same: first he gives me a cup of a liquid, whose colour changes every time and which I drink, then I have a vision and when I come back I ask questions about it. On another occasion twelve main Graha, or Demons, surround the ally. They represent the projections of the essence of all the hallucinations of evil or pain which can be experienced on Earth. By getting to know them, I am told, you can learn how to transform and heal yourself and the world.*

1   Osho, *The Orange Book,* Rajneesh Foundation, 1983, pp. 188-189. (This book, which contains a wide range of meditation techniques, is out of print and is currently replaced by Osho, *Meditation: The First and Last Freedom,* St. Martin's Press, New York, 1996).

2   See Sector One, note 4.

3   See Sector One, note 5.

SECTOR FIVE

~ Sign: Leo ~ House: 5th ~ Planet: 1) Sun 2) Sun ~
~ Ray: 1st (Will/Power), 5th (Concrete Knowledge/Science) ~
~ Element: Fire ~ Quality: Fixed ~
~ Direction: South ~ Season: Summer ~
~ Totem Spirit: Surahim Tahe ~
~ Epic States: Hartem, Metrah. ~

ANIMALS: Boar, cat, cock, crocodile, deer, dolphin, eagle, elk, firefly, hawk, lark, lion, lizard, lynx, nightingale, peacock, salmon, starfish, sturgeon, swan, turkey, and all feline animals.

PLANTS: Often with golden or orange colours, round shapes and strong smell. They have often annual cycles of growth and tend to move toward the Sun. Acacia, almond, angelica, anise, ash, calendula, camomile, cedar, centaury, chestnut, cinnamon, daffodil, date, frankincense, geranium, ginseng, grape, grapefruit, hazel, juniper, laurel, lavender, lemon, maize, marigold, marjoram, mint, musk, mustard, myrrh, nutmeg, olive, orange, palm, passion flower, peony, pineapple, rice, rosemary, rue, saffron, sage, sunflower, St. John's wort, tangerine, walnut, all aromatic herbs.

MINERALS: Amber, carnelian, cat's eye, chrysocolla, chrysolite, citrine, diamond, fire agate, garnet, pink tourmaline, rhodochrosite, ruby, sardonyx, topaz.

SPIRITS: Michael (*Angels*); Quetzalcoatl, Tonatiuh, Huitzilopochtli (*Aztec*); Shamash (*Babylonian*); Belanus, Lugh (*Celtic*); Jesus, St. Jerome, St. Mark (*Christian*); Ammon, Aton, Helius, Mendes, Osiris, Ra,

Sekhmet (*Egyptian*); Cautha (*Etruscan*), Asclepios, Apollo, Dianus, Dionysus, Helios, Heracles, Hyperion, Teia (*Greek*); Balarama, Indra, Pushan, Savitri, Surya, Vishnu, Varuna, Brahma (*Hindu*); Inti (*Incas*); Amaterasu (*Japan*); Itzamna (*Maya*); Thor (*Nordic*); Mithras, Zoroaster (*Persian*); Apollo, Hercules, Jupiter, Aesculapius, Sol (*Roman*); Strength, Sun (*Tarot*).

ANATOMY/
PHYSIOLOGY:

Heart, spine, back, circulatory system, thymus gland, spleen, right eye (male), left eye (female), brain, right testicle, immune system, individual cells, consciousness, vitality.

ASSOCIATIONS:

Procreation, self-expression, ambition, entertainment, play, honour, loyalty, pride, intent, leadership, monarchy, supreme authority, positions of rank, celebrities, powerful people, jewellers, actors.

COLOURS:

Yellow, gold, orange, red.

DETECTORS:

2nd brother/sister, partner of 4th son/daughter, 1st and 7th son/daughter, friends of partner, partners of friends, 2nd brother/sister of mother of father. 4-2, 3-3, 2-4, 1-5, 12-6, 11-7, 10-8, 9-9, 8-10, 7-11, 6-12.

GRIEVANCES:

Excess: arrogance, conceit, destructiveness, dominance, exhibitionism, intolerance, irony, narcissism, ostentation, pompousness, shallowness, tyranny. *Deficit:* fear of limelight, lack of ego or boundaries, low self-esteem, poor self-concept, self-effacing, self-hate. *Physical:* anaemia, heart and back problems, Hodgkin's disease, leukaemia, shingles.

QUALITIES:

Acknowledgement, appreciation, authority, celebration, confidence, creativity, excellence, generosity, joy, light, magnificence, open-heartedness, play, power, self-esteem, strength, triumph, vitality, will, worth.

Sector 5 represents the district, capital or residential area of the supreme authority of the horizontal axis. Here there is a royal dignity which stems from holding a spontaneous role of power. The king, unlike the prime minister or other political authorities, has no need to fight for a ruling position. He is relaxed, as his supremacy is undeniable. It emanates from the connection to a divine source and is a right of birth. And this is indeed the characteristic of true power in general. Sector 5 confronts me with the nature of this power and the ways in which I elect to use it.

In this sector I find the most prominent way of connection between Intent and Function: it is a high road moving from the awareness of my individual centre to that of the divine Centre.

As it is the main road, it is also the one with most side streets and diversions. Here the ego exhibits itself with all kinds of decoys and alluring lights. Such lights are at times so seducing and majestic that they can easily be mistaken and considered to mark the main road. Their purpose is often that of prolonging the journey in order to deal with the full exploration and release of complex grievances and major psychic *soap operas*. The disadvantage of diversions is that they are repetitive itineraries which end up revealing the same scenarios and scripts, multiplying frustrations and grievances. Their advantage is that they continue to teach me the same lessons until I have fully mastered them. When this is the case, I can move ahead. In this way everything serves an honourable purpose and diversions become sacred paths of teaching.

The blossoming of Sector 5 resides in my growing capacity to shine and generously dispense energy in all directions. It is based on the awareness of the connection between Intent and Function, and of my role as centre for all that exists within and without me. Such a situation develops a powerful natural magnetism, and a spontaneous self-esteem, emanating from the acknowledgement of my true identity. The exploration, and the direct relationship with Sector 5, enables me to play out all kinds of roles with pleasure and totality. The key is not to identify with the roles but to take them only for the purpose of their release. In Sector 5 I learn to lead the energies like the conductor of an orchestra. Here I am on the stage of life and proudly face the limelight. I find my potential to shine, and to go for my Intent, as I connect it with my Function.

Although each sector belongs to the horizontal axis and has equal value, Sector 5 and the Sun usually play a decisive role especially as a first stage. Once the connection with the Spirit Guide has been established, it is important to focus on the Intent and find out what are the major purposes of the fragmented part with which I identify myself. This means facing the Totem Spirit of Sector 5 and getting to know what his programme is, how is he dealing with it and most of all, whether such a programme is in harmony with my current Intent connected with the Function. According to this strategy this work is to be carried on in co-operation with the Guide. The basic structure of this interaction between me, the Guide and the Totem Spirit, is exemplified in the model given in the Introduction ('Basic Practices, Exploration of Sectors') and in Book One (Chapter 7, 'Connection with the Totem Spirit').

♌ *Leo:* This seasonal time represents the apex of summer. The heat of the Sun is strong and allows fruits and crops to reach their maximum ripeness before the harvest time of Virgo. Human beings slow down their activities and take some rest in preparation for the labours that will follow in Sector 6. For the Celts this time coincided with the harvest festival of *Lughnasad* (1st August), which also marked the sacrifice of the sun god.

After the identification with the collective traditions and the security of the past (Cancer), Leo moves its steps toward a path of individual creativity and self-affirmation. Here I can project my power into the world and allow it to be acknowledged by the environment. This implies the capacity of being creative, joyful, excited, proud, magnetic and of generously expressing oneself in the world, dwelling in the limelight and receiving admiration in response. When the Leo energy is lacking, people may fear to expose themselves, be low in self-esteem and blocked in the expression of their creativity. Too much Leo energy may result in the opposite effect with the person always demanding the central role and craving for constant attention.

Fifth House: This is the sphere where I can experience pleasure, entertainment, playful activities, games, and all kinds of creative work. How this is expressed is the result of the way in which the relationship to the Spirit of Sector 4 (Moon, immum coeli, fourth house, Cancer) has been dealt with. This means to be aware of, and properly work out, my roots and ancestral lineage, my inner child and its basic needs, my personal history connected to the collective history. Once the elements of the fourth house are assimilated and integrated, then enormous power becomes available for creative use and can be employed in Sector 5. In the history of human beings, creativity is essential, as it allows us to leave traces of our presence on Earth. It is a primary factor that expresses itself in various ways: bearing and bringing up children, having love affairs, building objects, producing inventions, leading political or idealistic enterprises, manifesting works of art, etc. At another level, the creative expression detaches itself from the ordinary models of the ego (Level 1) and relates to a wider awareness (Levels 2 and 3). The person becomes the agent for a collective intelligence, a channel for beings of other dimensions, a bridge between cosmic forces, a shaman. He is like a limpid and immaculate crystal through which various degrees of light are drawn and amplified. In this way the creative expression can gradually adjust to higher frequencies, releasing its subtle grievances and surrendering its Intent to the Function.

Sun: The position of the Sun in the natal chart can provide some clues about the basic type of energy available to the person, the general Intent, the areas of major creative expression and the *ego* according to the Freudian model of the psyche. It is important to notice that the Sun is just one of the Totem Spirits and, as such, is on the same horizontal level as the others. It is not to be confused with the Centre. If the Totem Spirit of the Sun is dominant and does not connect with the vertical axis, the active ego, as opposed to the passive ego of the Moon, takes over. In some way the Sun acts as mediator between the inner world and the outside world. If it is afflicted or weakly placed, it can have difficulties in fulfilling this role.

When the Sun is located below the horizon, in the lower part of the astrological chart, the Intent of the individual generally tends to develop through inner research, withdrawal, solitude or intimate and meditative activities. The Sun above the horizon may be an indication that the individual realises himself through actions in the outer world and relationships with others. If the Sun is situated in the eastern part of the chart, the Intent is often expressed through creative acts, initiative and use of power in the outer world. When it dwells in the western part, the person seems to face events produced by uncontrolled circumstances and tends to follow a path of acceptance. According to Raymond Merriman's evolutionary astrology,[1] the presence of the Sun in the first quadrant (from the immum coeli to the ascendant) shows a way of evolution through individual experience, meditation, intuition, self-mastering. The Sun in the second quadrant (from ascendant to medium coeli) gives a strong power of growth, initiative, yang, warrior attitude and creative expression. For such individuals it is essential to commit to specific objectives, be actively involved in the outer world and have a clear Intent. The Sun in the third quadrant (from medium coeli to descendant) indicates a path based on acceptance of others and self-transformation. These people are often involved in partnerships and social relationships. The Sun in the fourth quadrant (from descendant to immum coeli) shows a mystical, passive, female, predominantly *yin* path where the individual doesn't try to control events but accepts them instead. It is a path of faith and inner exploration.

Basic Practices

a. Using the guidelines (given in Book One, Chapter 7, 'Connection with the Totem Spirit' or Book Two, 'Introduction, Basic Practices, Exploring the Sectors') meet the Totem Spirit of Sector 5.

b. Activate the piece for Sector 5 of your Sacred Circle Pieces (see Book One, Chapter 4, 'The Sacred Circle Pieces' or Book Two, 'Introduction, Basic Practices, The Sacred Circle Pieces').

c. Choose one of the following practices ('Healing Tools') and do it daily, every other day or three times per week, for at least 21 days.

Healing Tools

1. **Attuning to the Sun:** Most religious traditions devote a lot of attention to the Sun. The custom of praying or meditating at dawn was very common in ancient times, as the rising Sun signified the emergence of light from darkness. The following meditation is used to attune to the Sun and its life-giving energy. Open the Sacred Circle and then sit or lie in a comfortable position. It is advisable to do this practice outside or in a place where you can feel the rays of the Sun on your body. If this is not possible due to climatic or other conditions, you can work in the inner world, and this is also perfectly all right. Take off your shoes, relax and be still. Ask your Guide to operate as filter between you and the Sun. Close your eyes and become aware of the light and heat of the Sun. Consider the position of the Sun in the universe, its relationship with the Earth and its location in your astrological chart. Then become aware of the inner aspects of the Sun: warmth, light, life, love, creativity, etc. Explore its qualities until you get the meaning they have for you. Extend this awareness to all parts of your body. Allow it to penetrate through each cell. Then begin to radiate it through your emotional, mental and spiritual bodies. When you have a full sensation of the energy of the Sun filling all your bodies, radiate it outward into the environment. Let it move in all directions. Finally, return to the awareness of your body, thank the Sun, open your eyes and take this energy with you throughout the day. If the heat of the Sun is strong, do not expose yourself to its light for more than ten minutes.

2. **Greeting the Sun:** Get up some minutes before the sunrise. Await the rising of the Sun as if you were waiting ardently for your beloved. As the Sun rises, feel that simultaneously something inside you is also rising. Once the Sun reaches the horizon, sense that it is close to your navel and continuing to rise. Practise for ten minutes. Then close your eyes and be still for another ten minutes. When your eyes are open the Sun creates a negative, so that when you close them you can see the Sun glowing inside.

3. **Expressing Appreciation:** A vital practice for Sector 5 is that of expressing appreciation and gratitude for all the beauty and light that you see in others. (One of the things that surprises me most is the fact that most people are not aware of their gifts. Perhaps this is so because certain qualities are so visible and taken for granted that nobody bothers to point them out. I have realised that, as a consequence, many people disregard their talents or, paradoxically, consider them as imperfections and defects that need to be changed.) To show appreciation and support for something positive that you see, is a most powerful healing practice. Also accepting compliments and appreciation without downplaying them is a major spiritual technique. A very common conditioning is the tendency of being modest, or of mistrusting compliments, and suspecting those who pay them of being after something. A group practice that encourages a different attitude is the *Circle of the Sun*. Participants gather in a circle and one of them starts by holding a talking piece. After connecting with his inner Sun, he looks at another person, says her name and gives the piece to her. Then he appreciates that person in some way. It can be a compliment, a pleasant comment, or something non-verbal, like a hug, a caress, etc. It is essential to give a wholehearted appreciation, without discounting it with feedback or ironic remarks. These deny or take back the healing effects of appreciation. An example of a discounting appreciation would be: 'You are really a loving person, full of care and tenderness for everyone. If you could only express the same love and care for yourself it would be perfect.' The person who receives the appreciation is invited to accept it, without giving it back or minimising it. After receiving, the person addresses someone else by name, throws him the talking piece and expresses her appreciation. The process continues until everyone has given and received at least two appreciations.

4. **Calling Your Name Using Only the Vowels:** This is a powerful practice related to Sector 5. For example, *FRANCO* becomes *AO*. The vowels of the name disclose the inner and sacred Intent of the individual. When I pronounce them I attune to my centre and connect it with the Centre. This is an effective practice also in groups. There each name can be chanted with vowels as a mantra. Singing names and hearing them resonate in the circle is a very deep experience of support for Sector 5.

5. **The Dances and Movements:** In Sector 5 these stimulate creativity, authority, generosity and power. Centre your energy in your head, shoulders and heart. Be radiant and focus on your in-breath. Feel that every time you breath, you fill your whole being with light and power. See yourself as a king, queen or emperor. Expand your chest and extend your walking stride, moving with high dignity.

6. **Playing a Role:** This technique exalts the dramatisation potential of Sector 5. First define the role you will be acting, possibly one whose characteristics are the opposite of those you show in your ordinary life. Then, once you have found your role, take some time to study it in detail. Be aware of how this character moves, speaks, feels and behaves. Consider also what he wears and his major habits. The next step is that of playing the role in certain moments of your life. Be aware that here you are the only one who is aware that you are acting. The outer world is to see you as that role. In all situations you need to behave according to the role. Perhaps you can go to a place where nobody knows you or just stay in your usual environment facing the challenge that friends or acquaintances might see you. If this is the case, just carry on playing your role. This was one of my favourite techniques. Once for many days I wore a long beard, moustache, a turban, and a long robe. I moved around the streets of my town with a black briefcase, pretending to be an Indian spiritual master. My involvement with the part was such that I received an invitation to perform a healing ritual and even began to attract some followers.

7. **The Paheka Sadohe Korah** (Chant of the Totem Spirits and Guides): For Sector 5 the chant is *Surahim Tahe Sadoh*. Please use this practice only if you intend to establish or support a regular relationship with the Totem Spirit of Sector 5. If you intend to use this chant, you can either sing it from

time to time to accompany a cycle of twelve shamanic journeys in Sector 5 or as a practice on its own to be done preferably once or twice a day for at least seven minutes during a period of 21 days.[2]

8. **The Scale and Chant of the Sun:** In order to activate or balance Sector 5, you can use this chant:

Oh Hay Yah, Oh Hay Yah, Oh Hay Yah, Oh Hay Yah, Oh

As you sing it, you can visualise the image of the Sun distributing its light towards all the planets orbiting around it. The Scale of the Sun is a powerful device for connecting with one's Intent and releasing grievances related to Sector 5. If you use the Sacred Circle, you can sit or stand in Sector 5 or the sector where the Sun is positioned in your natal chart. You can also stay in the sector where the Sun is transiting at the moment. Before beginning, if you wish, you can light a candle (preferably orange or yellow) and burn some incense. After calling your Guide, according to your habitual procedures, connect with your Intent. Ask your Guide to draw the energy of the Sun and the Totem Spirit of Sector 5. Then sing the chant (*Oh Hay Yah*, four times, followed by *Oh* at the end). It does not matter how you chant it, how many times and with what quality of voice. The Scale of the Sun is the main scale of the planetary scales. It represents the Intent and operates to connect the solar plexus with the heart centre. Witness what happens during the practice and, if you notice grievances, find your way to acknowledge or express them, without identifying yourself with their content. In the first stages open yourself to a situation of total block of the solar energy. Then experience the lower expressions of the Sun and Sector 5. As with all the scales, you are invited to express or channel the lower stages with maximum intensity and awareness. When you reach the peak of the lower stage, pause and find your way to gather all the energy and lift it up to the next stage. Then start and open up to the higher vibrations of the Sun. In the final stage simply be receptive to the energy of the Sun and see what happens. Conclude by singing the chant for the last time. Then ground yourself and take note of your insights. Another practice is that of singing the entire set of planetary chants from Sun to Pluto. This aims at strengthening the role of the Sun as the representation of the Intent of light and the expression of divine potential. In this practice, the Sun is the starting point and identifies with the body. After the chant of the Sun, move to Mercury, perceived as a small planet orbiting a few inches from the body (the Sun). Venus is also very close, whereas the Earth and the Moon are about half a meter away, and so on until you reach Uranus, Neptune and Pluto, which are much farther and can even be perceived out of the room.[3]

Astroshamanic Reports

In my astroshamanic work the relationship with the Totem Spirit of Sector 5 (the Sun) has a strong connection with that of Sector 4 (the Moon). The 144 combinations between the Sun and the Moon, as described in the annual lunar cycle, have taught me major experiential lessons in this life and have provided most of my basic astrological understanding. I am so grateful for having allowed the Moon and the Sun to be my teachers. When I started to study astrology, mythology and symbolism in general, I read a lot of books in order to get information and understanding. The more I read the more I felt confused and helpless. Something was missing and I didn't know how to find it. Upon asking for help from my Guide, all he would say was: 'If you want to know about the planets, the stars and the gods, go and ask the planets and the stars themselves.' His suggestion was too obvious and easy for my complicated mind to accept. I continued to move from one book to another and I gradually cut off the connection with the Guide. In the end I went into such a state of intellectual and emotional despair that I felt my life was useless. I didn't know what to do with all my potential. I had a lot of energy that wanted to be expressed. There was something to communicate and create. That something was not available in any book and I had no idea what it was and to whom I was supposed to communicate it. Nobody around me seemed to understand my condition. I felt like a complete alien and the only way out I could think of was that of death. It was in one of those dark moments that I was reminded of my Guide's advice. The situation was so grave that I was forced to heed his suggestions. 'All right,' I cried out, 'I will talk to the planets and their gods! I have nothing to lose after all, as at this stage I am indeed ready to lose everything. What shall I do?' The Guide replied: 'What god would you like to start with?' 'Let's start with Apollo as a representative of the Sun,' I answered. I thought I would have to go through a long period of training and demanding practices before even considering the idea of dealing with Apollo. I was therefore very surprised when my

Guide prompted me to meet him straight away. And it was then that my first astroshamanic relationship with a god, or Totem Spirit, officially started. Apollo empowered me and gave me lot of support as regards my first workshop. On that occasion Apollo told me: 'Connect with me and my sister Artemis. Bring what you find in the underworld to me. You have my blessings for your workshops. Stress the relationship between the Sun and the Moon.' When I heard these words at that time, I felt greatly energised but I did not get the sense of them. Upon reading them now, everything is perfectly clear and consistent.

The most important discovery during these early connections with planets and gods was realising that they were not after all the first connections. The major amazement was not that of being able to connect with gods, or Totem Spirits. What truly astonished me was the retrieval of hidden memories about previous relationships with such beings. These were not of past lives. During this life I had already had many interactions and long conversations with planets and gods. I had just forgotten about them. It was my decision to forget them, as they could not fit with my ordinary life. I am grateful to the crisis I went through, as it created the condition for the memories to come back. Meeting planets and stars was indeed a return to my home, and people, after a long time of absence. I would like to share with you a report which is very precious to me. It is a partial description of a shamanic voyage to my original source of power. That day a great shift occurred in my awareness and I was vividly confronted with my Intent and Function here on Earth. The report is incomplete and some technical details have been omitted. Moreover, as it was a most intense experiential journey, a great deal of information was communicated through sounds, images and vibrations that I could not convey in words.

For long time I have been asking the Guide about my Intent here on Earth, about what am I supposed to do. I have tried everything. I don't know what else to do or invent. All I have received so far are either enigmatic answers or the usual sense of peace, silence, love and acceptance that always emanates from my Guide. I treasure my connection with the Guide and I do understand that whenever I call upon him, I can receive all the support that I need. Yet, there is a part of me that is not satisfied. It is a part that wants to know in practical terms why I am here and what can I do to serve for the best. That part wants a strong vision, an answer that makes sense, that can wipe away all uncertainties. I want something which once I get it, I can say: 'That's it! This is my mission here. Now everything is clear. I don't have to move like a beggar any more. Now I know why I am here! Maybe the part that wants all this is just my inflated ego. And this is at least what I have thought so far. Now it doesn't matter whether it is the ego or not. What counts is that I want to know. I deserve to know. It is my right. I have a lot of energy and I don't know what to do with it. I am not going to spend another minute of life on this planet unless I get an answer. I realise that it depends on me and I take full responsibility. I am an adult now. I am ready to receive the truth about myself. To whoever is concerned I declare that I am available to open up to my highest Intent. I welcome it even if it is not going to please me. I understand that Guides are very sensitive. They take many precautions with human beings and are more than careful not to invade their space. This time I do invite you, Spirit Guide, to be frank and direct about me. All right?'

After this dynamic speech, I look at my Guide. He is contemplating me with such sweetness and grace. He knows everything about me and from his luminous gaze I can get something like: 'Your mission is to play and be happy. Do whatever makes you happy. I will support you.' I perceive such a wonderful sense of freedom. As I confront myself with my Guide I do not feel any obligation. I get only love, unconditional love. If I wish to embrace a great cause, if I am determined to accomplish heroic enterprises, well, I realise that the choice is only mine. 'If this makes you happy,' my Guide says, 'do it!' He always empowers me. I feel such power in his presence! But what can I do with all this power? How can I share it? It is so big! 'Can you suggest anything? Or, to put it better: could you allow me to find out what would be the best thing for me to do? I am asking this of you, beloved Guide. I can accept whatever. I promise that I will respect and treasure the answer if only I receive it. I will not question it. I surrender to it.' The Guide looks at me with an expression that conveys: 'Do you really mean what you say? Do you really want to know that? Will you accept it?' I look him straight in the eyes, as I take a deep breath and send out the most gigantic YES of my life. After that, without further explanations, I suddenly dash and fly with my Spirit Guide and animal spirit towards a whitish planet. It is all covered with a fog that looks like whipped cream. We land there. The fog gradually fades away. To my total astonishment I begin to see the shapes of a most familiar and yet most surprising environment. It is the place where I have spent most of my time since I was a child. A constant returning point of nourishing fantasies. A place that I have often judged as an addictive escape from my responsibilities in the world, a day-dream, an invention out of my frustrations, etc. I am amazed! I have spent years drawing maps of that place, with all its towns, lands, stars, planets, people. I have had endless secret conversations with its people.

Indeed that is the place where I have lived most of my life. Yet, I have never managed to accept it as something spiritual *or* shamanic. *Although it kept coming to me in every situation, I would dismiss it to search for something else. I wanted to have visions like the ones described by great shamans and spiritual leaders. Whenever I went into a journey, I kept meeting this* fantasy *world. But I could not take it seriously. I was looking for something else. How could I accept that what I had repeatedly been looking for has indeed always been available for me? Well, now indeed I do. I see the same places, landscapes and buildings which populated my fantasies. They are there and this time they are part of a shamanic experience. They have come as a result of an agreement with my Guide. I look at my Guide to check whether this is so and to receive a confirmation. To my further astonishment I notice that he is very familiar with that environment. He belongs to it and, moreover, he is indeed one of the major characters of that world! I have known him since I was a kid. This is marvellous! Everything fits so perfectly.*

With my Guide I land at Interspace Hartem Port: *the major interdimensional station of* Hartem, *the largest town of* Handor. *From there we have a priority access straight to the* Major Handorian Headquarters. *We get on a very special carriage of the* Hartem Transport System. *After a few seconds I find myself in the long corridor of a huge building. Everything looks familiar to me. With great determination and excitement I walk through the corridor. In the meantime many people gather. My visit seems to be something most unusual and unexpected. Everybody is staring at me with great amazement. It looks as if I am a very popular hero. I can sense such expressions of joy and surprise in the faces of the people around. It is as if they are saying: 'How did he manage to get here? How is it possible? What an incredible event! What joy! How grateful we are to him!' It is clear that it is a surprise both for me and them. It is also obvious that it is a most pleasant and joyful surprise. As I move through the corridor, I see well-known faces. They look at me silently with such respect, care and love. It is a scene of immense beauty. I cannot describe it. It is too much. I realise that for some technical reason I have to hasten my steps. It seems as if I cannot stay in this place for long. At least this is what I get from my Guide's gait. I need to see the* Interspace Principal Commander, *the one who deals with relationships from outer space. We are heading towards his bureau. He is the one from whom I am supposed to get the answers I want. We enter into his huge office. When I see him, I don't even introduce myself or say: 'Pleased to meet you,' or 'Hello'. I don't feel any sense of awe and that surprises me. I just witness myself bluntly asking: 'What's my original mission on Earth?' The*

Principal produces an ecstatic and yet very professional smile. He pauses for a while. Then he gently takes out a file from a drawer. He opens it and shows me a sheet with a picture. There I see something that puzzles me, for it is like the advertisement for an Italian ice-cream. It is the image of a brown cone with the apex downwards and a golden or yellow semicircle on top. The top is full of light with beams stretching out in many directions, making it very similar to a luminous torch. I ask what the significance is of this. The Principal replies: 'You're planting the seed as a living seed. This cone is about planting the seed. You plant the cone and that grows until the light is seen. You're a seed, you're a lighthouse.' Although the words of the Principal don't make any sense to my ordinary mind, I am well-acquainted with his tone. As I look at the cone, I realise it is very familiar. After a while I get an intuitive mastering of the whole story. 'How can I proceed with the work?' I ask, just to have a confirmation of what I am getting. The Principal answers: 'Keep constant contact with us. Daily. Go and perform with no concern and keep the connection. You connect daily, then hourly, every minute and finally all the time. First we need your information and then we send ours. Plant your seed. Wherever you go, plant it and forget about all local arguments.' Then I ask if I can receive something to support this connection. Before I can even finish my question, the Principal declares: 'You will now receive the Sacred Cone Seed.' He hands me a small luminous cone and then gives full instructions on how to operate it. He stresses that the purpose of the seed is release, or forgiveness. 'What you release,' says the Principal, 'are materials much needed here. It is your Function to send them. Send Earth's grievances and create conditions so that everybody can do this. We need them and in exchange we send those resources that are lacking on Earth, i.e. blessings, peace and love. Go on with your work! For the time being, there is nothing to explain about it. The explanations are beyond the understanding of human minds. To put it in simple terms, we need grievances to fertilise something here. Send the raw material. Earth has a lot of it, and we don't. Earth is a major productive field.' He then adds further detailed information which I omit here. 'Out of your constant research and asking,' continues the Principal, 'the content of your original mission is now available to you for development. Receive total acknowledgement. You can now organise yourself and start your operations. The time is ripe!' I look at him as if I were waking up from a long dream. There is something else that I need to get before I leap into this adventure. I do not feel totally convinced. The Principal then shows me a contract. There I can see a signature which I immediately recognise as mine. 'You were one of the main supporters of this Game and volunteered to go,' says the Principal. 'Now you're on the spot. Therefore, go on with the Game and play! And send grievances daily! That's what we mean by your coming here daily. That's your only Function as long as you are there. We bless and love you so much.' Then, after inserting the Sacred Cone Seed in my forehead, he calls some of his personnel. They all express their highest appreciation. They say such beautiful things about me and my role. Everything is clear. I cry with happiness and begin to sing with all of them. I continue to sing during my journey back. I keep on singing for the whole day. I continue to receive further information on the cone during the following days. I listen and see things so blissful and amazing that there is no naming them. They are beyond my ability to understand or know. I feel so blessed and filled with the vision that is finally going to set my life aright.

[1] Raymond Merriman, *Evolutionary Astrology: The Journey of the Soul Through States of Consciousness,* Seek-It Publications, 1991.

[2] See Sector One, note 4.

[3] See Sector One, note 5.

SECTOR SIX

~ Sign: Virgo ~ House: 6th ~
~ Planet: 1) Mercury; Asteroids, Ceres, Vesta; Chiron 2) Moon ~
~ Ray: 2nd (Love/Wisdom), 6th (Devotion/Idealism) ~
~ Element: Earth Quality: Mutable ~
~ Direction: South Season: Summer ~
~ Totem Spirit: Kahesepoh Sadeh ~
~ Epic States: Framg, Gmarf. ~

ANIMALS:	Ant, bear, dog, dolphin, donkey, fox, goose, mouse, pelican, sparrow, squirrel, swallow, whale, wolf, wryneck, domestic animals in general.
PLANTS:	Almond, barley, bean, caraway, celery, chicory, dill, endive, fennel, fig, hazelnut, lavender, lemongrass, marjoram, millet, oat, parsley, pecan, peanut, pistachio, pomegranate, rye, valerian, violet.
MINERALS:	Agate, amazonite, amber, aquamarine, carnelian, citrine, chrysocholla, crystals in general, flint, jasper, marble, sapphire, topaz, turquoise, zircon.
SPIRITS:	Raphael (*Angels*); Nidaba (*Babylonian*); St. Anthony of Egypt, Virgin Mary (*Christian*); Asclepios, Hermes, Astraea, Demeter, Hestia, Chiron (*Greek*); Ganga (*Hindu*); Mercury, Ceres, Vesta, Aesculapius (*Roman*); Hermit (*Tarot*).
ANATOMY/ PHYSIOLOGY:	Intestine, spleen, pancreas, digestive enzymes, sympathetic nervous system.
ASSOCIATIONS:	Analysis, classification, cleaning, details, discrimination, diets, nutrition, food, health, hygiene, purification, research, selection, service, work; accountants, craftsmen, critics, health officers, inspectors, teachers, masseurs, secretaries.

COLOURS:	Yellow-green; violet, brown.
DETECTORS:	1st and 7th brother/sister of mother, 4th brother/sister of father, partner of 1st brother/sister of father. 5-2, 4-3, 3-4, 2-5, 1-6, 12-7, 11-8, 10-9, 9-10, 8-11, 7-12.
GRIEVANCES:	*Excess:* fastidiousness, frustration, fussiness, guilt, hypochondria, hyper-criticism, inferiority, insecurity, nit-picking, over-modesty, over-perfectionism, over-specialisation, pedantry, pessimism, restlessness, self-denial, servility, unworthiness, work-addiction, worry. *Deficit:* confusion, lack of critical sense and analysis, superficiality. *Physical:* appendicitis, intestinal troubles, nervous disorders, obsession with diets and health, peritonitis.
QUALITIES:	Adaptability, attentiveness, availability, efficiency, gentleness, healing, humility, kindness, obedience, observation, purification, purpose, service, synthesis.

A major task in Sector 6 consists of finding out and defining the specific location, structure and correspondence of all energies, as they are perceived in each existing form, either seen or apparently unseen. Such huge consistency of forms, fragmented and separated by the hallucination of the ego, is retrieved and reconnected to its united matrix as represented by the Sacred Circle. Here all patterns move in a spiral and take their own position to contribute to the healing process. Healing takes place through releasing the source of all possible sickness: i.e. the belief in the perception of separate bodies and forms. Since shamanic healing is based on the fundamental assumption and experience that my true nature is spirit, and not the physical body (perceived as separated) or the ego personality, all kinds of sickness are regarded as sheer illusions. Whatever I accept into my mind is bound to become the reality for me. If I enthrone the belief in separate bodies in my mind, then I am likely to be affected by sickness. This means that I am going to enter into a forlorn battle with the physical reality. Here I can either be the prey of sickness, addiction and eventually succumb to that, or live a healthy life in which I keep my body in good form. Indeed, as long as I consider myself as separate, there is no real difference between these two options. My being healthy is simply the result of the projection of sickness and death towards what I perceive as unhealthy. For this purpose I build a pseudo-reality based on the avoidance of something with which I will inevitably have to deal, sooner or later. Although I can insist on such insane belief, deep in myself, I am aware that I am simply delaying the effects of an inevitable outcome. And this creates anger, fear, guilt and all the sickness that I may perceive either within or without.

Sector 6 corresponds to the phase of selection and assimilation in the cycle of sectors. It is a stage that requires the attentive work of discrimination between what is useful and what needs to be released. Discipline, critical capacity, an eye for flaws and the ability to take things apart and reorder them in better shape are called for. Everything is carefully analysed, classified and allocated to its specific and best usage. This involves filtering or storing the essence of every form and discarding the rest. Here it is essential to focus on the resources that are extracted rather than on the wastes that are expelled. Otherwise, waste material risks being held on to, blocking the process of assimilation and producing toxic effects.

In the astroshamanic cosmology, Sector 6 is also the place where all records and information are kept. It is a sort of cosmic multimedia library that contains all possible documents and files as regards life in this and other dimensions. Large dossiers related to all the beings that live or have ever lived on Earth can be found here. The access to such data requires a level of spiritual integrity, power and purity which is virtually out of reach for most human beings. By regularly working with the Spirit Guide and the Totem Spirits, the information related to my own dossier can gradually become available and allow me to uncover my primary role at all levels of existence. Once I decide to abide by this role, then I am confronted with a huge process of discrimination. This involves releasing all the parasitic and conventional roles that I have inherited out of the collective and individual fear to face my primary role, i.e. my Intent connected with the Function. In Sector 6, I can become squarely aware of the portion of work that represents my contribution to the whole. When this occurs, all that I need to do is simply to go on with the work, without questioning any more the nature of my Intent or pretending to be confused. The power of Sector 6 lies in accepting my part and taking no other. Such acknowledgement gives a sense of immediate peace and safety.

Before receiving the revelation of the *Sacred Cone*, which brought major clarity on this matter, I had a major experience about my primary role, during a training on experiential astrology in Poona (India). In the course of a meditation, where I was investigating the overall purpose of my life, I felt myself descending onto the Earth as an engineer. I had been called to repair something. With my bag full of maintenance tools, I reached the machines which were out of order. Peacefully undisturbed by all the activities and turmoil around me, I fixed the machines, made sure that they worked properly and then returned to my base in space, ready to answer another call. Although at that time most of my thought system considered that vision as metaphoric science fiction, I did realise that, on a deep as well as practical level, it made much more sense than anything I had experienced so far in my life. That call had been there since I was a small kid, although I had always seen it as a fantasy. Whenever I went into that *fantasy* I sensed such joy, peace and clarity. Yet, I felt it was an invention, a day-dream, an addiction or a sort of insanity. From the part of my mind conditioned by the social environment I would receive feedback such as: 'It is not real, you have made it all up. You must face real life. You must take on your responsibilities in this world. You are trying to escape from something. You are afraid to face life.' I spent many years trying to find out what I was escaping from. I thought it was the so-called *reality* as opposed to my *fantasy*. As a consequence I did my best to face the consensus reality and comply with it. Putting to good use my abundant Virgo and Scorpio traits, I dissected all components of that reality, experientially analysing every part, going to its roots and moving to the minutest details. The more I faced and went into the *reality*, the more I found it unreal and insane. I would then return to my original fantasy and then back again to consensus reality to explore something else that I had missed before. I continued with this to and fro movement, until I was finally confronted with the startling experiential fact that the consensus reality was also a fantasy of mine. In that decisive and powerful moment, I acknowledged that my life had been a constant swing between two *fantasies*. It was not a question of finding out what was the reality and trying to adapt myself to its laws. This could not apply any more. Now I had the power to choose between two options, and I was totally entitled to make such a choice. Electing my original fantasy would inevitably imply the gradual undoing and release of the other fantasy. That is indeed the breakdown that I have come to repair as an engineer, out of my adherence to the original fantasy.

Whatever happens in the ordinary reality is but the rough version of what is taking place in non-ordinary or subtler realities. For example, as regards work and employment, which is a typical theme for Sector 6, each occupation has a specific correspondence in other dimensions. This means that through my work – it does not matter what it is – I can find a connection with other realms. According to Sector 6, work is the sacred practice par excellence and is meant as *seva*, a Sanskrit word which means 'unconditional service'. Here I find out what is the part in the whole that I can play to be truly of service and what action is needed to comply with it.

♍ *Virgo:* The seasonal period of this sign is that of the summer harvest. Human beings, after taking some rest in the previous months, have gathered strength to go back to hard work and store the fruits of the Earth. It is a time of great attention, discrimination and care, as the quality of this labour will have decisive repercussions in the following autumn and winter seasons. This work requires time, patience, mental discrimination and ceaseless release of blocks to the perception of what is meant to emerge. It is a state that often causes a sacred restlessness and anxiety in Virgo people. The perfection of the reality that they experience in their mind apparently requires major labours and activities to be manifested outside. There is absolutely no problem for Virgo to face hard work when there is clarity of Intent and, as a matter of fact, this is what makes life wonderful for this sign. Yet, when they are disconnected from their Intent, existence can sometimes be very bitter, boring, and unhappy. Here they risk turning their analytical faculty against others or themselves, rather than using it in their higher service. Virgo, together with Capricorn, is a practical and hard-working sign. Its potentials flower in the realm of work and service, and Virgo people may at times feel out of place and experience discomfort in social life.

Sixth House: It is traditionally related to healing, work, service, health, hygiene, cleaning, nutrition, domestic animals. In the sixth house (as the seasonal time of Virgo generally indicates) I go back to work once the holiday time is over. This house represents a time of purification through a direct relation with matter and practical work, meant as an act of service for the community and the whole. Here any activity can be transformed into a ritual work and become an opportunity for major healing. The sixth house is also connected with situations of inner crisis and with those apparent difficult times in life that occur whenever processes of transformation are activated.

☿ *Mercury:* Virgo traditionally shares the rulership of Mercury with Gemini. Virgo's Mercury expresses its qualities in concrete and practical ways. This sign represents the introverted and analytical inner aspect of thoughts, the capacity for classification, selection, definition and order of the mind. It is related to Hermes as inventor of astronomy, written music, alphabets, weights and measures. Mercury in Virgo is also associated with healing as represented by the *caduceus* (a staff with two serpents spiralling in opposite directions), signifying the vertical axis and Sacred Cone structure, and to Mercury's function as *Hermes Psychopomp*, the guide of dead souls into the Lower World.

Asteroids: They are a belt of thousands of minor planets orbiting between Mars and Jupiter. Although ways of considering asteroids differ among astrologers, I am inclined to assign all to Virgo and Sector 6. The four main asteroids are Ceres (⚳), Vesta (⚶), Pallas (⚴) and Juno (⚵). Those that are most related to Sector 6 are Ceres and Vesta. *Ceres* is the largest asteroid and represents the nourishing, fertile and personal side of Sector 6. It depicts the practical aspect of the mother figure (providing food, working in the house, healing, educating, etc.) rather than the emotional (Moon). The prominence of Ceres in the natal chart can indicate major healing potentials and talents in the area of nutrition, medicine, agriculture and service in general. *Vesta* is an asteroid named after the virgin Roman goddess of the sacred flame and home altars. The position of Vesta can indicate the areas where the individual is likely to commit to something greater than himself and joyously sacrifice aspects of his life for the benefit of the whole. It can also give a clue as to how sexual energy can be employed in a sacred way. Many individuals that experience apparent limitations, frustration or deviations in their sexuality, as it is perceived according to the models of conventional reality, have often made a precise choice at the level of their soul, which is essential they understand, in order for them to express their potential and enjoy their true purpose in life. The relationship with Vesta can help and support the acknowledgement of their true sexual nature and empower shamanic and healing potentials, releasing guilt and conditioning generated by conventional ideas and prejudices. The transits of Vesta often indicate a time of retreat and solitude, or the beginning of a specific work which is likely to become a sacred service or mission in one's life.

Chiron (δ) is a planetoid discovered in 1977 with an eccentric orbit crossing those of Saturn and Uranus. This makes it appear as a bridge between the energies of these two planets. Chiron expresses the energy of Mars at a higher octave, shifting action from a focus on behalf of the individual to that in the interest of a cosmic Intent and the whole. A prominent position of Chiron in the chart (i.e. conjunct to one of the angles, the Sun or Moon) is typical of healers, spiritual teachers, shamans and whoever is subject to apparent suffering and deep crisis as a form of release and transformation. This is, by the way, the most common initiation for most healers. Chiron triggers us into the deepest wounds and grievances so that they can be acknowledged and cleared. Together with Pluto, it represents the most intense and devastating force in life. Chiron, by transit, often identifies the times of maximum pressure during a lifetime and, at the same time, the periods of highest illumination: those which enable the access to other dimensions. When Chiron transits any natal planet, it brings the possibility of a radical shift of consciousness and a quantum leap as regards the energy of that planet. The rulership of Chiron has been attributed to Scorpio, Sagittarius and Virgo. This last rulership may provide a deeper explanation of the nature of Virgo than Mercury alone seems able to provide.[1]

Basic Practices

a. Using the guidelines (given in Book One, Chapter 7, 'Connection with the Totem Spirit' or Book Two, 'Introduction, Basic Practices, Exploring the Sectors') meet the Totem Spirit of Sector 6.

b. Activate the piece for Sector 6 of your Sacred Circle Pieces (see Book One, Chapter 4, 'The Sacred Circle Pieces' or Book Two, 'Introduction, Basic Practices, The Sacred Circle Pieces').

c. Choose one of the following practices ('Healing Tools') and do it daily, every other day or three times per week, for at least 21 days.

Healing Tools

1. **Storing Information:** One of the major practices in astroshamanism consists of recording, selecting and storing information received during inner journeys, rituals,

workshops, connections with the Spirit Guide. Tools such as the *Astroshamanic Journal* or the *Map of the Journey* (see 'Introduction, The Astroshamanic Journal' or Book One, Chapter 5, 'The Astroshamanic Journal' and Book One, Chapter 7, 'The Map of the Journey') can be immensely useful in this process. They allow the recording of data that can easily be lost or forgotten, due to the strong disturbing and diversionary effects of the ego system. I am always amazed whenever I read my old journals and discover that already twenty or more years ago I had received most precious guidance. The information received in deep shamanic experiences belongs to a dimension of *eternal present,* or *here and now.* This means that they continue to be available and bestow their gifts in any moment of my life and every time I decide to revisit them. Indeed there is nothing so valuable as such experiences. And I am very grateful to Sector 6 for providing the determination to keep track of them. For this purpose, during shamanic journeys I often employ a tape recorder. There I record the live description of what is happening. In this way I can then write down the integral sequence of the journey without missing precious details. When I listen to the tape, sometimes only a few minutes after the journey, I am often surprised to hear things that I have already forgotten. A more subtle way of storing information consists of *using special stones.* Quartzes, hematites or other gems can be programmed to record the contents of journeys. Care in keeping data that I receive during shamanic experiences is also a sign of respect for the Spirit Guide and other unseen beings. This does not mean that they are going to be offended if I don't take note of my shamanic experiences. The act of recording information (in whatever way I choose to do it: by writing, drawing, using a tape, etc.) is a safety precaution for advancement with shamanic work. It makes things easier. It is indeed the act of erecting a bridge between non-ordinary and ordinary reality. The first shamanic experiences are only the outer layer of deeper experiences that can only be disclosed if I build a strong foundation, i.e. if I learn the first lessons. This work is like putting together a puzzle. The picture defines itself as I continue gathering the pieces. Nothing will ever come up if I take a new piece and do not consider the previous ones. When I start a puzzle made up of many pieces and begin to collect the first ten or twenty pieces, the picture is still likely to be a mystery. Maybe one piece belongs to the upper right corner and the other to the centre. Yet, as I move along, the first pieces will help me track the arrangement of the whole picture. The shamanic experiences that you have in your journeys, dreams or other practices are most precious pieces. You cannot find anything of such value either in the world or from any person you meet there (including spiritual masters and enlightened ones). Patience and diligence are needed here, and Sector 6 is a great teacher.

2. **Work: Releasing Grievances:** How you feel about your work or the way you serve in your community and environment has a deep impact on health at all levels. In Sector 6 the essence of work is not remuneration, but the feeling of doing something good, of contributing with one's craftsmanship and producing tangible and acknowledged effects. Whenever you feel grumpy, bored or annoyed that you have to go to work, before discharging an avalanche of complaints and grievances on your environment or mind, stop for a while. Pause and exhale deeply. Feel with the exhalation that you are releasing grievances. Do not focus your attention on the nature of your grievances. Avoid going into any rationalisation about them. Simply allow them to be experienced and released. Continue to let go of all grievances, disregarding their appearance. What is the point if they are nauseating and revolting? Why should you involve yourself with them if you have decided to let them be and go? Own them and empty yourself. You will be surprised to notice a change within five minutes.

3. **Identifying, Prioritising, Accomplishing and Releasing Tasks:** Those who have Sector 6 emphasised in their energy system can easily get involved in huge amounts of work activities. This can often cause anxiety, stress, frustration and many worries, as the attitude of Sector 6 is not only that of taking on a lot of work, but also of carrying it out in the best way. A practice which I find useful is that of identifying all work, tasks and chores that I can think of, both professional and domestic, or short and long term. I write them down on a sheet of paper, prioritising them with a number according to their importance and setting an expiry date for their completion. A good time for drawing up this list is around New Moon. During that period it is good practice to withdraw from major involvement and take one or two days

to connect within. This allows me to explore what are the best ways to employ energy in accordance with my Intent. The list is a tool to put order in the mind and also to discriminate about what is essential and non-essential. If I realise that a certain task has been postponed for a long time, I confront myself with the decision either to complete or release it. All the resolutions that I have made in my life, even the most trivial, continue to hang on in the mind until either I manifest them or let them go. Simple affirmations like 'I want to write a letter to him', 'I want to repair the bike', 'I want to go to India' or whatever, will literally haunt me and deplete my energy unless I take a clear position regarding them. Also it is important to be aware of and alter the thoughts which are repeatedly used to sustain negative and grieving trances. The technique of *telling lies to yourself* described in Sector 3 can be very useful here.

4. **Abstaining from Judging:** Another typical attitude of Sector 6, on which I used to be an authority, consists of magnifying problems, judgements, criticisms and complaints both towards oneself and others. A useful practice is that of abstaining from judging. Spend a whole day avoiding all expressions and thoughts of complaint and judgement. Live a day accepting everything and everyone, without making any exception. It does not matter whether you truly feel like that or if you pretend. Simply do it as if you were an actor. Play with it. Then continue the same practice every other day for 21 days. You do not necessarily have to take this up as your style of life forever. It is just a strategy or game. If you have spent most of your life criticising and blaming yourself or others, and this has not brought anything good to you, what do you have to lose if you avoid doing it just for one day or a week? See what happens when you stop wasting your energy in search of faults and mistakes, and concentrate instead on the beauty, love or anything valuable that exists within and without you. Always remember that what you see in others is what you choose to see. The awareness of your ego to the errors of other egos is not the kind of practice that is required in spiritual work. To the ego it is perfectly all right to point out mistakes. Errors belong to the ego and correction of errors lies in the release of the ego. 'When a brother behaves insanely, you can heal him only by perceiving the sanity in him. If you perceive his errors and accept them, you are accepting yours. If you want to give yours over to the Holy

Spirit, you must do this with his. Unless this becomes the one way in which you handle all errors, you cannot understand how all errors are undone.'[2] When I first began the practice of abstaining from judgements, I realised that I didn't really know what to talk about with people. I became aware that the absolute majority of my conversation was based on judgement or complaint toward something or someone. It could be the government, the church, the neighbours, my work, my health, my friends, myself. Abstaining from judgement was therefore tantamount to being silent. It was amazing to notice that both in myself and others. It was also astonishing to discover how healing were the effects of my abstention. When I stop criticising and judging others, accepting them as they are, without wanting them to be different, I begin to accept myself. Often, the hardest and most cruel judgements are expressed indirectly through irony and jokes. It is a way of avoiding the embarrassment of a fierce confrontation which, although it is not considered aggressive or offensive in conventional life, does not make any difference for the unconscious and emotional side. That side is simple and direct. There, my words are accepted as they are and do not have obscure implications. The unconscious does not understand irony, nor does it have any sense of humour. It is incapable of seeing separation and totally alien to personal pronouns. If I say something unpleasant about somebody, all that is acknowledged are just the unpleasant words, and, as there is no understanding of pronouns or jokes, they will be directed both to me, the other and everyone. The abstention from judgement becomes complete when I also avoid being involved in situations that provoke judgement, even if I don't take part directly in the process. For this purpose it can be useful to shun the company of people who indulge in judgements and also to avoid reading newspapers, watching television and the like.

5. **Fasting:** This is one of the most ancient healing practices and is very typical of Sector 6. It is an effective way of cleansing the physical body and keeping it healthy by emptying it of stored toxins and blocks that prevent an effective flow of energy. When you take no food for a day or more, the body is released from the labour of processing and allocating nutritive substances. The abundant storage of reserve energy is finally employed and this prevents its contents from becoming useless and stagnated. Fasting is also

a major spiritual practice, used by many traditions to commune more directly with Spirit. Whenever I choose to let go of something that is considered essential in this dimension, I open myself to other realms. By fasting I also release my urge to fill the body with something. Through abstaining from food, I communicate my willingness to *die temporarily*. In this way I can be totally present in the here and now and focus on what is being activated at a subtle level. For some people fasting for a long period can really feel like dying, while for others it can be a most pleasant opportunity for getting some rest from all the labour involved with buying or collecting and cooking food, washing up dishes and digesting. It is not the purpose of fasting to cause sufferance and pain. On the contrary it is a joyous experience and a graceful opportunity to connect with other levels of perception. It is good practice to fast with an Intent and do a simple ritual or invocation to open and close the period of the fast.

6. **Discrimination:** One of the basic qualities of Sector 6 is the capacity of discrimination. This function, when applied to the internal monologue and the external dialogue, can allow me to retrieve and value information that supports my highest Intent and release whatever curtails it. By holding a neutral stance, through meditation and shamanic practices, I can check out the data in my mind before allowing it to circulate and coming to automatic conclusions. According to the tradition of the Sacred Cone Circle, *negative* thoughts, or grievances, are voiced out and released in specific shamanic practices, such as the *Basic Ritual* (see Book One, Chapter 4, 'The Astroshamanic Basic Ritual of the Sacred Cone'). When grievances are directed as an offer toward specific areas of the vertical axis, they reach dimensions that employ them for the highest. Conversely, if they are expressed in the horizontal axis (i.e. in the ordinary environment, both within and without), they create damage and spread like viruses. Some tribal traditions have a strong awareness of what serves best at a horizontal level and manifest it in their conventional phrases. For example, when some of these people notice in their thoughts or conversation anything that supports an Intent of love and unity they say, 'This is a story that needs to be told'. On the other hand, if they hear themselves or someone saying words or expressing thoughts of judgement, grievance or guilt, they say instead, 'That is a story that

doesn't need to be told'. For the latter case, in the *Sacred Cone Circle*, we say, often with a most delightful expression, '*Grahe Ilibisi Pahai!*' or 'This is an exquisite delicacy for the *Sacred Cone!*'

7. **The Paheka Sadohe Korah** (Chant of the Totem Spirits and Guides): For Sector 6 the chant is *Kahesepoh Sadeh Sadoh*. Please use this practice only if you intend to establish or support a regular relationship with the Totem Spirit of Sector 6. If you intend to use this chant, you can either sing it from time to time to accompany a cycle of twelve shamanic journeys in Sector 6 or as a practice on its own to be done preferably once or twice a day for at least seven minutes during a period of 21 days.[3]

8. **The Chant and Scale of the Asteroids:** This chant refers to the entire band of asteroids and is employed to heal situations of separation, fragmentation, confusion, worry, lack of clarity and focus. It also operates on the archives of the mind, releasing data that blocks the connection with higher levels of awareness. The chant is:

Si Ti Yah Kah, Si Ti Yah Kah, Si Ti Yah Kah, Si Ti Yah Kah,
Mah Si Kah

Unlike the other chants, besides having an opening (*Si ti Yah Kah*) and a closing (*Mah Si Kah*) expression, it also uses a final one:

Ai Hey Poh

This is chanted to indicate the conclusion of the chant.[4]

Astroshamanic Reports

The following voyage takes place during a Full Moon in Virgo and is aimed at connecting with the Spirit of Sector 6, *Kahesepoh Sadeh Sadoh*. Both the energies of Sector 12 (Pisces) and 6 (Virgo) are at work and melt with each other. The Spirit of Sector 6 reveals itself mainly through feelings and at a certain stage (when the subject changes from *I* to *we*) is channelled by the voyager himself.

I sense an extraordinary white light radiating from my centre. Upon opening the Sacred Circle I envisage a representative for each direction and sector. This white energy reaches everywhere and everyone: situations and persons of the past, present and future. It's a great dance of love and power. I sing the Asteroid Chant *and take everything back to its original common matrix. Whatever has been lost or stranded is being reunited: a great variety of energies, emanating from the same centre, becoming a whole again; first, watching and considering the differences, happily classifying all kinds of characters, seeing their own place in the universe; then, finding the point of emanation, the very same Great Tree which shows up the basic unity. I'm going to meet the Spirit of Sector 6. I invite the Guide to be with me as I say: 'Stay with me every moment in all deeds. The sacred dream is becoming a reality. What is radiating inside is taking form outside and more and more the world I see becomes a place of delight, a paradise, a place of power. I accept this challenge to see the real face of the world, the face of my loving Guide. The time has come for the vision of Pisces to be grounded into Virgo, to be given form and become tangible. The time has come for sacred dreams to be real and part of this life as I perceive it. We, as a team, are determined to get to this. All our deeds are aimed at this basic Intent that dwells in our hearts. We'll get at it with the sacred help of all divine alliances known and unknown. We go, we go and see beyond until we get to that dwelling place. We're determined to find the space of love wherever we move and wander in this life. We're the heroes of this age: a new age of understanding, reawakening and transformation. And we go and clean, that's our Function. And in this cleaning we rejoice. We don't care where the dirt comes from. That's not our business. We clean whatever, whenever and wherever. We enjoy the period of cleanliness and, when the dirt comes, we clean again. That's our Function. Keep on cleaning. We are happy cleaners. We don't care about the waste; we let it go through the Sacred Cone. We celebrate what is being received out of this exchange. We let all dirt go through the channel so that it can be used for the Plan of Salvation. We do that! And enjoy the ecstasy of sacred cleaners. This dance continues all the time in every sector.'*

The following are connections made with the Spirit Guide to receive guidance on Sector 6.

Today I have created a deeper connection with my Spirit Guide. He summons all Spirits and Guides needed. He acts as a basic reference point between me and non-ordinary reality. He's been with me for ages, attempting to connect and express himself. He's the driving craziness, the uncontainable sex urge, the anger, the restlessness, the craving heart, the excitement. He's pure energy and I welcome him at last. We're going to work for a basic purpose. Together we explore each sector. I ask him about Sector 6 and he explains that 'the Totem Spirit of Sector 6 is the silent worker who operates behind the scenes, who sends energy everywhere without seeking recognition. The Spirit of Sector 6 is being nourished by the same act of serving and is not interested in being seen. He knows that his work can be effective at any moment. He knows that he can operate now! The present moment is the most adequate condition for his work. He works now as he's aware that he can die now. He is willing to express his heart's desire in this moment to accomplish his Intent connected with the Function with no further delay. He performs now! He works now as this is the most perfect moment. Now, now, now, now! And as you chant the Asteroid Scale you summon all the units spread in the universe and make them into one single force. They dance together and are finally united, celebrating with joy the ecstasy of divine communion. It's a great re-encounter and everything is being channelled through your Intent connected with the Function.'

And now I would like to pay a brief tribute to my old occupation. I worked for thirteen years in the hotel business as night porter. That time was a major blessing for me, as those long nocturnal shifts supported the connection with a different reality. My rhythms of life were upside down compared to those of ordinary human beings. I would go to bed when most people got up and be awake when they slept. I received such valuable teachings from all those nights. The amount of actual hotel work required only a couple of hours and this left ample time for me to do whatever I wanted. Mostly I would use those hours for studying, meditating, sleeping, eating delicious food from the restaurant, relating with and opening up to other realms or even giving healing sessions and meeting members of my Circle. Hotel nights were a major shamanic formation time. It was there that I received some of the guidance that allowed me to develop astroshamanism. I am very grateful to all the hotels where I worked. The last one was a luxurious old villa in the midst of a wonderful park full of ancient trees. By midnight everybody was already in bed and from then until the end of my shift, I was the king of the place. I was virtually paid just to be there and rest or do my own things. During my period of employment I had many non-ordinary experiences and visions that fitted perfectly into my being in that place. Then I realised my time in that hotel was coming to an end. One night as I was outside, gently caressing the trunk of my favourite tree and admiring the beauty of the house, I exclaimed: 'It is like heaven here. What a blessing! I do feel uncomfortable though. What is it?' The reply came straight away, as I sighed: 'If I could only be in a spiritual hotel! I wish I were in a place where people come in search of Spirit, to heal themselves and the world. This would make me very happy. I am sure you will understand, beloved trees. I am grateful for the joy and peace we have shared together.' That night I took the decision to leave my hotel profession. 'If ever I go back to work in a hotel,' I promised, 'it has to be a spiritual hotel.' As I write now, I look out from the window of my room overlooking the forest around Cluny Hill College.[5] Soon I will start my shift at reception... And my mouth gently widens into a big smile.

[1] Barbara Hand Clow is one of the major supporters of Chiron as ruler of Virgo and the sixth house. For further information see: Barbara Hand Clow, *Chiron: Rainbow Bridge Between the Inner and Outer Planets*, Llewellyn, 1995.

[2] *A Course in Miracles, Text*, pp. 167–168.

[3] See Sector One, note 4.

[4] See Sector One, note 5.

[5] *Cluny Hill College* is the educational campus and main workshop-accommodation centre of the spiritual community of the *Findhorn Foundation*. It was formerly the hotel (*Cluny Hill Hotel*) where Peter and Eileen Caddy with Dorothy Maclean (the three historical founders of the *Findhorn Foundation*) used to work.

DIRECTION WEST

~ Element: Water ~ Season: Autumn ~ Body: Emotional ~
~ Kingdom: Vegetal ~ Part of day: Dusk or sunset ~
~ Signs: Libra, Scorpio, Sagittarius ~ Sectors: 7, 8, 9 ~
~ Human age: Adulthood ~
~ Totem Spirit Keeper: Rogah Sadoh ~ Colours: Blue, black ~
~ Celestial bodies: Moon ~
~ Journey: Way of the Spiritual Warrior ~
~ Spirit Pathways: Strength, experience, introspection. ~

ANIMALS:	All fish and water creatures, all reptiles, bat, bear, crow, elk, frog, magpie, owl, raven, snake.
QUALITIES:	Balance, co-operation, courage, empowerment, forgiveness, intimacy, intuition, power, rebirth, relationship, release, self-discipline, sharing, transformation.
GRIEVANCES:	Attachment, confusion, control, fear, hiding, intolerance, judgement, manipulation, obsession, vindictiveness.
HEALING TOOLS:	Bhakti yoga, cathartic work, creativity, death/rebirth experiences, dream work, rebalancing, rituals of release, silence, soul retrieval, standing meditations, trance dance, work with ancestors and power animals.
INSTRUMENTS:	Cauldron, cup and grail, click sticks and bones, conch shell, didgeridoo, masks.
MINERALS:	Amethyst, aquamarine, hematite, lapis lazuli, obsidian, opal, river stones, silver, smoky quartz.
PLANTS:	Algae, camomile, hibiscus, jasmine, nettle, sagebrush, vanilla, violet, willow.
SPIRITS:	Quetzalcoatl (*Aztec*); Arianrhod (*Celtic*); Archangel Gabriel (*Christian*); Isis (*Egyptian*); Poseidon (*Greek*); Neptune, Diana, Selene, Hecate (*Roman*); Undines, Sprites, Nymphs, Naiads, Mermaids, Nereids, Oceanids, Potamides (*Nature Spirits*).
FESTIVALS:	Fall/Autumn Equinox (20/23 September); *Michaelmas* (29 September); *Samhain* or *Halloween* (31 October).

The path of the West represents the fall and death of an old cycle and of all that has been familiar so far. It is a most intense and blessed time. Here I have the opportunity to relinquish my conventional ego identification, as the centre of my awareness, and move into dimensions where I can get a wider perspective of who else I am. As the sky gradually shifts into more darkness, and physical nature apparently dies, a time of obscurity and death at an emotional, mental and spiritual level descends. This process of *initiatory death* is often called the *Way of the Spiritual Warrior*, or *shamanic death*. As such, it can cause trepidation in the habitual ego which tends to hold on to things because of its terror of what lies ahead. By cultivating introspection and connecting with the Sacred Circle and Spirit Guide, I can withdraw from the fears generated by the insane belief in separation and gather the love and support which I need to advance along the path of transformation. Being aware of, and accepting, the strategy of initiatory death, and the rebirth that follows as a natural development makes it easier to accelerate deep changes without going into the fiction of suffering, pain or loss. The major challenge in the West is to learn to die well to what no longer serves and be open to receive what honestly supports my Intent connected with the Function. Good questions here are: 'What is there in my life that wants or needs to die? What ways of being in the world do not serve my current Intent and all that I am discovering through my shamanic work? What no longer serves me, my loving companions, the community where I live, the planet and the universe?'

When I look at the world only through the perspective of my personal identity or of the culture I apparently belong to, I let the invention of my personal or collective ego rule as the centre of the universe rather than allowing the Spirit Circle, and all it represents, to be at the centre. This attitude may be useful in the early years spent on this planet, so as to build boundaries and a strong strategic ego structure. If this phase degenerates into an idolatry of my individuality, family, country, people, etc., as something separate or identified with a physical form, then the whole meaning of the strategy is lost. This is a very controversial area which can cause major confusion, if I lose track of my connection with the Guide and get enmeshed in the fragmented thought system of the personal or collective ego. 'The ego is insane. In fear it stands beyond the Everywhere, apart from all, in separation from the Infinite. In its insanity it thinks it has become a victor over God Himself. And in its terrible autonomy it "sees" the Will of God has been destroyed. It dreams of punishment, and trembles at the figures in its dreams; its enemies, who seek to murder it before it can ensure its safety by attacking them.'[1]

To serve my Intent connected with the Function is to let go of my attachments to pain, to release the tendency of wanting to be *right* at the expense of being happy, and to be available to explore other dimensions or ways of existing in the universe. I need to become aware of my role as channel and meeting place for energies of multiple realities and worlds. I need to understand that in every single moment I can elect whether to contribute to unity or separation, and that this choice involves being aware of the quality of my thoughts.

The West is an area of gradual withdrawal where shifts are experienced in the nature of social relationships as well as in dreams, shamanic journeys and connections with the inner world. Discovering and exploring the linking agents, or *Bhi Jinah*, that make up the web of life and uncovering the correspondences of the *Sector Detectors* (see Book One, Chapter 7, 'Sector Detectors and Shamanic Forms') are powerful practices for this season. The connection with the Totem Spirits and power animals of the West is also very helpful, as it provides essential energy to cross this major time of transformation. Facing the topic of death is another important feature as it gives major insights that open gaps into the shallowness of ordinary consciousness. Visiting cemeteries, considering people or relatives who have left their bodies, living each day as if it were the last, writing a strategic or actual testament, supporting terminally ill people are just some examples of connection with death. The release stage of the *Basic Ritual* (see Book One, Chapter 4, 'The Astroshamanic Basic Ritual of the Sacred Cone') is especially related to the West, and it would be helpful to practise it more often during this time of the year. In order to receive something new, I am asked to relinquish what is old and no longer needed. Release and death are an integral part of the cycle of nature at all levels. In shamanic work it is essential to be aware of this crucial phase of life which is often feared or kept unconscious in conventional reality. I need to learn how to dispose of what does not contribute to, or support, my Intent. I need also to be open to receive the assistance which is available at all times from the Spirit Guide and other seen and unseen beings. While this process develops, the ego senses that the framework of its hallucination is threatened and its reactions may become extremely intense. Certain situations in life may appear confused, fearful, earnest, precarious, painful or sad. And yet, a major transformation is taking place and incredible blessings blossom. Faith is required. Be with your Spirit Guide and have faith in him in what but seems to be a trying time. Go on with your practices, now that the rewards of your work are at hand. Allow yourself to be nourished by a new perception and accept the support that is there for you to receive.

The Bhi Jinah: According to the *Epic of the Sacred Cone*, *Bhi Jinah* are strategic beings that populate the gaps among the forms seen by ordinary human beings. They dwell in areas commonly defined as *nothing, emptiness* or *vacuum*. Their aim is that of drawing the attention to the fullness of such nothingness and making human beings aware of the connection and unity that exists among everyone and everything. Bhi Jinah are a sort of spiritual glue that joins all fragmented parts. They constitute the linking agent of the web of life. As the West, according to this tradition, corresponds to the water element, Bhi Jinah operate here as a primordial ocean that keeps whatever exists together. Their role is essential in all kinds of relationship. If partners are aware of such beings and encourage them to join in their relationship, ecstatic shifts can happen. To perceive Bhi Jinah, the only condition is that of being willing to see them and letting go of the hallucination of separation. Certain conditions or practices easily enhance this process. I usually experience Bhi Jinah as living joyful puppets or cartoons of different forms and size. Most of them wear a conic hat and also, at times, a tee-shirt with a cone printed on it. I often see them smiling and having fun. At times, depending on the sector they belong to and the situation of their environment, they can also be rather noisy and restless. Besides Bhi Jinah, there are also other beings too, such as *Graha, Sadoha* and *Paheka*. Well, I am not going into these now... One thing to keep in mind, as we step into the West, is that all I see is the result of what I have chosen to see. Bhi Jinah have taught me this lesson. If I look around, I can notice that the majority of the spaces that I see are apparently *empty* and not occupied by forms. Actually, from a spiritual perspective as well as from a scientific view, nothing is really empty or meaningless. It is just the conventional mind that accepts seeing only what supports its hallucination and refuses to acknowledge what would threaten it. This is the reason why Bhi Jinah are not usually seen: they would virtually blow up the entire foundation of the perception of separation.

Since I was a child I have noticed things and beings that my parents, relatives and whoever was around me did not appear to see. At the beginning I was sure that, as I was just a small boy, they shut me up or pretended that such things did not exist simply because it was a matter for adult people only. I felt that such mysteries were kept secret on purpose and disclosed only when one was of age. There were many things that could only be done after reaching the age of 18, like driving a car, voting, getting married, being allowed to watch certain movies. Thus, I thought that receiving direct information about Bhi Jinah or other beings and also about my true purpose in this world was only a question of coming of age. On my 18th birthday I envisaged that a special authority would arrange a meeting for me. There I would go, accompanied by my parents, and all the secrets of life would be revealed to me. I just had to be patient and wait. In the meantime, I could relax and be with the boys of my age. They did not seem to show much interest in these issues and would rather involve themselves with weird activities (such as soccer, basketball, motorcycles) in which I could hardly understand the sense. The only exception was a small group of friends who lived in my block at *via Oslavia 5* in Bologna. I used to play one of my favourite games with them. It was about sitting together on a low window-sill and pretending to be aboard a big starship moving into space. That was so exciting! Actually my understanding of the whole building was that it was indeed a starship. For me it was not a fiction, but a rare occasion in which I could share my perception of life. Hence it did not make any sense to stop the game, forget all about it and start deeds like homework, going to school or visiting relatives. I would try hard and do such things only to be entitled to adulthood, and to the supposed revelation of all secrets. At last, when I was alone, I could enjoy the starship and company of Bhi Jinah without any limitation. I would spend long hours talking to those beings, drawing maps of stars and planets, holding meetings with the starship crew, etc. So as not to create suspicion in adult people, I would pretend to do my homework or to play with some silly toys. I was very intrigued by Bhi Jinah and other non-ordinary topics, and would often ask questions of my parents. They would reply giving queer explanations or saying that I had to wait until I grew older. As a result I used to listen with much interest to my parents' conversations with their adult relatives and friends. What they said was gibberish to me, especially when my mother spoke the Bologna dialect with her relatives or my father the Sicilian dialect with his. When I heard such discussions, I was sure that they were about the issues I was craving to have explanations about. Hence I was really looking forward to becoming an adult. The first step, I was told, consisted of going to school and studying hard. My parents kept repeating this. One day they also explained that in their times they could not go to school for their families were very poor and also because of the war. They said, 'Franco, our parents could not afford to send us to school. We have worked since we were young and cannot provide the answers you ask. Yet, we are going to do the best for you so that you can study and get to know all you want.' How honest of them to admit that! I realised that I could not expect my parents to teach me certain things. Yet I would learn them at school. When eventually my school years began, I was quite disappointed to realise that nobody really cared about starships, Bhi Jinah and alike. I thought that perhaps it was a matter for more advanced schools. I looked forward to stepping into secondary school and university. When I did, I was even more dissatisfied and frustrated. I have no words to describe the pain, confusion and isolation experienced in my school years. I was puzzled about what was going on. The things I was required to study did not make any sense to me, although they appeared valuable for others At the same time what made sense for me did not seem to make any sense to others. Only years later, through the connection with my Spirit Guide, I began to get the first answers to my questions. Much to my amazement they did not come from school, parents, relatives or religious or state authorities. I had the first major glimpse of them in 1976. It is a long story and I am still trying to put it together. Upon looking back at my life now, I can only rejoice at the fact that my past is now making a lot of sense. I regard it as part of a comprehensive set of lessons that I have chosen to receive. Thank you Bhi Jinah. Thank you Spirit Guide. Thank you beloved parents and all my relationships at all possible levels!

[1] *A Course in Miracles, Workbook,* p. 467.

SECTOR SEVEN

~ **SIGN:** Libra ~ **HOUSE:** 7th ~ **PLANET:** 1) Venus 2) Uranus ~
~ **RAY:** 3rd (Active Intelligence/Adaptability) ~
~ **ELEMENT:** Air ~ **QUALITY:** Cardinal ~
~ **DIRECTION:** West ~ **SEASON:** Autumn ~
~ **TOTEM SPIRIT:** Ataherah ~
~ **EPIC STATES:** Hanmar, Ramnah. ~

ANIMALS:
Bee, butterfly, camel, cat, crow, deer, dolphin, dove, duck, frog, hen, lobster, kingfisher, owl, panther, peacock, pheasant, rabbit, salmon, sparrow, swallow, swan, trout, turtledove, wren.

PLANTS:
Usually with very attractive flowers and pleasant smell, smooth leaves and green fruit. Almond, apple, apricot, archangel, artichoke, asparagus, beans, birch, bramble, carob, cherry, chestnut, chickpea, clove, cypress, daffodil, daisy, dandelion, fern, fig, goldenrod, gooseberry, grape, ivy, lentil, lily, mint, myrtle, oak, parsley, parsnip, passion flower, peach, pear, pea, plum, pomegranate, rhubarb, rose, rye, strawberry, tansy, tea tree, thyme, vanilla, violet, wheat, yarrow, all sweet smelling spices and perfumes.

MINERALS:
Alabaster, aquamarine, beryl, blue sapphire, bronze, brass, carnelian, chrysolite, chrysoprase, copper, coral, diamond, emerald, jade, kunzite, lapis lazuli, moss-agate, pink tourmaline, turquoise.

SPIRITS:
Anaele, Lucipher (*Angels*); Quetzalcoatl (*Aztec*); Ishtar (*Babylonian*); St. Mary Magdalen (*Christian*); Isis, Maat (*Egyptian*); Turan (*Etruscan*); Aphrodite, Hera, Athena, Adonis, Themis (*Greek*); Krishna, Shakti, Lakshmi

	(*Hindu*); Freya (*Nordic*); Venus, Juno, Pallas, Vulcan (*Roman*); Justice (*Tarot*).
ANATOMY/ PHYSIOLOGY:	Chin, complexion, facial features, hair, lips (esp. upper), kidneys, navel, parathyroid glands, skin, venous circulation.
ASSOCIATIONS:	Love and romance, marriage, partnerships, social life, love affairs, beauty, pleasures, entertainment, festivities, arts, dance, rhythm, harmony, money, beautiful possessions, cosmetics, jewellery, co-operation, diplomacy.
COLOURS:	Green, soft yellows, turquoise.
DETECTORS:	Partner, ex-partner, paternal grandfather, maternal grandmother, 2nd son/daughter, 3rd and 7th brother/sister, 1st son/daughter of 1st brother/sister, roommate, friends of father. 6-2, 5-3, 4-4, 3-5, 2-6, 1-7. 12-8, 11-9, 10-10, 9-11, 8-12.
GRIEVANCES:	*Excess:* ambivalence, compromise, dependence, exploitation of relationships and sexuality for ego gain, extravagance, frivolity, gossiping, indecisiveness, indolence, laziness, narcissism, procrastination, wastefulness. *Deficit:* destructive relationships, fear of intimacy, incapacity or unwillingness to establish long-term relationships, lack of balance and sense of beauty. *Physical:* acne, kidney and bladder troubles, nephritis, skin disorders, spices or sugar addictions.
QUALITIES:	Balance, beauty, charm, co-operation, gentleness, grace, harmony, love, partnership, peace, relationship, sharing.

In Sector 7, I draw the power that allows me to create harmonious relationships among the various sectors and to connect different Intents to the same Function. It is a territory where balance is a major aim and all necessary actions are taken to foster peace, co-operation, agreements and loving relationships. Here it is easy to experience the interrelation of all parts and how their gentle combination contributes to the benefit of the whole. The expression of this sector requires patience, adaptation, diplomacy and practice in a constant search for equilibrium between one polarity and the other, or what is outside and inside: a delicate enterprise where points of accord are emphasised and contrasts are kindly released. In this area of the Sacred Circle I learn to accept myself through the acceptance of others, to understand what is the true significance of whoever is around me and how I am supposed to relate with them according to my Intent connected with the Function.

Ordinary ways of activating Sector 7 include the awareness of aesthetic value (clothes, furniture, art, beauty, etc.) and partnerships or relationships with others. This sector is also related with the *shadow*: that which I project outside and which follows me just like the physical shadow does, when I walk across a field on a sunny day. This side manifests itself in the people who are frequently close to me. As Sector 7 tends to absorb so much energy in outer relationships, it can sometimes be a difficult area to explore in the shamanic world and, as a consequence, a place which easily becomes unbalanced. One of the major causes of power loss here consists of investing conspicuous dosages of energies in nourishing thoughts and emotions of yearning, sadness, torment, jealousy, conflict, morbidity, obsession and all other kinds of grievances for past, present and future partners or lovers. This is a most customary parasitic practice for many human beings. Its consequence is to deprive one of vital energies that could be profitably employed to achieve shamanic states of consciousness, directly face the *shamanic forms* (see Book One, Chapter 7, 'Sector Detectors and Shamanic Forms') and therefore truly improve relationships in the ordinary reality.

In astroshamanism, the connection with Guides, Totem Spirits and shamanic forms allows the energies that are wasted or suffocated in ordinary relationships to be balanced and healed. The way in which I experience my relationship with others illustrates the reflection of my interaction with shamanic states of consciousness. Usually, when I am unable to create fulfilling or harmonious relationships in my outer life, it is because I do not live those relationships in my inner life. An intimate connection with the Spirit Guide and the states of consciousness that lie beyond ordinary awareness is what is truly searched for in outer relationships. The Spirit Guide is indeed the only figure that is capable of offering constant love, support and fidelity. Nevertheless, as his presence is discreet and non-invasive, I am the one who needs to take the first step toward him.

Libra: This sign begins with the autumn equinox: the time when the Sun passes from the northern to the southern hemisphere, making night and day of almost equal length all over the planet. The seasonal time of Libra is the declining cycle of nature. Trees lose their leaves and days become shorter, although this is still happening slowly and gradually. As the Earth produces landscapes of rare beauty, there is still time for relishing soothing moments of harmony and calmness. At the same time activities intensify: animals gather their winter supplies or get ready to migrate, and at all levels agreements and preparations are made for the next season to come.

With Libra the individual moves into the second half of the Zodiac and reaches a turning point. Here he starts being involved with a reality which goes beyond the personal level and expands in the social order. The first step is to move from one to two and this process regards relationships and partnerships between two or more beings and the realisation of harmonic interactions through conscious or unconscious contracts. This brings a desire for justice and accord through equal considerations of both sides. Such attention is meant to build bridges between polarities, to lay aside differences and support connections.

Seventh House: The cusp of the seventh house corresponds to the *descendant*, located opposite to the ascendant. The descendant relates to the people, energies or situations that I meet as I apply my Intent connected with the Function. These can be employed in two possible ways: to support and nourish the ego hallucination or to release such an illusion through forgiveness. Here some of the major repeated scripts of human beings can be found, especially as regards relationships. Certain people and circumstances in life respond to my work of refining and focusing of my Intent. The planets close to the descendant, the zodiacal sign of the descendant, its position and the aspects of its ruler define the energies of those people and situations that contribute to my release of grievances or the reception of blessings.

Traditionally the seventh house corresponds to relationships and partnerships of all kinds, including those with enemies. The experiences in this house can either refer to special and separated relationships or to sacred relationships aimed at forgiveness and unity. In this area, enemies or people who I tend to dislike are very useful as they help me uncover and release the grievances that my friends or lovers would politely ignore.

Venus: The position of Venus in the natal chart can be a key as regards the way in which I express my feelings towards others. Here I identify the types of person, things or situation that attract me or bring me pleasure, what I project on others, how I feel I can bestow affection, the way I behave and the strategy I employ in order to be loved, what

I may give in relationships and the way in which I perceive love. Love is one of the most misunderstood energies and, as such, it often finds destructive expressions. This is the case when I disassociate from my Intent connected with the Function or with my Spirit Guide, and I project that on another person. If this occurs I move away from my sacred centre and transfer it into the precariousness of someone else, as I perceive that in his/her physical form: this is inevitably going to produce and nourish fears and pain when that physical form, for some reason, is not with me any more. In a woman the position of Venus generally depicts the particular feminine archetype she identifies with or aspire to, whereas in a man it may be similar to Jung's concept of the *anima* or to the features of Demons (see Book One, Chapter 7, 'Demons and *Graha*'). The position of Venus in a man's chart tends to show what aspects of the feminine archetype cause most attraction or are projected onto external partners. Astroshamanic work in this area has to do with the retrieval of these qualities and the development of the *holy relationship*, that is, a state in which the inner partner is fully integrated and acknowledged, no matter with whom I am in an external relationship or whether I am in such a relationship at all.

Basic Practices

a. Using the guidelines (given in Book One, Chapter 7, 'Connection with the Totem Spirit' or Book Two, 'Introduction, Basic Practices, Exploring the Sectors') meet the Totem Spirit of Sector 7.

b. Activate the piece for Sector 7 of your Sacred Circle Pieces (see Book One, Chapter 4, 'The Sacred Circle Pieces' or Book Two, 'Introduction, Basic Practices, The Sacred Circle Pieces').

c. Choose one of the following practices ('Healing Tools') and do it daily, every other day or three times per week, for at least 21 days.

Healing Tools

1. **Greetings:** The use of simple and pleasant forms of greeting addressed to people, animals, vegetables, minerals, or anything seen and unseen is a most powerful practice of healing. Simply welcoming somebody with a heartfelt 'Good

morning' followed by his or her name is enough to exchange great amounts of energy and heal major conflicts. The words and the movements that I employ when meeting somebody are important. In real life there is nothing like an accidental or insignificant meeting. In every circumstance, through whomever I meet, both within and without, I have the opportunity to discover my authentic nature. 'When you meet anyone, remember it is a holy encounter. As you see him you will see yourself. As you treat him you will treat yourself. As you think of him you will think of yourself. Never forget this, for in him you will find yourself or lose yourself.'[1] Many forms of salutation employed by various traditions are expressions of this awareness. In India the form *Namasté* is often used. It means something like 'I bow to the Light that is in you' and is accompanied by an actual bow with the hands joined at the level of the heart. In Central Africa a way of greeting someone is to say 'I am here to be seen' to which the other replies 'I see you'. An old form of Gnostic salutation is 'I am the Light in you'. In the Maya tradition there is the expression *En lak'ech/A lak'en* that means 'I am another you. You are another me'. In some ancient Sufi dances, the participants meet the other dancers many times, moving around in two circles and greeting each other with specific movements and saying *Ya Azim. Ill Allah Hu*, 'You are wonderful. Nothing but God the One'. The use of the body as a form of salutation finds its most intense expression through hugging. Holding someone in the arms allows a visible connection with the energy of the other. It can also be substituted by other forms like shaking hands or kissing. It does not really matter what form of salutation is chosen. It can even be a silent movement of the head or a gentle smile. What counts is always the Intent and its connection with a Function of love and forgiveness.

2. **Shamanic Forms:** The relationship with *shamanic forms* (see Book One, Chapter 7, 'Sector Detectors and Shamanic Forms') is a most typical practice of astroshamanic healing. Here follows a brief example. Go to your Spirit Circle and call upon your Guide. Ask him to summon the shamanic form of a person with whom you have problems. Allow the image of that person to be translated into what that person corresponds to in your inner world. Do not relate with the image of the person as you see it in your daily life. Simply face the shamanic form. For example, if you have decided to deal

with your former partner, do not identify that person with his or her physical body. Open up to the energy that he or she has in your inner world. This is the true energy that is manipulating your former partner as a puppet. You could see this energy as an animal, an archetype, a dragon, a Totem Spirit, etc. What matters is that you do not use the image of the person as you perceive it in your outer life. When you see the shamanic form, tell it what you feel and the nature of your problems. If you are not comfortable, ask support from your Guide. You can also invite this form to take up another form with whom you can feel more at ease. Be aware that you are the master of your inner world and can create whatever you want. For example, if the shamanic form appears aggressive or dangerous, you can call a group of brawny guards to calm it down or surround it with a sphere of pink light. Useful work to do with shamanic forms is that of sending love to them through the Guide. You can also give permission to the form to relax and express the love it feels for you. It is up to you to do whatever you consider appropriate in order to create harmony. Once you have established a good relationship with the shamanic form, you can ask questions such as: 'What role do you play in my inner world? What lessons are you teaching me? What lessons am I teaching you? With what Totem Spirit are you related to? What other people or situations are related to you? What can we do together in order to bring love and peace into our lives? How can we harmoniously contribute to our highest Intent?'. Answers to such questions come either verbally or through images, feelings, thoughts, etc. If the dialogue does not work, find another strategy, ask your Guide to work as mediator, use your gifts, send love and light and, most of all, allow the shamanic form itself to send you love and light. Avoid getting nervous or frustrated if you do not achieve immediate results. The work with shamanic forms requires patience, devotion, diplomacy. In my experience I find that the best way to relate with them is to send light and love, and to allow them also to reply with love and light. Whatever appears to attack or disturb me always indicates an area within myself where I need to work. Every attack, as I perceive it, is always a request for love. In the outer life it is sometimes difficult to be aware of this. When I face the shamanic form, I can more directly relate to the outer persons and acknowledge them as parts of me.

3. **What Do I Like?** Reflect on the question *What do I like?* In the course of one week write as many sentences as you want beginning with *I like...* or *I enjoy...* Please be honest about all this and let go of any conditioning or judgement about whether it is right, spiritual or good to like something or not. If you tend to think of what you dislike or fear, consider the opposite and write it down. After one week read all your answers and discover their essential core. Organise them so that you come up with some basic statements about what you like.

4. **Focusing on Gaps and silences**: Every day for one week, I invite you to focus on the gaps that exist between objects or people around you, rather than on the objects or people themselves. Shift your perception by emphasising what is usually disregarded as meaningless. You can decide to spend a certain amount of time doing this every day and also to continue the practice throughout the day whenever you feel it appropriate or you have nothing specific to do. Pay attention to the gaps that apparently separate all the forms that you see. Such gaps are so important in astroshamanic work! Those places between the physical forms are the dwelling places of *Bhi Jinah*, strategic joyful beings of love and unity. When you start to become aware of them, you can rest assured that the hallucination of separation is close to being pierced. As you experiment with all these practices, go slowly, do not rush, take it gently, trust your intuition, take note of all your discoveries, allow the Spirit Guide to support you and open up to receive all you need. Please do not do this exercise while driving or doing anything that requires full attention to ordinary reality! Do the same practice with sounds. Bring your attention to the gaps of silence between words or sounds. For example, you can listen to the spaces between the words of someone who is talking and to the gaps of silence between the sounds that you hear as you walk in the countryside or in a town. You can also focus on the space of silence between the sounds that you make when you speak, sing or play an instrument. When you talk be aware of the gap between each word. Try and fill those gaps with energy and significance. And finally be very aware of the void that exist around you.

5. **Sector Detectors, Shadows:** Autumn is a major time for taking an inventory of your life and gently releasing

whatever or whoever no longer serves your Intent connected with the Function. As you move into the path of the West, attention to information coming from Sector Detectors is likely to increase (see Book One, Chapter 7, 'Sector Detectors and Shamanic Forms'). Have a look around! See what is being mirrored back in all that happens to you every day. Consider the places where you live and work, your job, friends, family, relationships. Look at everything. Whatever you see, you have created it in order to learn some lessons. Is this what you want? Is this the way in which you wish to live? Is your current life connected with your Intent? These questions are not aimed at making you feel bad, depressed or worthless. On the contrary their purpose is to give you power. By being honest and considering the reality of what you have created around you, without playing the victim or making excuses, you move along the best way to transform your life according to your highest Intent. Beware of your projections! Consider them carefully with neutral and non-judgmental eyes. Be willing to see what you are putting on others that you can own yourself. Shadows are reflections of yourself and give a wider perspective of what exists at various levels. Autumn is an excellent time to work with shadows, for when the sun begins to lower itself in the sky, longer and clearer shadows are cast around physical forms. Shadows are gateways to other dimensions. Take time to be aware of shadows. Simply look at them, breathing deeply and paying attention to what happens within and without you. If possible, spend an evening or night alone in the woods or in your home with all the lights turned off. Let the natural darkness of the night embrace you wherever you are. Watch how you feel. Are you afraid? If yes, what are you afraid of? Do you like the darkness? What do you like? Sounds also have shadow aspects and these are found in the spaces between each word or phrase or between the steady beat of your heart or of a drum. You can also decide to spend some time paying attention to those short instants of silence that exist in whatever you hear, as in the previously described practice.

6. **The Paheka Sadohe Korah** (Chant of the Totem Spirits and Guides): For Sector 7 the chant is *Ataherah Sadoh*. Please use this practice only if you intend to establish or support a regular relationship with the Totem Spirit of Sector 7. If you intend to use this chant, you can either sing it from time to

time to accompany a cycle of twelve shamanic journeys in Sector 7 or as a practice on its own to be done preferably once or twice a day for at least seven minutes during a period of 21 days.[2]

7. **The Chant and Scale of Venus:** This can be a valuable tool for activating or balancing Sector 7:

Nah Ti Nah, Nah Ti Nah, Nah Ti Nah, Nah Ti Nah, Oh

The Scale of Venus is a powerful device for releasing and transforming grievances based on relationship issues. If you use the Sacred Circle, you can sit or stand in Sector 7 or the sector where Venus is positioned in your natal chart. You can also stay in the sector where Venus is transiting at the moment. Before beginning, if you wish, you can light a candle (preferably pink or green) and burn some incense (for example, rose, patchouli, sage, cedar). After calling your Guide, according to your habitual procedures, connect with your Intent and Function. Ask your Guide to draw the energy of Venus and the Totem Spirit of Sector 7. Then sing the chant (*Nah Ti Nah*, four times, followed by *Oh* at the end). It does not matter how you chant it, how many times and with what quality of voice. The Scale of Venus operates mainly on the Heart centre, or *Anahata*. Witness what happens during the practice and, if you notice grievances, find your way to acknowledge or express them, without identifying yourself with their content. In the first stages open yourself to a situation of total block of the heart centre. Then experience the lower expressions of Venus and Sector 7. As with all the scales, you are invited to express or channel the lower stages with maximum intensity and awareness. When you reach the peak of the lower stage, pause and find your way to gather all the energy and lift it up to the next stage. Then start and open up to the higher vibrations of Venus. The stages usually involve the following themes: block of the heart, predatory search for love, romantic love or special relationships, forgiveness, holy relationship. In the final stage simply be receptive to the energy of Venus and see what happens. Conclude by singing the chant for the last time. Then ground yourself and take note of your insights.[3]

Astroshamanic Reports

Together with my Guide, I move to Sector 7 to receive guidance about sacred relationships. To the Totem Spirit of this sector, I ask how I can create a sacred relationship. I am pervaded by a sphere of pink light. From its centre the following answer reaches me: 'A sacred relationship is not a relationship between two partners. It is a relationship that involves three parties. In contrast to special relationships, that consider only two polarities, a sacred relationship opens up to the conscious presence and active participation of the third pole. It is indeed this third pole that keeps the relationship together. A sacred relationship starts when, as a mutual agreement, the third pole is invited. It is a process of initiation that requires careful and patient work. A sacred relationship is undisturbed by time and space. It dwells in the eternal present and continues also when the partner is far away or is not in the physical reality any more. The relationship goes on forever. Remember! Whenever you meet somebody in your thoughts, dreams or imagination, that is an actual meeting. Cease giving so much importance to physical forms. In a sacred relationship the connection at an emotional, mental and spiritual level is as real as that at a physical level. Employ the flow of subtle energy. Do not condense it, or separate it. It is the way of Sector 7, that of the harmonic and balanced flow of love. Surrender to the beauty and charm of this sector. Produce thoughts related to this energy and use the following practice: send out messages of love without saying anything, use the silence of your heart to talk, do not waste its energy through words or facial expressions. Avoid the display of your feelings, let them be a secret of love between you and me. And see what happens...'

I reach a large tipee *where Guides, elders, shamans and other holy beings gather in a circle. I enter and sit among them. Then I say with determination: 'I have come to receive instructions and get tangible signs of your presence. I am ready to surrender to my authentic Intent.' I notice that there is a fire in the centre of the circle. All those beings stand up and move around the fire. They gently wave their bodies as the shape of a horned animal takes form. The animal invites me to sit at a table with two of my Guides. I ask them: 'What can I do?' They answer: 'Operate in accordance with what you have established. Connect constantly with us. We are here to give you the support that you require. Great things are about to occur and only your availability can allow them to be part of your awareness. We cannot favour such a process if you are not consciously available. That is feasible only through your regular focus on your Intent and the related Trust. Remember: Intent and Trust.' I tell them that I am ready to do that and encourage them to give me further instructions. They reply: 'Be a channel through which our conjunct force can circulate. Look at all of us. Do you trust us?' I carefully watch each one of them... Then I give my official yes. I receive information about sacred relationships. [...] 'Such relationships come from the connection with us. If this is not the case you are just mocking yourself and entering into the role of the manipulator. It is only a matter of relating with us. In a sacred relationship you cannot relate directly with what is perceived as separate (i.e. the other) for, from the perspective of the sacred, nothing is separate. It is only possible to let it flow and release through the Function of forgiveness. When you are not directly connected and operate on the horizontal level, it is acceptable to employ strategic structures and forms of energy condensation. This is important, as, for human beings, condensation is a way of learning. What is essential is to be aware that condensation is just a strategy or symbol that needs to be released once the true force is there.'*

'The meeting with the Guide is an actual meeting of love, the peak love experience for a human being. It is the acknowledgement of the relationship which has always been with you, tenderly following you throughout all ages, partaking of the secrets and intimate movements of your heart. The connection with the Guide is the highest love experience. It reveals the true face of every being and situation, it teaches you to respect your true nature; it reminds you of who you are. Its bliss is so boundless that, in order to be accessible to the awareness of your limited perception, it has to use fragmented ways of expressions. In the Guide you find that love you have always looked for: an eternal love, which cannot be halted. This relationship is so easy and simple and spontaneous. Yet, to the insane perception of human beings, accustomed to effort, strife, competition, pain and suffering, such simplicity can be distorted as an intricate and unfathomable mystery. The major difficulty in relating with the Guide consists of accepting, and being aware of, what has always been there and always will be. This involves realising that the power of decision as regards the consent to this relationship merely relies on you. The Guide is available at all times, waiting for you in the glorious land that exists beyond the insanity of this world. The place where you go whenever, either out of exhaustion or conscious choice, you leave your toys of separation and choose to look within, effortlessly receiving the essence of love. Such essence is unconditional. It does not require you to do anything special to deserve it. You are entitled to it as long as you decide that this is so. You know how to connect with the Guide. All this is spontaneous as the authentic expression of love. Simply follow the natural élan of your heart. Each

human relationship is indeed the symbolic representation of that with the Guide. As long as there is this awareness, human relationships are sacred. If this is not the case, what follows is inevitably pain, loss, and all kinds of grievance. It is not possible for a single human body to contain the overflowing abundance of the Guide. Sacred relationships between human beings involve the active participation of the Guide. In this way each relationship is acknowledged as part of the whole and you release the hallucination of separation. If you have problems with a partner or friend, ask your Guide to relate with the Guide of the person involved. Guides know what is to be done and how to heal a relationship. In astroshamanism you do not operate on the outer person, but solely in the shamanic world through your Guide. Your power consists of being a channel and allowing the energies to do their work. As far as I know, for the time being, there is no other function reserved to you.'

[1]   *A Course in Miracles, Text p.142.*
[2]   See Sector One, note 4.
[3]   See Sector One, note 5.

SECTOR EIGHT

~ SIGN: Scorpio ~ HOUSE: 8th ~ PLANET: 1) Pluto, Mars 2) Mars ~
~ RAY: 4th (Harmony/Beauty/Art) ~ ELEMENT: Water ~
~ QUALITY: Fixed ~ DIRECTION: West ~ SEASON: Autumn ~
~ TOTEM SPIRIT: Harassadoah ~
~ EPIC STATES: Friaan, Naairf~

ANIMALS: Bat, butterfly, chameleon, coyote, dog, eagle,
            frog, lynx, phoenix, raven, scorpion, snake,
            spider, toad, vulture, wolf, woodpecker, animals
            involved in deep processes of transformation,
            serpents and poisonous creatures, repulsive
            insects.

PLANTS: Artichoke, asparagus, basil, belladonna, carob,
            carrot, charlock, coriander, cumin, cypress,
            elderberry, garlic, ginger, heather, leek, mustard,
            narcissus, onion, pepper, petunia, pimento,
            pomegranate, pumpkin, rose of Jericho, rue,
            shallot.

MINERALS: Agate, albite, aquamarine, bloodstone, hematite,
            emerald, garnet, green tourmaline, malachite,
            moonstone, obsidian, ruby, smoky quartz, topaz.

SPIRITS: Azrael (*Angels*); Mitlontecutli, Mictlancihuatl,
            Tezcatlipoca, Tlazolteotl (*Aztec*); Ereshigal
            (*Babylonian*); Don, Epona, Gwydion (*Celtic*); St.
            Thomas, St. Martin (*Christian*); Anubis, Hosiris,
            Selket (*Egyptian*); Alpanu, Mantus (*Etruscan*);

Hades, Hecate, Persephone, Orion, Orpheus (*Greek*); Shiva, Kali, Kama, Bali, Yama (*Hindu*); Yima (*Persian*); Pluto, Mars, Vulcan (*Roman*); Death, Judgement (*Tarot*).

ANATOMY/
PHYSIOLOGY:
Anus, defecation, reproduction, reproductive and elimination organs, sexual hormones, urinary system.

ASSOCIATIONS:
Regeneration, transformation, transition, renewal, resurrection, crisis, destruction, cataclysms, volcanic eruptions, atomic energy, crime, violence, war, terrorism, secrets, death, rebirth, drains, translation, collectiveness, group work, secret societies, colossal enterprises, dictatorship, religious conversion, sexual act, finance, insurance, research, psychotherapy.

COLOURS:
Green-blue, dark red, purple, black.

DETECTORS:
Partner of 2nd brother/sister of father, 2nd brother/sister of mother, 5th brother/sister of father. 7-2, 6-3, 5-4, 4-5, 3-6, 2-7, 1-812-9, 11-10, 10-11, 9-12.

GRIEVANCES:
Excess: control, cruelty, defensiveness, guilt, inflexibility, isolation, jealousy, manipulation, morbidity, obsession, obstinacy, possessiveness, resentment, ruthlessness, secretiveness, self-hate, stiffness, suspect, symbiotic relationships, vindictiveness. *Deficit:* fear or denial of death and shadow aspects; lack of intensity, passion or commitment; projections of negative emotions; resistance and incapacity to explore inner world or unconscious; unwillingness to release and transform pent-up feelings. *Physical:* afflictions of reproductive and eliminatory organs, blindness, haemorrhoids, homicide, sexual abuse or addiction, suicide, torture, tumours, venereal diseases.

QUALITIES:
Empowerment, forgiveness, intimacy, passion, perceptiveness, rebirth, release, thoroughness, transformation.

With Sector 8, I penetrate into the most profound layers of elimination, release and metamorphosis on the horizontal level: those related to death and total regeneration at a physical, emotional, mental and spiritual level. Here my inflamed yearning is not quenched by the visible surfaces of what surrounds me. Ardently I search for the covert roots, the recondite plot, the primal genesis. I am haunted by a febrile and ultimate urge to fiercely seep into the most arcane recesses of the mind. And there I slither, impregnating all, annihilating myself into the ultimate abyss of consciousness. Disasters, calamities, obsession, abhorrence, desolation, infatuation and even more unmentionable grievances yield manure for this implacable quest. Through the cryptic ordeals of Sector 8, I confront myself with grievances resonating far beyond any personal or collective history which the ordinary mind can conceive. What appear as my grievances or hers, his, theirs, ours and yours are merely the remote echo of most ancient spasms. As I work in this sector, I am not concerned with chasing the causes of this pain and whoever is responsible. Here I become aware of the deep transformational power of grievances and acknowledge the unfathomable reality of my Intent connected with the Function.

Sector 8 corresponds physically to the genitals and anus. In the majority of societies that have populated the Earth in the latter ages, these areas are usually hidden and subject to many taboos. They symbolise major zones of power existing at subtle levels and unseen by human eyes. Their revelation is bound to frighten unless I create an adamant connection with the Spirit Guide and my Function. Those areas are concealed with a symbolic layer, then cloaked with further layers until I find myself trapped in an endless sequence of symbolism. I am scared to death and I run away. It is a forlorn flight, since the memory of that fear continues to haunt me. Fragments of my mind cling to a slim layer of fiction. However, sporadic fragments manage to reach the authentic core. There they are in their glorious reality. And here I am, ready to retrieve all possible fragments. Now I do recognise that what I have been afraid of is my Spirit Guide and Circle with all the love that emanates from them, inward as well as outward. Love is the sole reality I have been hiding from, as only love is real. Therefore, what can I do but willingly and strenuously release whatever I have created to separate myself from this original reality?

Release is the basic word in Sector 8. And it is exactly what the corresponding physical organs of this sector emphasise. The presence of draining and release systems for sewage has always been one of the main requisites for the survival of all societies. It is a feature common to all forms of life on Earth. Each of them employs specific channels through which waste or toxic materials are disposed of. This function is essential at a physical and also at an emotional, mental and spiritual level. Unfortunately, in latter ages, the awareness of waste material has been confined almost exclusively to the physical level. This has lead to massive contamination and is indeed the fundamental cause of the current pollution of the earthly environment. One of the main traits of astroshamanic work regards the holistic release of waste material at all levels of existence and the retrieval of the tools and awareness that render this possible.

Sector 8 is a much misunderstood area in the horizontal level and the key screen for deep or hidden projections. Here, others – and especially the objects of my highest and lowest passions – become a mirror reflecting back the disowned parts that I avoid recognising in myself. With Sector 8 I learn to take back all that I have projected and to accept myself completely even in the most obscure and controversial states. Here I face fearful shadow zones, opening the doors of sullen vaults left unattended for ages. When I relate with others from this perspective, I learn to share authentically and intimately. Then it is easy to know myself through what I am deeply shown by others and to look direct into the eyes of what is no longer useful, rapturously allowing that to be released to its final glory. This includes relinquishing ancient emotions which continue to be activated by events that are no longer there, dealing with the mystery of death and learning to let go of grievances in a safe way.

The main spiritual traditions and nature itself teach me that in order to create something new it is necessary to let go and transform the old. When I allow what is no longer needed to die, I create the space to receive new visions and blessings. It is essential that I learn to constantly regenerate myself by facing little deaths and releases every day with the same regularity that I use to go to the bathroom. Toilets, latrines, urinals, loos, WC are merely the current degraded denominations used to indicate what were once among the most arcane and sacramental temples erected on Earth. Since I was a child I have spent a lot of time in those places. They have taught me their precious secrets and offered me treasured guidance. Thus, I have made it a basic existential and spiritual priority on this planet to spend abundant time every day in a decent and undisturbed toilet.

Sector 8 is related with the mystery of death and the connection with *ancestors*. By this term I identify here my entire lineage of relatives down into the origin of the human species and all the beings that have lived on Earth, the solar system, this galaxy, universe, and Grey Sphere, not to mention what is beyond that. Yes, there are quite a lot! Some are close and others are remote ancestors. Yet they all make up that huge puzzle of which my ordinary awareness is just a minuscule fragment. According to different perspectives, close ancestors can be related with *past lives* or express through historical beings or archetypes that either inspire or disturb me. The quality of being a close ancestor can be extended to divine beings, animals, plants, minerals, geographical areas, etc. In shamanic and tribal cultures ancestors are honoured with great respect. An ideal time for connecting with them is autumn, or fall, especially during the days in which the Sun is in Scorpio, and also winter. Ancient people were much aware of their close ancestors and all their decisions were made by consulting with them. When I address my ancestors I relate with the most ancient parts of myself. In such occasions I can retrieve images, events, memories and situations that help me understand who and what I am now. In this way I become conscious that I am the product of a past which is not limited to what has happened to me since I was born. If I authentically wish to explore the past and connect with my roots, it is essential that I am open to include all, especially those people and situations that I tend not to acknowledge.

Ancestors, besides giving me support and guidance, can also hold major grievances and pass down destructive models of behaviour or belief systems. Such grievances constitute the root cause of all my current, as well as collective, problems in life. In order to effectively heal them it is necessary to be aware that they emanate from an ancient heritage. When strong conflicts and tension develop among couples, lovers, friends, relatives, colleagues or people *casually* met, what actually happens is that the same conditions that once engendered separation and pain are being reproduced in the present for correction. These situations are momentous, as they confront me with the opportunity to invert the trend of separation, to forgive and open up portals in my conscience. These openings have inevitable effects on the collective awareness and on present or future generations.

Scorpio: The seasonal time of Scorpio marks the definitive development of the involutive process in nature and the prevalence of night over day. Leaves die, while many animals and men are forced to abandon their fields because of lack of light or cold weather. This is a splendid chance for the Earth to have some rest so that the process of regeneration can be properly activated for the next cycle to come. This period of the year coincides with *Samhain*: a leading festival for many ancient traditions, celebrated from the sunset of 31 October to that of 1 November (or at the closest New or Full Moon). To the Celts this day was the start of the New Year and also the moment when the connection between the Middle and the Lower Worlds was strongest. As such, it was the best time to honour ancestors and the dead. On those occasions Celts used to bring abundant flowers to the burial places and spend the whole night celebrating in the company of their ancestors. The Christian religion then transformed this festival into *All Saints'* and *All Souls'* day. Another feature of Samhain were the fires. They were lit at sunset and had the function of destroying the negative residues of the past year in order to open up to the new annual cycle. The period of Scorpio is a fundamental time for creating a bridge between the reality of my fellow travellers on Earth and those who have left their physical bodies to move into other worlds. Here funerals and mourning play a major role. These practices can be powerful shamanic and transformative tools when employed with sacredness and focused Intent. In many tribal cultures funerals are major cathartic rituals where all kinds of grievances are released – and not only those related to the departed.

These borderline aspects between the world of light and darkness, life and death, often manifest in Scorpio through apparent destructive and perverted tendencies, obsessive swings of mood or with the sublimation of acute conflicts and passions into outstanding creative enterprises. Scorpio is connected with ending and learning to let go. It is about discovering what is good and can be kept. It is about finding out what is no longer useful or that which is indeed toxic and cannot be kept unless I decide to poison myself.

Eighth House: It is traditionally related to transformation, property and business affairs of partners or other people, to birth, death, separation, legacies, transpersonal sex, power plays, finances, occult studies, rituals and shamanism. This house shows the attitude, passions and turmoil related to sex and pleasure intended as transpersonal and shamanic strategies. The expression of such energies is often blocked or misguided, as it opposes the models of identification of the individual (as they are generally shown by the ascendant). The eighth house shows how I can empty and regenerate myself, let go of poisoning energies and open up to a new life. Each sign experiences this differently. The planets and related Totem Spirits in this house carry strong dynamics which are hard to control and are usually kept hidden unless I make a conscious choice to relate with them in the company of the Spirit Guide. The path of this house is based on the recognition and acceptance of whatever tends to destabilise my preconceived visions of myself and the world. This means being able to face and integrate those emotions concerning death, sex, animal instincts, life after death, etc., that the ego belief systems repress, project or misinterpret.

P **Pluto:** Just as Pluto is the most recently discovered planet of the solar system, it is connected with the furthest point in human awareness: an area where what has significance for the ordinary mind does not make any sense at all. By reaching this location, I can truly communicate with the Spirit Guide and acknowledge the reality which dwells beyond the veil of illusion. The function of Pluto is that of urging me to recognise the hidden, radical and underground motivation of my perception. It is connected with the most ancient collective unconscious. The personal and the ordinary collective unconscious are walled off from the most ancient unconscious. Its energy is underneath and wants to move up, while the personal unconscious tries to put a lid on it. This creates a strong tension that is inevitably going to erupt in unpleasant ways if it is not purposefully dealt with. It is energy which needs to be handled with caution, as it is difficult to integrate in ordinary life. Pluto can appear ruthless and cruel to those who have a limited perception of reality. It is a transpersonal force which crumbles, tears and burns away all outworn components whose time is done, without moral regard of any sort.

In the natal chart Pluto corresponds to fossilised thought forms and emotions that manifest themselves as obsessions and addictions which do not find any explanation or justification in terms of the ordinary mind. The true nature of the original cause is not clear and although the mind fights to find a way out, all its attempts are hopeless. The position of Pluto in the chart indicates those areas of darkness and the way in which I can confront myself with them.

Pluto's transits allow what needs to be released and transformed to emerge. They help or force me to recognise my

Function, to let go of the past, to connect with my true Intent and get ready for rebirth. Sometimes it is possible for symptoms of illness or of whatever has been secretively dwelling within to manifest outside. Although this can appear painful or unpleasant, it always indicates that a process of healing is taking place. During this time it can be useful to retreat into a safe environment and devote all the time that is required to the process of transformation.

Basic Practices

a. Using the guidelines (given in Book One, Chapter 7, 'Connection with the Totem Spirit' or Book Two, 'Introduction, Basic Practices, Exploring the Sectors') meet the Totem Spirit of Sector 8.

b. Activate the piece for Sector 8 of your Sacred Circle Pieces (see Book One, Chapter 4, 'The Sacred Circle Pieces' or Book Two, 'Introduction, Basic Practices, The Sacred Circle Pieces').

c. Choose one of the following practices ('Healing Tools') and do it daily, every other day or three times per week, for at least 21 days.

Healing Tools

1. **Pretending to Die:** A very deep crisis and period of despair, often operated through Pluto's transits, may be dealt with using the major remedy of Sector 8: death! (i.e. pretending to die). When I feel worn-out by emotional problems, upset by unpleasant situations in daily life, deeply concerned about the future, then it is essential for me to take a break out of the dynamics of my routine to examine what is happening in the perspective of my imminent death. The technique consists in considering all my situations as if I were on my last day of life. Facing death I can truly see what really counts for me. Many teachers admit that death is the only wise adviser we have. Confronting death allows me to test the quality of my Intent for, as AFS Bogus says, 'Only the Intent that in the face of death does not sneak away is a veracious one'.[1] Shamanic work involves an immersion into the mystery of death in order to master a full experience of what life is truly about.

During a period of 21 days, as you wake up in the morning and throughout the whole day, whenever you remember it, take a few moments from the routine of your daily events. Use them to consider the reality of your existence and measure it against the fact of your inevitable death. Pretend that it is the last day in your life. Feel what it might be to die. Go through the different phases and details of your death. Write your own epitaph and also imagine how people around you comment on your death. See what parts of you are dying. Experience the detachment that comes from death and feel it working in your daily life.

2. **The Graha Chest:** This is a practice that consists of employing a box to insert notes with all thoughts of fear, worry, depression, obsession and all kinds of grievance that occur during a lunar cycle (28 days). The act of writing is in itself a major process of release and detachment from grievances. If I write down something about my grievances, I literally relinquish them. This is a powerful way of releasing mental and emotional waste material. In this case the box operates as a toilet at that level. At the end of the cycle I can read the contents of each note and then dispose of them in a sacred way. Upon checking the contents of the box, I usually realise that what, at the moment of writing, seemed to be a most dramatic problem, is now totally solved, forgotten or does not make any sense.

3. **Relationships:** When strong Sector 8 factors are at work, it is easy to move from times of total isolation to a suffocating and symbiotic relationship where neither of the partners manages to survive without the presence of the other. The terror of being abandoned, and returning to the previous isolation, is such that the partner is constantly controlled. If I hold him or her tightly enough, I believe that they won't leave me. Yet, the exasperation of this situation is often bound to cause that abandonment which the partners were desperately trying to avoid. Special relationships in Sector 8 can reach their most tragic levels of drama. Their scenes emanate a constant smell of inevitable death and calamity. Although such relationships are aimed at finding relief from gloomy consequences, the load of grievances can be so strong that, unless they are consciously dealt with, their poisoning potential is bound to explode. In Sector 8 grievances reach some of the most glamorous expressions: their causes are so

ancient and obscure that even the ego is puzzled in its attempt to find a culprit (in this case it often ends up embroiling past lives, the Devil or God Himself). When the demon (Mahagraha) is acknowledged and dealt with, these relationships can be major blessings and opportunities for healing, forgiveness and miracles. They can also bring unmentionable pain when all thoughts tend to centre obsessively around the significant person. Here the mind is vampirised by the fantasy of the lover and is unable to attend to any other business. If you are or were involved in such relationships and still find it hard to let go, you can employ the following affirmation whenever you meet, or think of, your partners (current or former): 'God is the love in which I forgive you...' Then add 'God is the love in which I forgive myself'. You can also ask your Spirit Guide to send out a ray of pink light from your heart to that of the other person and say something like: 'I bless you... to your higher good'. Do this even if it seems a hypocritical blessing on someone that you would rather curse.

4. **Shamanic Trance Posture:** Sector 8 is related to the process of elimination of waste material and is intimately connected with the secret power that comes from the recognition of its value. Such often repulsive material is a most precious source of prosperity. For many traditions the meaning of gold and excrement is in very close relationship, whereas for many psychics their vibrations seem to be identical. For example, among the Bambara (Mali, Africa) gold is considered a sublimation of copper, i.e. the excrement of the god Faro, the organiser of the world. In this context waste material is burned and its ashes thrown into the river Niger as an offering to Faro, who will then return beneficial rain as a form of exchange. The Aztec Goddess Tlazolteotl, who is the object of the shamanic trance posture of *Tlazolteotl*, was Goddess of Love or Fertility as well as Goddess of Excrement and Garbage. One of her functions was that of receiving the last confessions of those who were about to die. The verbal and emotional evocation of grievances assumed a form that the goddess would eat. The posture, along with others, works as a multilevel release device and allows relief from ancient waste material. It is practised by standing with your feet parallel and your knees slightly bent. The hands are brought together in front of the chest and curled as if they were holding heavy breasts. The fingernails face forward and point

upward. The face is straight ahead and the upper teeth are extended over the lower lip, whereas the upper lip is raised enough to prominently display the teeth. (See Book One, Chapter 9, 'Shamanic Trance Postures'.

5. **Forgiveness Ritual with Water:** You can do this ritual at any time, when you have a shower or bath, outside by the sea or any source of water, and even in the shamanic realm of your Spirit Circle. Throw water over your shoulders seven times. Feel that it washes away all that obscures good friendship with your partner, family, community or friends. Make a statement like: 'I wash away fear, doubt, isolation and all sense of separation. I release guilt and sorrow. I let go of anger. I rejoice in the glory of accepting my Intent connected with the Function.' Feel a beam of light moving from your heart and radiating to all the hearts of those with whom you have experienced grievances. Allow that light to reach them and then return back to your heart. Gradually step away from the water and affirm your Intent through a song or strong statement.

6. **Releasing**: Set your Sacred Circle and place a white candle at the centre. Pour a small amount of aromatic oil (preferably lavender) on a dish or bowl and place it to the left of the candle. Position one of your power objects on the right of the candle. Enter the Sacred Circle from the East and move anticlockwise to the West facing the candle at the centre. Open the Sacred Circle according to the usual procedures. Light the candle and smudge all parts of your body (including the bottom of your feet), all the directions, the four corners of the room (if you are working indoor), all the objects involved in the ritual and the entire area of work. Then stand and focus on your Intent connected with the Function. Solemnly declare that only what is related to your highest Intent is allowed in your environment. Demand that all other energies be relinquished and returned to the love where they truly belong. See yourself and the entire space where you work filled with bright white light. Touch the aromatic oil with the side of your right thumb and caress the top of the head, the centre of your forehead, your throat, heart, the base of your spine, the back of your knees and the bottoms of your feet. Say a prayer of thanksgiving and close the Sacred Circle.

7. **Death and Life**: Before going to sleep, lie down and relax yourself. Then pretend that you are dying. Feel that you

cannot move your body because you are dead. Do this for ten or fifteen minutes and allow this process to turn into sleep. In the morning, as you start to wake up, feel that life is coming back to you. Start moving, stretching like a cat, swaying but still keeping your eyes closed. Open to a luminous flow of energy in your body. Take deep breaths and allow joy, light and laughter to enter into your system. Do this for ten or fifteen minutes and then get up.

8. **Death, the Teacher:** Whenever you remember it, look past your left shoulder and see the presence of Death there. Let it teach you about death. Ask Death what it has to teach you at this time in your life and bravely listen.

9. **Grievance Signal:** Learn to detect a signal in your body that informs you about hidden or denied grievances which occur in your life. It could be a shiver of your head, a pain in your stomach, an unpleasant vibration in your genitals. When you recognise this signal, be aware of it and take some time to examine what is going on. If possible write down what you were doing shortly before or right at the moment of the signal. Reflect on that and try to discover what the grievance is about.

10. **The Paheka Sadohe Korah** (Chant of the Totem Spirits and Guides): For Sector 8, the chant is *Harassadoah Sadoh*. Please use this practice only if you intend to establish or support a regular relationship with the Totem Spirit of Sector 8. If you intend to use this chant, you can either sing it from time to time to accompany a cycle of twelve shamanic journeys in Sector 8 or as a practice on its own to be done preferably once or twice a day for at least seven minutes during a period of 21 days.[2]

Astroshamanic Reports

Here is a typical situation of Sector 8 in which I was confronted with the choice either to succumb or wake up. The language of the experience below has been translated and adapted so that it can be more understandable.

I ask my Guide: 'How can I face and go through this current state of fear that I am experiencing?' The Guide solemnly and gently replies: 'The only way is that of focusing on love and all that you desire at your highest. This has inevitably to do with the Sacred Cone. Whenever you experience fear, despair and other assorted grievances, please remember: you are in a state of great power. The moment you encounter the lowest emotions, please be still. You have not done anything wrong. Nothing wrong has been done to you either. Please be motionless and remember your Function. You are here to release the old nightmare and open up to the happy dream. It took you ages to arrive in that precise moment where you can make such decision and manifest the most loving desires of your Etnai [holy and sacred people]. It is part of the agreement that you are to experience grievances and, when they do transit through your system, it is a sign that you are working properly, as long as you do accept to let them go. The old nightmare joyfully comes to you to be released. And when it is close to the happy moment in which it finds its final freedom, then it celebrates with hymns that, to the distorted echoes of this dimension, turn out in the form of acute grievances and pain. In those moments, please be aware that you do not walk alone. My love and that of your Etnai accompanies you if only you are open to accept and treasure it. Please release your stubbornness of being isolated. You are not alone. You have never been. Salvation is a co-operative enterprise. You do need our help as we need yours. Open the gate of your channel. You are a sacred pipe. All you need to do is to allow waste material to move through your conduit. When this occurs it is obvious that you are going to experience grievances. This is part of the work. This does not mean that you are to suffer. Pain comes out of the misunderstanding of your Function. And your Function is a most joyful and ecstatic one. Therefore, whenever the pain is steady and strong, it is because you are trying to block the flow of grievances and are closing up to the experience of bliss. That is part of the customs of the ancient traditions of misery which it is your Function to release. Please be still in those moments and remember. Avoid forlorn interpretations and discussions, as they are all attempts to preserve the state of separation and prevent grievances from reaching their final goal. Please stop and offer all you are experiencing to us. Forget everything else and call us. We will be there immediately and operate the Sacred Cone with you. This is what you teach and what you are. Once you allow the activation of the Sacred Cone and release grievances, the work is done. It is very simple. Then grievances are not there any more. And you can open up to the love which has always been there. Support the Plan of Salvation. Transform all your life into deeds that promote such a Plan. Use your vehicles to represent unity at all times and levels.' [...] I then ask the Spirit Guide to receive information about my sacred relationship. 'This relationship,' explains the Guide, 'is going to draw high dosages of love which are going to make the Graha people so exultant. In this sacred *relationship there is a mutual acceptance of the Sacred Cone. You are both in a condition to work for the same Function and remind yourself of what that Function is. There is a part which has to do with your responsibility and that you need to operate in order to contribute to the sacred relationship. Please do not be decoyed by the ancient nightmare into what a sacred relationship is about. Partnerships were originally created as a way to spread the plan of separation. It was a most effective method to cut off from us and the Etnai so as to proliferate segregated realms of fear and guilt. It is obvious that when two join with us and our common Function, major grievances are going to use us as a gateway to find their ultimate liberation. At once major blessings are going to move in the opposite direction and manifest themselves in all possible realities. Please be confident and use the tools you have been given. Do not expect the other to do it for you. Be a demonstrator. It is only by demonstrating that you teach.'*

The following is one of my early shamanic journeys in Sector 8.

I slink into a cavern lit by feeble torches. A titanic chameleon suddenly emerges. Its appearance is so excessively striking and sensational that, far from engendering fear, it almost makes me laugh. I feel a lot of power and understand that all I see is a creation of mine. Chameleon takes me on a sightseeing tour to show me places and situations that I have created in my ancient lives. I explore different sequences: stakes where people are burning alive, battlefields saturated with blood, stinking lazarets crammed with putrefying bodies, and all sorts of horror movie scenes. The whole tour is so appalling that it becomes almost ridiculous. The Totem Spirit of Sector 8, Harassadoah Sadoh, then booms throughout the cavern: 'These are the grievances that you have begot!' I ask what I can do to release them, and I hardly manage to hold my hilarity when her overemphasised dreadful voice replies: 'Release them!' I decide to heed her command. In a few instants all the appalling scenes fade away and become celestial visions. Chameleon turns into a luminous butterfly while the Totem Spirit solemnly declares: 'This is the power that comes to you once you claim your fatherhood. Would you like some more?' It looks like a challenge and I feel so powerful that I cannot help saying yes. I tell the Spirit that I am determined to transform a controversial relationship. Together with the Spirit Guide we all move through a small underground passage that leads to a misty lake. We take a boat and drift out into a spectral watery environment until we reach a rocky islet. I climb it until I get to the big tree which is on top of the main rock. There I see the form of the person concerned. She is tied up to the tree and cannot move. Her appearance is pale and weak, yet she also expresses rage and sourness. I shiver at the sight of her and begin to feel inadequate and to go through a long menu of grievances. I ask the Spirit Guide what to do. 'Claim the fatherhood of what you see. It is a creation of yours. You produced it for strategic reasons related to the plan of separation. You imprisoned her and can create the basic conditions to set her free. Do this in three stages. [...] Remember that it is only by connecting with me that the release can finally take place.'

[1] AFS Bogus, 'Letter to Francesko Saint on 2 November 1986' in *Provordo Etnai Pratinindhe Pradhikara's Southern Europe Archives, year 1986.*

[2] See Sector One, note 4.

SECTOR NINE

~ SIGN: Sagittarius ~ HOUSE: 9th ~ PLANETS: 1) Jupiter 2) Earth ~
~ ELEMENT: Fire ~ QUALITY: Mutable ~ DIRECTION: West ~
~ SEASON: Autumn ~ TOTEM SPIRIT: Nivaya Sadhu ~
~ EPIC STATES: Santjul, Lujtnas. ~

ANIMALS: Cuckoo, deer, dolphin, eagle, elephant, heron, horse, partridge, peacock, pheasant, porcupine, quail, stag, swallow, whale, wild boar, zebra.

PLANTS: Generally abundant, big, edible, good-smelling and full of fruits. Like the cycle of Jupiter, they tend to live twelve years. Almond, anise, apricot, ash, asparagus, betony, birch, bilberry, borage, buck wheat, carnation, chestnut, cinnamon, clove, daisy, dandelion, endive, fig, fir, ginseng, iris, jasmine, laurel, leek, lime, mallow, maple, mint, nutmeg, oak, olive, rhubarb, sage, sandal, sassafras, spinach, strawberry, sugar cane, tea tree, tomato.

MINERALS: Amethyst, azurite, carbuncle, emerald, hyacinth, lapis lazuli, marble, moonstone, pink tourmaline, ruby, sapphire, sodalite.

SPIRITS: Sachiel (*Angels*); Marduk (*Babylonian*); Bussumarus, Dagda (*Celtic*); St. James, St. Sebastian (*Christian*); Tina (*Etruscan*); Zeus, Chiron, Ixion, Themis, Artemis (*Greek*); Ganesha, Indra (*Hindu*); Thor, Donar (*Nordic*); Jupiter, Fortuna, Diana (*Roman*); Wheel of Fortune, Temperance (*Tarot*).

ANATOMY: Hips, liver, thighs.

ASSOCIATIONS:	Religion, clergy, philosophy, higher education, law, sport, gambling, stock market, prosperity, abundance, development, growth, wealth, luxury, profit, good fortune, prestige, opportunity, success, optimism, happiness, philanthropy, foreign affairs, distant travel, gluttony, obesity, inflation, fulfilment.
COLOURS:	Blue, deep purple, violet, soft lavender.
DETECTORS:	3rd son/daughter, 1st brother/sister of partner, partner of 1st brother/sister, 1st son/daughter, 4th brother/sister, 2nd son/daughter of 1st brother/sister, friends of friends. 8-2, 7-3, 6-4, 5-5, 4-6, 3-7, 2-8, 1-9, 12-10, 11-11, 10-12.
GRIEVANCES:	*Excess:* conceit, dissipation, exaggeration, exhibitionism, extravagance, fanaticism, gullibility, ill-judgement, , inflation, irresponsibility, laziness, lust, over-optimism, pretentiousness, procrastination, recklessness, restlessness, self-righteousness, self-indulgence, superficiality. *Deficit:* fear of risks; lack of faith, excitement and humour; pessimism. *Physical:* cramps, gall-stones, gout, liver troubles, obesity, over-eating, sciatica, swellings, travel-addiction.
QUALITIES:	Abundance, adventure, cheerfulness, compassion, discovery, education, encouragement, enrichment, faith, fulfilment, fun, honesty, hope, humour, knowledge, laughter, open-mindedness, opportunity, optimism, prosperity, risk-taking, success, trust, truth, wealth.

As I emerge from the obscurity of Sector 8 and move my first steps into Sector 9, I find myself in an oasis of such brilliance. Joy and celebration transpire all around. I meet cheerful faces on my way. They smile at me and everything is so gentle and carefree. I am encircled by such contentment, felicity and exuberance. Everything is going so well! What can I do but open up to this blissful glee? How was it possible to forget about this place? 'No need to get concerned about that. Enjoy the beauty of this moment. You are fully entitled to be with us. This is your true inheritance. Breathe it in and out. Take and share it. Let it flow abundantly.' I have such joy now! Whatever I see contributes to comfort me. I laugh, sing, smile, and even shout. I am in the land of infinite possibilities. My body is growing and expanding and amplifying and dilating and enlarging. And, as I witness this process, I realise that I am hopping and capering and galloping. Freely! Totally nude, on a sandy beach, I run wildly and exultant, raising my hands towards the sky, lifting my thighs and gently bumping them against my belly. What liberty! I flit from one landscape to another, beaming a festive welcome and spreading gladness on whatever I see. Where is all this joy coming from? Just a few moments ago, I was right in the middle of an agonising tragedy, congested by sludge and gloom, trapped into a marshy hollow, paralysed with fear and on the verge of succumbing to a dismal fate. And now, here I am, spilling joy from all the cells of my body. Isn't it incredible? How is such a shift possible? How come sheer despair can change into jubilant euphoria in a twinkling of an eye? 'O beings of the Spirit Circle, please let me know.' At such a question all the Guides and Totem Spirits begin to roar with laughter. 'Are you mocking me? Is it a joke? A Game?' And as I add this, the laughter becomes even louder. I have gone through the terror of Sector 8. I have looked straight into the eyes of death, passing through the darkest valleys of hell. And now all that is over. I only catch sight of happy faces around me. My dreadful past is not there any more. Has it ever really existed? Was it just a nightmare? What can I do but laugh at this absurdity? I realise that I am surrounded by wonderful and loving beings. Everything is going in my way. Everyone is supporting me.

With Sector 9 I dash into an adventurous quest for truth, in the field of creeds, ideas and faith. I confront myself with old and new beliefs and let go of what is not needed any more. Through Sector 9, I enter into the realm of spiritual search and absorb nourishment and strength from each religious tradition, receiving unconditional support and trust. Here I can sense such paramount enthusiasm! And I want even more. Yet, I am also overwhelmed by all these abundant possibilities and roads. I pause and reflect, looking for guidance. I need a master, somebody who can escort me along the path of knowledge, a *guru* (which in Sanskrit is the name given to the planet Jupiter), an enlightened one, a wise teacher, and finally my Spirit Guide. Yes, there he is. He neither invades nor controls. He simply indicates the path, leaving it up to me to follow his gentle direction.

Sector 9 is the realm of beliefs. Whatever I believe, whether I am aware of it or not, and no matter if it is sane or insane, becomes my reality. If I have a specific vision of the world and believe it, I perceive life in that way even if, in practical terms, my experiences are the same as those who hold another vision. For example, whoever has a confident and optimist view of life evaluates as fortunate and happy the same experiences that a pessimist would regard as negative and unfortunate. I create my ill fate as well as my good fate. What I believe determines the joys and satisfactions that I encounter in life. According to this premise, care and awareness are required about my beliefs. In Sector 9, I question myself as follows: 'Where do I get this belief from? Is it from my experience of life? Or is it something that I have taken for granted? Does it really serve my Intent and Function?' If this is not the case, it does not count who is the source of this belief. I am here to find my truth. I am not satisfied with any borrowed or second-hand knowledge.

In the shamanic spiritual traditions there are two major paths: the *Way of the Warrior* – characterised by self-discipline, asceticism, strenuous combat with antagonistic forces and powerful alliances with Totem Spirits and Guides – and the *Way of the Adventurer* – based on the playful exploration of life, the search for harmony, trust, ecstasy and pleasure. The warrior is very typical of Sector 1. He moves into the reality of a hostile world inhabited by predatory forces. His main effort has to do with acquiring more power so as to face and overcome the adversities that he finds along the path. His motto is: 'The world is a most dangerous place, full of dreadful monsters, yet I can get the power to overcome them'. The warrior moves from a state of impotence and victimisation to one of power and glory. As for the adventurer, whose path is typical of Sector 9, although he is aware that there can be some problems in life, he will never perceive existence as something dangerous. On the contrary, life is wonderful, full of ecstatic opportunities and thriving with joy. His basic belief is 'I am the creator of the world and, as a result, all dangers, pleasures and any kind of experience are generated by me'. The adventurer is also a being of power. This power is employed to create an ecstatic perception of life and to help others do the same. Belief systems and mental attitudes determine personal reality. These attitudes correspond to specific psychic territories identified by the Twelve Sectors. Shamans of both paths (warriors and adventurers) have the knowledge of most of these territories and the ability to move within them for healing purposes. Please be aware that both ways aim at the same sacred goal. As a matter of fact they are not truly different, and they appear as such only to a limited mind. They are strategies, or *provisional orders,* and not absolute truths. What matters is that they can serve the purpose of achieving specific Intents and connecting them with the Function. In this process it is possible to stick to one strategy or use two or even more. Again it is not a question of supporting this or that tradition. The sole concern is that of releasing the illusion of separation and giving space to the reality of unity. Anything, as long as it works, is shamanically fine.

According to some shamanic traditions our energetic bodies were separated from us at birth and taken away by antagonistic forces. This explains the situation of human beings and our limited spiritual awareness. Another way to see this, which is the other side of the same story, is that I have chosen to be separated and those *antagonistic forces* are only creations of mine which function as defences so as to preserve that choice. I can provide different explanations for something which has occurred in the past depending on the traditions or belief systems I adhere to. As far as I can understand, these explanations, however brilliant or accurate, do not matter much. What counts is whether they are going to help me manifest my true potential or contribute to keep me in chains, whether they can give me real power or not. A state of power always implies that the choice to transform myself and to create what I want is only mine. It doesn't depend on somebody else. In this context all ideologies and belief systems, no matter how different they purport to be, can be divided into two categories: those that *empower* and those that *victimise* me. The latter group includes the supreme ego ideologies of all times. Although they take infinite forms and do their best to distinguish themselves one from the other, their thought system is always based on a fundamental premise: *someone* or *something* is the cause of what has happened to somebody else. It can be parents, capitalists, communists, the education system, the Church, patriarchal societies, the devil, past lives, the Mafia, politics, males, females, a specific race or country, the ego or – and this is perhaps who in the end is intimately considered the ultimate culprit – God Himself. The identity of that *someone* or *something* is however irrelevant. What matters is that there be *someone* or *something* who can uphold the status of culprit and be therefore the cause of all my problems. This condition, although I could find many reasons to justify it, will never allow me to heal and empower myself. Its function is only that of postponing the problems and therefore prolonging my agony. There comes a time when I get tired of playing the same game over and over again. Only when that time arrives can I truly begin to recover my original identity. Then I discover that this identity goes far beyond my limited perception and embraces many other parts which I once considered as separated from me. In that brilliant moment I become aware of the Game which has gone on since this dimension started to develop and expand. Many names have been given to this Game. I call it the *Game of the Sacred Cone.* As a matter of fact, its name does not really matter. What counts is the determination to play it and abide by its agreements until the whole Game is over. It is a provisional Game. It is not going to continue forever. Like all games, this one uses a specific time and space structure. Once the players are in the arena, they know the rules. They are aware of the perimeter of the field and the time they have. There they are, playing with integrity, humour, totality, excitement, passion, joy. And here I am, playing with them with a wide smile on my face. 'Play and laugh,' my teacher Ur Ichi would say. And it is his precious advice that I heed as I move my way into the fields of Sector 9.

Sagittarius: The seasonal time of this sign is the darkest of the year, yet it is a most promising period, as it heralds the coming of the winter solstice and the gradual return of the light. As such it is a phase of deep trust that reflects in the preparation for the religious and social celebrations of the end of the year. Human beings make resolutions, devote time to their family and tribe, connect with their religious traditions and give thanks for the return of the Sun. Just as the position of the Sun is at its lowest now, so the Sagittarius fire glows deep within, smouldering all residues of grievances and kindling the transmutation into the higher spiritual flames.

After dwelling in the subterranean obscurity of Scorpio, the individual emerges and voyages along the terrestrial surface on a quest for his higher aspirations, which does not exclude the appreciation of mundane pleasures. In Sagittarius all that belongs to the Earth (the higher ruler of this sign according to the writings of Alice Bailey) is exalted and thoroughly enjoyed. In the apparent conflict between matter and spirit, Sagittarius faces an inevitable choice: that of finding a target on which to direct its powerful energies. And it is here that, following the direction of his arrow, the individual is called to confront the challenge of faith and light.

Ninth House: It is related to philosophy, deep thought systems, long journeys, travels abroad, spiritual guides and teachers, law, religion, higher education, knowledge and also any path or training that involves expansion of perception. It is connected with all those experiences that allow me to develop and define my vision of the world, to search for the truth within and without. For those who begin to approach the shamanic dimensions, this house is significant for it identifies the ideal characteristics and the most distinctive traits given to the Spirit Guide as they are perceived in the early stages of work. According to Edwin C. Steinbrecher, '*The personality and physical appearance of one's Inner Guide always corresponds to the ninth house (or horoscopic section) of the natal pattern* (when Koch birthplace house cusps, not Placidean, are used). This is traditionally the section called the *House of God and Religion* and the area describing your philosophical and spiritual views, as well as your own ability to act as a guide or way-shower for others.'[1]

♃ *Jupiter:* Jupiter represents expansion, growth and integration in the world, especially from a social point of view. It is the urge to expand my individual radius and share my resources with others. This planet expresses the attempt to absorb and include as much as possible of what is perceived as separate so as to retrieve the experience of the original unity.

The position of Jupiter in the natal chart indicates the opportunities of expansion and growth, what can allow me to feel *greater*, give me confidence, fulfilment and satisfaction. It will also describe the areas of life where I can be fruitful, abundant and outgoing, if I choose to take those ways and manifest their potentials. From the shamanic perspective Jupiter's location provides information on the type of ceremonies, initiation practices and experiences that can allow the individual to clarify his vision and reach the goal on the spiritual path. The force of this planet is based on an attitude of trust toward life, on a spontaneous optimism that transforms each situation into an exciting adventure. It is a path of abundance and prosperity that, as long as I am in this dimension, can easily divert into exaggeration and over-inflation. Unless I employ a structural container and place strategic limits upon this energy, I am likely to jeopardise and waste it. The planet Saturn stands beyond Jupiter to remind me of this.

The transits of Jupiter are traditionally related to opportunities, success, abundance, and also to waste, risks, laziness and exaggeration. This planet activates and amplifies whatever it touches. When it transits over harmonious areas of the chart,

Jupiter works as energiser and draws experiences of well-being and good fortune. This amplification trend applies also to challenging areas and in this case the related issues will be exacerbated.

Basic Practices

a. Using the guidelines (given in Book One, Chapter 7, 'Connection with the Totem Spirit' or Book Two, 'Introduction, Basic Practices, Exploring the Sectors') meet the Totem Spirit of Sector 9.

b. Activate the piece for Sector 9 of your Sacred Circle Pieces (see Book One, Chapter 4, 'The Sacred Circle Pieces' or Book Two, 'Introduction, Basic Practices, The Sacred Circle Pieces').

c. Choose one of the following practices ('Healing Tools') and do it daily, every other day or three times per week, for at least 21 days.

Healing Tools

1. **Spiritual Travels:** All situations that allow me to move and open up to new horizons and discoveries are connected with Sector 9. Mountain walks, trekking, journeys to foreign countries, adventurous travels, pilgrimages, visits to sacred sites or museums, etc. are all effective medicines for this sector. Take some time to go on a journey and visit a place you have never seen before. You can go for a weekend, one day, an afternoon or even an outing of a couple of hours, and visit a temple, a forest, a sacred site, a place of pilgrimage, etc. What matters is that you go to an area which is totally new for you and that gives you a sense of discovery, excitement or search for truth. Do this as a spiritual practice: tuning in or praying before leaving, performing a brief ritual upon reaching the spot, connecting with the spirits of the place, tuning out at the end of the trip.

2. **One Belief:** Imagine you have the power to make the world believe in one basic concept. Something that you strongly believe. What will you choose? And why? How does it feel to you? What will the world be like when everyone believes in that concept? How fully do you believe in that concept

yourself? How does it manifest in your life? If you decide to opt for this exercise, write down all that you come up with in the course of 21 days. At first consider all possible beliefs that reach your awareness, make a list of them, try them out and see how you truly feel about them. Then make a selection, until you end up with your basic and core belief, the one you are sincerely ready to use and expand.

3. **Laughter:** One of the most pleasant spiritual practices, as I perceive it, is that of spending at least five minutes laughing upon waking up. Before opening my eyes, I stretch myself like a cat and begin to make some strange sounds. Then after doing this, still with eyes closed, I begin to laugh. Try it! At first it will require an effort and the laughter is likely not to be truly genuine. Then, if you persevere, things are going to change. You will retrieve memories of past laughter and cosmic jokes. And you will laugh at what is happening right in the here and now. You will soon begin to see how absurd life is. You will also gradually enter into the playful mode of the *Game of the Sacred Cone*. When I start a morning like that, I plant the seed of laughter right from the beginning and I let it grow throughout the day. This usually implies moving into a process of consistent transmutation, with grievances being drawn and released through unpredictable series of laughter that can blow up at any moment during the day. Laughing is such a powerful energy that nothing else is needed. The technique consists of laughing deeply for no reason at all. Here I am not laughing because of something that is going on or because of a joke.

The first time I began to use laughter as meditation and was trying hard to capture something that would help me laugh, I wondered: 'Do I need to have a reason for laughing?' Well, now it is impossible to describe in words what happened. As soon as I asked myself that question, something shifted within me. After some seconds a roaring laugh erupted from my belly. It continued for almost an hour. The energy was so strong that my body started to shake and I had to roll on the carpet in the attempt to release its drive. Even now when I think of this question I cannot help laughing. Believe me, it is one of the most powerful techniques I have ever used. When I consider all the time I spent using the most complicated and lengthy practices of meditation, the pain and effort I went through in my sacred journey, all the spiritual questions I chewed over in my mind... And then just out of laughter and being totally involved in having a good time... Isn't it incredible? Laughter retrieves the potential which was lost at the moment when the first glimpses of the process of separation took place. This is why it is so healing and most beneficial in the work with the Sacred Cone. 'Into eternity, where all is one, there crept a tiny, mad idea, at which the Son of God remembered not to laugh. In his forgetting did the thought become a serious idea, and possible of both accomplishment and real effects.'[2] In my work with Sector 9, I am constantly confronted with this choice: to laugh or not to laugh, to release or not to release. Most of my Guides and spiritual teachers have a terrific sense of humour. The first instruction I was given in the initial meeting with my Guide was 'Smile!', whereas the last words was 'Go and play'. AFS Bogus, the *ProvOrdo Etnai Supply Vicar*, has the capacity of causing laughter in the most serious situations. Being with him means seeing life upside down. I met him in 1982 during one of the worst moments in my life. He didn't say anything. As he was writing some papers, he just looked at me through his glasses without moving a single feature of his face. As a matter of fact he appeared very serious. Yet his seriousness was so candid and innocent! There was something in him that made me feel totally ridiculous in my pain. Nevertheless Bogus was looking at me with a lot of respect. And it was probably such profuse sense of respect that generated a burst of laughter in me. I laughed so much that in the end I totally forgot why I was feeling so bad before. Then I stopped, as this did not seem to make any sense. I felt ashamed and disdainful. What would the Supply Vicar think about me? How could I laugh at pain? How could I forget all about the misery of my life and that of the world? Therefore I began to make a strenuous effort in order to retrieve the reasons I had been in pain for more than one month. As I was toiling to remember, I became very frustrated for my hurtful memories seemed to have vanished. I looked at Bogus in the attempt to receive succour. Again, there he was as before, staring at me, this time with an air that appeared as gently puzzled. I was enchanted by his expression. He didn't say a single word. He continued to discreetly scrutinise me as if I were an unidentified mobile object. Then he carefully and slowly took his glasses off, exposed his fiery eyes, and suddenly started to laugh so wildly that his face turned red, then turned orange, yellow, green and all the remaining colours of the rainbow. And then after a while, he put his glasses on again and suddenly returned to his state of seriousness. As if nothing had happened, he continued to write his papers. This was one of the greatest teachings I have ever received. That day Bogus saved my life.

4. **Running:** Run on the road or in the countryside or in your own room on the spot. As you run, employ all your body: feet, legs, arms, hands, belly, head. Breathe deeply. Run for at least fifteen minutes. Be total in your running. Use all your energy. Do not save yourself. Then stop and sit down. Be silent and still for no less than ten minutes. Allow the movement to develop within. Retrieve all the energy that you gave out and allow it to lead you toward your Centre.

5. **Sacred Circle Dances:** These dances are a typical way of expressing the energy of Sector 9. They celebrate major sacred and social events, like weddings, funerals, births, agricultural cycles, connection with ancestors, God, or the Mother Earth. An original collection of these dances was gathered by Bernhard Wosien, a German dance professor, who in 1976 was invited to share his work with the spiritual community of the *Findhorn Foundation*. In such a context the dances found fertile ground and currently continue to represent a most prominent feature of the local community life. Besides being significant opportunities to create harmony among people, sacred dances have very deep healing effects and echo the spirit of most ancient traditions. 'One has to dance them and be totally present to discover their meaning and healing power. Only then does their religious origin reveal itself – the way to Oneness, from separation to community to vibrant togetherness.'[3] Sacred Dances also give the chance of connecting with the energy of other cultures and feeling intimately close to their spirit without physically visiting their countries. A practice for this month could be to attend Sacred Circle Dances or to do them on your own, inviting your Spirit Guide and the Totem Spirits to dance with you.

6. **Choosing a Country:** Sector 9 tends to reproduce the astroshamanic structures in the geographical and political arrangement of planet Earth. This is one of the reasons why human beings with strong Sector 9 values are very fond of

travelling and moving abroad. Thus, in this perspective, each geographical country corresponds to a specific sector or combinations of sectors. Moving to, or connecting with, certain geographical areas is in this case tantamount to having an astroshamanic voyage to a particular sector. Acknowledging the correspondences that exist between locations in the outer world and areas of the inner world is one of the major skills in Sector 9. Choose a country of the world to which you feel attracted. Find some music for that country and use it as the background to one of your shamanic voyages. You can also choose to dance or do a special ritual. Explore that country with your Guide and see what it energetically represents for you. Other ways to tune in to that country are, for example, by eating its typical food, using its objects or clothes, looking at its geographical map, learning its language, watching movies or reading books about it, meeting people from that place and, of course, physically travelling to the country itself.

7. **The Paheka Sadohe Korah** (Chant of the Totem Spirits and Guides): For Sector 9, the chant is *Nivaya Sadhu Sadoh*. Please use this practice only if you intend to establish or support a regular relationship with the Totem Spirit of Sector 9. If you intend to use this chant, you can either sing it from time to time to accompany a cycle of twelve shamanic journeys in Sector 9 or as a practice on its own to be done preferably once or twice a day for at least seven minutes during a period of 21 days.[4]

8. **The Chant and Scale of Jupiter:** In order to activate or balance the energy of Sector 9, you can employ the scale of Jupiter and its chant:

Hi Su Mayo, Hi Su Mayo, Hi Su Mayo, Hi Su Mayo, Ay

Upon singing it, you can visualise the image of Jupiter with all its colourful bands. If you use the Sacred Circle, you can sit or stand in Sector 9 or the sector where Jupiter is positioned in your natal chart. After calling your Guide, connect with your Intent and Function. Ask your Guide to draw the energy of Jupiter and the Spirit of Sector 9. Then sing the chant (*Hi Su Mayo*, four times, followed by *Ay* at the end). It does not matter how you chant it, how many times and with what degree of voice. The Scale of Jupiter creates strong emissions of energy from all over the body and releases beliefs based on fear and separation. Witness what happens during the practice and, if you notice grievances, find your way to acknowledge or express them, without identifying yourself with their content. In the first stages open yourself to the lower expression of Jupiter: dogmatism, fanaticism, irresponsibility, excesses with food and drinks, etc. You can also focus on the White Demon (*Hagraha*) and see yourself surrounded by happy, buoyant, optimistic, lucky, wealthy, cheerful beings, while you are miserable, depressed, sad, poor. (See Book One, Chapter 7, 'White Demons'.) As with all the scales, you are invited to express or channel the lower stages with maximum intensity and awareness. When you reach the apex of the lower stage, pause and find your way to gather all the energy and lift it up to the next stage. Then start and open up to the higher vibrations of Jupiter: benevolence, wisdom, faith, trust, connection with the Guide. Find your connection also with all those beliefs that support your current Intent. In the final stage be receptive to the energy of Jupiter and to what is necessary now for your path. Conclude by singing the chant for the last time.[5]

Astroshamanic Reports

At the Spirit Circle, by the Spirit Tree, I usually find one of my three Guides. One of them has the most direct relationship with the Spirit Tree. At times he seems to hide just behind the Tree itself, and comes out in full sight the moment I call upon him. He is the one that I consider to be my basic Spirit Guide. He belongs to the Middle World. In the shamanic world he corresponds to the trunk of the Spirit Tree, whereas in my body he relates to the heart centre. In my tradition this Guide is called *Urai Sadoh*. On one of our early meetings some years ago, he showed me the Tree for the first time. In our initial interactions I could not see his face, as it was covered by a mask – that of a sort of bull or horned animal. Then, one day, out of my passionate insistence, he revealed his visage. What a joy to see his face! And what a beaming smile! His main activities seem to be that of laughing, dancing, gesticulating, chanting or sitting perfectly still doing absolutely nothing. He has the quality of providing answers that way. His hair is black and long and he sometimes wears a maroon robe. He works in a team with the Guide of the Lower World, a black tribal man located at the roots or belly centre, and with the Guide of the Higher World, located in the top section of the Tree or Head Centre. On one of my voyages I met a tribe of black men and exchanged screams, dances and savage movements with them. Then I began to talk about my experiences in the outer world. For an instant I felt that it was stupid to speak about such things. It seemed to me as if I didn't have the authority. I then asked my Guide of the Lower World to take the lead with this tribe, but he insisted that I had to be their leader and show them my power. I accepted that and called the four directional Guides and created a spherical field of energy. I asked the whole tribe to come with me and pay tribute to the Tree. A great festival took place. My Guide was there by the Tree with his usual laughter. I didn't know what to do, but I felt that I had to perform something. I then decided to use some of the Spirit Medicines given by the Totem Spirits. I felt full of power and asked the Guide to indicate a place where I could send it for healing. I was shown a triangle pointing downward which was quite familiar to me and what followed was a most euphoric experience.

I entered into the Spirit Circle, and I moved towards the Great Tree. I firmly embraced it and sensed its robust bark. A potent flow of energy moved within the trunk and allowed me to experience the connection between the Higher and the Lower Worlds. I was confronted with my Function as a bridge between these realms. I acknowledged my role and became a hollow golden pipe that surrendered to God. As I did that, I detected a silent invitation. It had to do with my Intent, or target. I was being encouraged to define it. My target was that of the Etnai, the Spirit Circle, Spirit People and God. It was in that direction that I moved at all times. I felt as if there was something missing though. I was not really connected with the Guide, the Spirit People and God. 'How can I relate more thoroughly with you?', I asked, 'How can I actually hear your voice and distinguish it from that of the ego? In which direction do I have to go so that I can truly find you?' The Guide responded: 'Be quiet and still and simply define your target.' 'What is my vision? What is my target?' I asked myself. I get so involved with actions and searching and questing and seeking that I forget about it. I am pushed here and there. Then at the end of the day I am worn out. And here I am, asking myself: what is my target? Well, as soon as I asked, I could see a circle of holy beings. I was with them and we sat within a double cone of light. We were so joyful and ecstatic. Each one wore a different coloured robe and represented a different energy. There was so much love and radiance among us. We were twelve and One at the same time. The Guides were also there. God was there too. We were the Spirit People. We were the

Etnai. This was the target! O Beloved Guide I asked, 'How can I manifest this vision?' He replied: 'Well, simply be it. You have found the target. Just allow the arrow to stay on the target and lay aside your bow. Relax. You aimed at the target and shot. That required concentration and energy. Now that the target is being reached, enjoy it. Be the target! Be your vision. What else could you be?'

1   Edwin C. Steinbrecher, *The Inner Guide Meditation: A Transformational Journey to Enlightenment and Awareness,* Aquarian Press, 1982, p. 58.

2   *A Course in Miracles, Text,* pp. 586–587.

3   Bernhard Wosien, 'A Life Lived for Dance', quoted in Lynn Frances and Richard Bryant-Jefferies, *The Sevenfold Circle: Selfawareness in Dance,* Findhorn Press, 1998, p. 41.

4   See Sector One, note 4.

5   See Sector One, note 5.

DIRECTION NORTH

~ ELEMENT: Air ~ SEASON: Winter ~ BODY: Mental ~
~ KINGDOM: Animal ~ PART OF DAY: Midnight ~
~ SIGNS: Capricorn, Aquarius, Pisces ~
~ SECTORS: 10, 11, 12 ~ HUMAN AGE: Old age ~
~ TOTEM SPIRIT KEEPER: Riallah Sadoh ~
~ COLOURS: Yellow, white ~ CELESTIAL BODIES: Stars ~
~ JOURNEY: Way of the Teacher ~
~ SPIRIT PATHWAYS: Cleansing, renewal, purity. ~

ANIMALS:	Buffalo, dolphin, dragon, earthworm, goose, moose, mountain lion, otter, racoon, salmon, seagull, wolf, all winged creatures.
QUALITIES:	Clarity, commitment, communication, community, completion, detachment, discipline, honour, leadership, maturity, order, respect, responsibility, revelation, synchronicity, wisdom.
GRIEVANCES:	Abuse of authority, arrogance, ignorance, confusion, doubts, concealment, hysteria, rebelliousness.
HEALING TOOLS:	Brainstorming, breathing, council, dance, divination, mountain walking, sacred texts, sitting meditation, group and network of lights meditation.
INSTRUMENTS:	Fan, feathers, flute, rattle, sacred pipe, wand.
MINERALS:	Alabaster, amethyst, crystals, herkimer diamond, peridote, rhodochrosite, sodalite, topaz.
PLANTS:	Amaranth, hazelnut, lavender, mint, nettle, oak, pine, rosemary, sweetgrass.
SPIRITS:	Tezcatlipoca (*Aztec*); Danu (*Celtic*); Archangel Uriel (*Christian*); Nuit, Amun (*Egyptian*); Hermes, Athena (*Greek*); Mercury, Pallas (*Roman*); Fairies, Sylphs (*Nature Spirits*).
FESTIVALS:	Winter Solstice or *Yule* (20–23 December), *Candlemas* or *Imbolc* (1 February).

When I travel towards the ivory chill of the North, I leave behind the obscurity of the West with all my redundant and outworn garments. The entrance to this direction, at first sight desolate and austere, reveals itself in the solemn stillness of a landscape where the essential persists and all the rest dissolves. The North is a basic area of expression for my highest and most authentic nature, the setting of the inner leader and teacher. Here I have the chance of acknowledging and accepting my true responsibilities in life. The time spent in this direction offers precious opportunities for the understanding of my genuine inner potentials. It is also the place where I uncover and release my shadow sides, identify errors as false and unreal, correct them, perceive light, and take on my highest inheritance of glory. If I open myself to my Spirit Guide and Circle, here I can speak from a position of power, allowing my heart to express its true yearning, facing challenges in the physical world, and moving along in accordance with my original vision.

As the North is the place of the Teacher and Leader, it is the area where I accept total responsibility for all aspects of my life. I cannot be a leader if I continue to identify myself in the role of the victim of circumstances set up by something that exists outside, be it my partner, family, country or the whole universe. 'Responsibility does not mean that we are required to take on all the world's dilemmas and burdens and make them our own. Rather it means that we should be "aware witnesses" of what we are putting into our personal computers and what we are sending out into the world. [...] Responsible people are those who are accountable for their actions. Irresponsible people are those who try to place the blame for their actions, large or small, on somebody else. We have all made "mistakes" and we will continue to make many more, especially if we are on a path of growth and transformation. Making mistakes simply means missing the mark. The real waste is if we do not learn from our "missings" and make adjustments in our life patterns.'[1]

A major feature of responsibility is *discipline,* a word that indeed means 'being a disciple unto oneself'. The place of the North is also the point where I accept myself as I am and include all aspects of my being no matter how positive or negative they appear. Wisdom comes from getting to know my role in the world, accepting the limitations of living in a physical dimension, honouring my own rhythm and cultivating my potentials and gifts.

In the West I celebrate the epic of the *Satame Saike* – the quest for the Beloved, the Spirit Relationship, the Sacred Marriage – whereas in the North I move into another perspective and encompass an apparently wider arena. Here I honour the *Etnai Saike* – the quest for the Spirit People or Tribe. The Game takes on another strategy as it spreads into the social environment of groups, communities, nations, planets, galaxies and universes. As I proceed with my quest, I realise that the true longing of the realm of form and human perception is that of relating with what is unseen, a reality from which what is visible in my ordinary perception has separated itself. This is the cause of all the pain and suffering and guilt and grievances. The *ProvOrdo Etnai* is the brotherhood and sisterhood who accept the return to the original land of unity and join the Spirit Tribe (*Etnai*), letting go of their toys of separation and consolidating together to achieve purposefully the release of all illusory multidimensional blocks. Handor, exemplified by light, void and empty spaces, meets Rodnah, represented by darkness, form and filled spaces. Epically, this is the only possible partnership. In this context I realise that my deeper motivation in creating relationships with lovers, partners, friends, communities, guides is that of retrieving parts of myself so that I, and we, can ultimately and thoroughly embrace the void, Spirit, God. It is calling upon all my people, including everyone, inviting them on the path that will lead us to the original land of ecstasy and glory. In this process, I am aware of the time and space location where I operate, yet I look at whatever surrounds me as if it had already gone into that ultimate ecstatic dimension. Here it does not matter if this seems to be far beyond the current actual achievements of the other as I perceive it. My willingness is to learn to respond to all perceivable forms of error, both outside and inside, solely and unequivocally with my acceptance to release the illusion of separation. This will eventually transform the tribe of misery into the Spirit Tribe. As I progress along the path of the North I become aware of my ultimate transcendental lineage. There it is, easily available whenever I connect with my shamanic world. This is a customary experience for many people who work with shamanic journeys, especially on their first attempt. It is so nourishing to connect with the Spirit Tribe. There I can see all the people I have met in the outside world. They are all united, at peace, joyful, singing and playing together. I often experience them as a group of beautiful children. We are all together, united. There is no separation. For Handor's sake, this is indeed the world I want! It is the happy dream that I am determined to manifest. This is the genuine aspiration of the *ProvOrdo Etnai*. That Spirit Tribe is there, available at all times, beyond the gloomy veil of all insane tribes and families the ego illusion has generated in its forlorn attempt to escape from the power of love. In the North I learn to release ancient tribal grievances and open up to the dimension of the Sky, to all those people who managed to move at another level. As a matter of fact, the disappearance or extinction of many nations and races (Etruscans, Toltecs, Picts, Skidni Pawnee, for example), far from being a regretful occurrence, may be a major triumph in the light of this path. They continue to live and inspire us in a dimension far more comfortable and luminous. They have managed to take a quantum leap, to pierce the dense veil of this deceptive location, to march ahead along the path of return. They are the beacons, the heralding magnets that draw us into the ecstatic love of our true inheritance. Thank you valiant and generous beings. Be with us and inspire our journey. Let the North be a time for nourishing our need of true spiritual community, for acknowledging the unseen members of the tribe, allowing them to take the lead and be with us, dwelling in the empty spaces, exalting the Bhi Jinah. What glory! What beauty!

The following story belongs to the *Trudeh Etnaie Korah*, the popular ballads of the *ProvOrdo Etnai* aimed at evoking the energy of traditional mythic heroes. It narrates the enterprises of Harda, the hero of Uriah Tapeh, the Clan of Sector 11. It is in *sacred idiom* and, as it is often the case with such language, the attempt to translate it is in itself an enterprise.[2] Well I will have a try at it and be aware that this is just a rough synopsis. Harda wanders for years all over the vast territories of the North hemisphere. He looks for his lover. The lover he has been guided to serve. All he knows about her is the name: Etnai.[3] He also knows that she abides somewhere in the North. Unceasingly he wanders, days and nights. Then one day he reaches the summit above a valley. From there he sees a large village. 'This is Etnai!' He goes to the village. At the gate they ask him what is the purpose of his visit. 'I am here to serve you,' he replies. He is admitted. For years he works hard and does all that is needed. The village is his lover. With her he spends all his time. Harda is happy. He has reached his goal. He serves so beautifully. Although he is an outlander, the villagers are fond of him. Harda is very popular. All that he does is simply to love Etnai. She is his lover. The lover he has been guided to serve. One day the chief of the village decides to give him his daughter as spouse. Her name is Etnai... Well, this is the way of Harda. His lover is Etnai, the People, the village, the spouse...

---

[1]   Mattie Davis-Wolfe and David Thomson, 'The North Gate', p.5, in *Walking the Sacred Wheel*, Sacred Circles Institute.

[2]   The story could be translated in many ways and this is just an amateurish attempt. Please be aware that in *sacred idiom* there is no true reference to gender. This means that all subjects involved could be defined as men or women or both.

[3]   Etnai means something like 'people', 'large community' or 'tribe'.

SECTOR TEN

~ SIGN: Capricorn ~ HOUSE: 10th ~ PLANET: 1) Saturn 2) Saturn ~
~ RAY: 1st (Will/Power), 3rd (Active Intelligence/Adaptability),
7th (Ceremonial Order/Magic) ~
~ ELEMENT: Earth ~ QUALITY: Cardinal ~ DIRECTION: North ~
~ SEASON: December ~
~ TOTEM SPIRIT: Sauter Kitaya ~ EPIC STATES: Haxar, Raxah~

ANIMALS:	Tend to spend long time underground or in environments full of limitations and hard conditions. Ass, bat, bear, beetle, camel, cat, crane, crocodile, crow, donkey, eel, goat, hare, lion, mole, mouse, owl, pelican, rat, snow goose, stork, spider, tortoise, underground animals and insects, vulture, wolf.
PLANTS:	Usually have a long life and are seldom attractive, with grey or very dark leaves and trunks, unpleasant smell and taste, hard barks. Saturn is also associated with the roots of plants in general. Barley, beech, beet, belladonna, cannabis, comfrey, cypress, cumin, elm, eupatorium, fumitory, holly, horseradish, ivy, mandrake, moss, potato, rue, rye, spinach, yew, willow.
MINERALS:	Amber, amethyst, beryl, carnelian, coal, dross, fire agate, garnet, green tourmaline, jet, labradorite, lapis lazuli, lead, onyx, peridot, ruby, sapphire, toadstone, stones of black, sand and grey colour, rough stones and minerals in general.
SPIRITS:	Kassiel (*Angels*); Ninurta (*Babylonian*); St. Matthew (*Christian*); Consentes, Min (*Egyptian*); Cronus,

Medusa, Pan, Amalthea, Atlas, Rhea (*Greek*); Kali, Shiva (*Hindu*); Saturn, Janus, Vesta (*Roman*); Devil, World (*Tarot*).

ANATOMY/
PHYSIOLOGY: Hearing, knee, ossification, skeletal system, skin, teeth.

ASSOCIATIONS: Authority, manifestation, social status, career, coldness, refrigeration, limitation, frustration, restriction, frigidness, obstruction, delay, crystallisation, coherence, imprisonment, consolidation, weightiness, decay, deficiency, deterioration, loss, famine, caves, chronic ailments, long illness, suffering, old age, time, form, routine, monotony, drudgery, hard work, adversity, depression, melancholy, misfortune, failure, poverty, budgeting, debts, responsibility, property, mining, agriculture, land.

COLOURS: Blue-violet, indigo, black, grey, dark brown.

DETECTORS: Father, partner of mother, father of paternal grandmother or of maternal grandfather, mother of maternal grandmother, mother of partner, 3rd brother/sister of mother, 6th brother/sister of father, 1st son/daughter of 1st brother/sister of mother. 9-2, 8-3, 7-4, 6-5, 5-6, 4-7, 3-8, 2-9, 1-10, 12-11, 11-12.

GRIEVANCES: *Excess:* apprehensiveness, coldness, depression, dogmatism, fear of change, frigidity, maliciousness, mania for order, manipulation, melancholia, mistrustfulness, narrow-mindedness, nervousness, over-materialism, pessimism, rigidity, scepticism, secretiveness, self-repression, shyness, sorrow, stubbornness, suspiciousness, touchiness. *Deficit:* chaos, confusion, immaturity, incapacity to function in the physical world, incapacity to plan and set goals, incompetence, irresponsibility, lack of boundaries and structure, poor self-discipline. *Physical:* arthritis, chronic ailments, fractures, gout, infanticide, insomnia, orthopaedic and teeth troubles, rheumatism, stones.

QUALITIES: Aspiration, authority, commitment, completion, discipline, focus, growth, integrity, manifestation, maturity, motivation, order, perseverance, realisation, resourcefulness, responsibility, results.

Learning the lessons of Sector 10 implies the capacity and the responsibility to create the conditions for the manifestation of my highest Intent and to be willing to connect it with the Function. In this context I confront myself with the productive managing and employment of material and spiritual resources aimed at the realisation of specific objectives. In Sector 10 contracts are clear and there is no possibility of misunderstanding. Here business is business. When I treat the Totem Spirit of this sector with integrity and respect, I can rest assured that things get done. The goal, no matter how distant it may seem, is certain. It is only a question of moving forward, with commitment, step after step, patiently and confidently, honestly aiming at the Intent agreed upon and disregarding all possible diversions found on the path. There is a long road ahead and this requires a strenuous and persevering motion. This path is arranged in different stages and develops through the progressive achievement of short and medium term objectives. Here there is no time for easy exaltations, cheap enthusiasm, emotional attachments or other distractions. There is space for responsibility, hard work, endeavour and whatever supports the attainment of the desired result. This is the power of Sector 10, things are bound to get done, no matter what. Such a certainty gives an immediate sense of grounding and security. Here I am confronted with my responsibilities as regards my goals. If I truly want to bring about a given situation or result, all I need to do is to connect with this sector and make an agreement. Saturn is called the *Lord of Karma,* as it provides the means to face and release all the desires that keep clogging the mind. There is no room for complaints, fantasies, or statements such as 'if only I could be,' 'if I had... I could..., but as I don't have..., I can't,' or 'I wish I were...'. In Sector 10 it is only a question of being genuinely willing to manifest the desired result. Once a goal has been identified and there is commitment to accomplish it, a whole machine sets in motion and operates relentlessly until realisation is reached.

Many successful business people think in this way: 'I don't have a clue about how I will manage to achieve that result. Yet, in the meantime, this is what I can do'. This attitude focuses my mind on the present and allows each action, even the most modest (like getting up, washing up, doing up one's shoes, etc.) to be placed in the context of a wider perspective: that of the manifestation of my highest Intent. Here it is necessary to release the grievance of wanting everything at once and cultivate the art of patience. There are cycles that need to be completed and it is not possible to proceed according to rhythms based on anxiety and avidity. At times Sector 10 confronts delay and limits that, far from being obstacles, can be precious opportunities to prepare myself and acquire more experience. Usually they mean that my Intent needs more time to focus, that the tree is not ready to bear its fruits. In this case I can employ the time generated by the delay to get more consensus towards my Intent and develop the skills that I lack.

Some people, especially those with high ideals and spiritual aspirations, are often frustrated by the constant difficulties they encounter on their path. It does not matter how big my goals are, if I agree to connect with Sector 10 and consent to take up my responsibilities, I will either manifest the desired result or choose to release it upon realising that I do not wish that result any more. The ego has developed many tactics to avoid taking responsibility: blaming society, parents, religion, partners, bad karma, etc. The word *responsibility* is often associated with the word *guilt*. In the context of Sector 10, the association changes from *guilt* to *power*. It is one thing to feel guilty, another thing to feel responsible. I am not responsible to my family, society, work, etc. I am only and truly responsible to my inner world and Spirit Circle. Responsibility is true freedom. It means I am ready to master my life.

The hallucination of the ego is based on the conviction that existence proceeds through separated components which are often defined as *individualities*. Such disjoined entities purport to have a life of their own, shut off from their environment and growing autonomously at a physical, emotional, mental and spiritual level. In this context the ego ranges far and wide, pursuing all kinds of goals and contemplating the ultimate aim of attaining an individual spiritual enlightenment. This is perhaps the most imbecile goal ever thought by the mind. Yet it is, as I see it, what many human beings on a spiritual path are misled to strive for and achieve. The investment in this creed of being an individual entity, treated as separate from the whole, generates an inevitable sense of insecurity and the consequent need to exercise endless control, defence and manipulation on whatever threatens the belief itself. This attitude is at the root of authority problems. The acquisition of control starts from the very first years: on one hand I learn to exert control over my body or general behaviour, on the other I begin to control, or be controlled by, what is outside of my supposed individuality. My parents, teachers, elders, or authorities of any kind tell me what to do. If I want to be accepted or receive their love, I must obey. If this is not the case, I will pay the consequences and be punished. In this bitter scenario the illusory idea that is constantly absorbed is that of believing that the measure of maturity and power consists in exercising control over the outside world. This attitude amplifies in adult life as the whole life transforms itself in a continuous fight to achieve positions of power and control over things, people, nature, money, sex, etc. Here even my little or big rebellious acts towards those who keep the power are bound to enter into the same vicious circle. The sole true authority with whom I can confront myself exists within. It is not external. It is internal or at a level of perception which goes beyond the fiction of individuality.

The abuse of positions of authority derives from the belief that the source of love, peace, light or power is outside. When this happens, I enter into a predatory circuit where the roles of victim and persecutor cyclically continue to alternate. The Spirit of Sector 10 forces me to confront, at times bitterly, with problems related to authority figures. Parents, teachers, bosses, policemen, politicians, spiritual masters, partners are all examples of authorities on whom I project my grievances. They often appear in my ordinary life, dreams or shamanic journeys, to allow me to release and heal ancient wounds. Sometimes the temptation to see them as antagonistic forces and begin to fight can be very strong. 'What is the point of fighting a fight you cannot win. It is as useful as pushing against a river,' a wise elder said. This does not mean that I have to become a doormat. It signifies that if I operate with the energies of Sector 10, I need to be aware of the limits involved and not waste time in hopeless battles. Here it is again the question of connecting the Intent with the Function and employing the energies with integrity, without dissipating them in dubious deeds. Examples of common ways of wasting energy are: blaming myself or others, complaining and generalising about things (like 'Men are *always* like that', 'I *never* manage to do it'), worrying, wanting to be right at all costs, emphasising problems without leaving space for solutions, procrastinating, avoiding conclusions, manipulating or being manipulated, indulging in addictions, being addicted to creativity and the chronic expansion of forms.

According to the strategic perspective of the *Sacred Cone Circle*, the whole universe has been created in the desperate attempt to escape from the reality of unity and produce the mirage of separation. Since this process started, an opposite Plan was also set in motion. Many names have been used to describe it. I employ terms such as *Plan of Salvation,* or *Game Resolution*. The aim of this Plan is to gradually release whatever has been created in the process of fragmentation promoted by the ego so as to give space to the reality of unity and love. As a consequence, it is in the ego's best interests to use its resources of defence to strenuously oppose this Plan. The basic policy in this regard is that of protecting and holding on to all that is connected with the body. The ultimate attempt of the ego is to maintain that the development of physical forms is mandatory in order to achieve salvation. The fact that this is not the case, according to the Plan's perspective, does not imply that the Plan rejects the body. On the contrary its policy is that of recycling whatever the ego creates and using it as a means for attaining its goal. And as the body is the tool par excellence in the support of the illusion of separation, it is essential to pay major attention to it. In this process the body becomes a temple, a Sacred Circle, a teaching device which is meant to be released or employed quite differently once the learning has taken place. For this purpose I am not supposed to invest copious energies into embellishing a temple. It is just a temporary asset, a *Provisional Order*. The purpose of a temple is that of containing the Centre, the Inner Altar or Spirit. Striving and investing tremendous resources, high-tech devices and time to glamorise the temple may be a typical sign of the unwillingness to reach the Centre and to bring the Game to an end. Yet, if the Game is the conscious result of my free choice and through it I do experience love or what I truly desire, there may be indeed no need to bring the Game to an end.

Capricorn: The seasonal period of Capricorn coincides with the arrival of the winter sleep and the quietness that facilitates inner work and planning for the next seasons to come. It is the phase when trees are like skeletons and the Earth appears naked, although in its depth the seeds are at work aiming at a remote as well as certain goal. From a spiritual perspective this is indeed the time of the highest flowering, as the seeds of Aries reach the end of their nine months' labour. This sign starts with the winter solstice, also called *Sol Invictus* and the *Gate of Heaven*. According to some esoteric traditions there are two major gates: the Gate of Cancer *(Gate of Men)*, which leads into the physical dimension of separation and illusory perceptions of this planet, and the Gate of Capricorn *(Gate of Heaven)*, the one leading to the spiritual kingdom of unity. It is during the darkest moment of life that enlightening experiences can take place, as well as the possibility to move to another level. Summer is apparently the most abundant, luminous and happy time of the year. Actually this is only what the physical body perceives. Winter is a time of coldness, darkness, introversion and withdrawal. Physical energy is at its lowest and this weakens the ego which thrives on the available exuberance of matter. It is in this context that spiritual energy may easily reach its peak. It is part of the awareness of many esoteric traditions that darkness, depression, grievances and fear heralds the arrival of light, love and joy. When the Sun enters Capricorn it reaches its lowest position on the northern hemisphere horizon and this also starts the solar cycle of ascension. This event is the cause of major celebrations in all traditions. It marks the birth of the new solar year and of all significant gods who have inspired or conditioned mankind in the past ages: Jesus, Dionysus, Mithra, Quetzalcoatl, Apollo, Horus, Baal, Bel, Attis, Chango, Tammuz and many others. For the Mayan cosmology, this time, whose symbol is the spiral, represents the number zero and the most critical period of the year. In the Hindu tradition, Capricorn is considered the symbol of *pralaya*, that is, the process of demanifestation of the universe which occurs at the end of each cosmic age.

Tenth House: The cusp of the tenth house corresponds to the *zenith,* or *medium coeli,* that is, the point of intersection between the higher meridian and the ecliptic, or the position of the Sun at noon. The medium coeli, opposed to the *immum coeli,* is located at the top of the natal chart and represents the peak achievement of the soul on Earth and its doorway into spirit. Whereas in the immum coeli the soul has its seed, in the medium coeli it reaches its highest flowering. The medium coeli is the potential apex of the soul and the direct result of the development of the nature of the immum coeli. Through the seed of the immum coeli a structure can be built allowing the soul, as well as all those with whom it is connected, to move on to the path of transformation. This structure is represented by the vertical axis of the Sacred Circle, of which immum coeli and medium coeli astroshamanically constitute the polarities of the Higher and the Lower Worlds, respectively. When I align to the energy of this axis I connect with my true Intent according to my authentic multidimensional nature.

The tenth house is traditionally related to social status, career, reputation, ambitions, those in authority (bosses, officials, the father, etc.). According to astroshamanic cosmology this area hosts the authorities who preside over the executive running of political and administrative power: a location that can represent both the governmental headquarters of the ego and the board of directors of the gods on Earth.

ℏ *Saturn:* Saturn is notorious for its bad reputation and gloomy energy. Its aspect however, as it can be observed through a telescope, is very attractive. It is hard to consider it a malefic planet. According to one's perspective its rings can either suggest the presence of limitations or be seen as a sacred halo. Also its fame of being a heavy and cold planet, devoid of emotions and feelings, does not seem convincing. Saturn is the only planet whose density is less than that of water and, even though it is 95 times the size of the Earth, its weight is so light that it would float in one of our oceans if we could set it there.

Saturn is the main keeper of the different structures that make up the illusion of separation. Its task is to preserve each one of them until I am ready to move beyond and finally retrieve the knowledge of who I really am. Saturn represents the power that derives from commitment, responsibility and discipline. The first step in the acquisition of true power is experientially acknowledging that the world of polarities, conflicts, illusion and suffering is a world that needs to be released. This requires a commitment, a determination to let go of all that distracts from the ultimate goal of unity.

Saturn is the last of the traditional planets: the *superego* according to the Freudian model of the psyche, the conscience, the dweller on the threshold or doorkeeper between my space-time location and what lies beyond. It stays in the border zone between Level 1 and Level 2, ordinary and non-ordinary reality. No one manages to truly pass into Level 2 until they have faced Saturn. From Saturn onwards I enter into a dimension which is totally different. There all my habitual vision of life and the world blows up. That is why Saturn can be so scary. As a matter of fact I am perhaps the one who tends to scare Saturn. Among all the Totem Spirits of the Spirit Circle it is probably the most unappreciated and hated. For those who dare to move beyond the veil of appearances, Saturn shows itself in its candid, sweet and thoughtful presence. Acquiring this perception of Saturn allows access to the liberating power of Uranus. Such transcendental energy is harmoniously achieved through enduring and disciplined work, the acceptance of realistic limits in pursuing my Intent and the release of those self-imposed by negative beliefs.

The house and sign placement of Saturn in the chart indicates the type of responsibilities the individual will face in his life, his limits, inadequacies, weaknesses, fears, how and where the tests of his spiritual training take place. It is sometimes a troublesome area where delays and obstacles are experienced. Yet simultaneously, when I accept the meeting of adversities and work hard, keeping my connection with the Intent aligned with the Function, Saturn's placement can lead to major blessings.

The transits of Saturn have a cycle of seven years and represent basic confrontations in the spiritual journey. They force us to face the practical reality and to acknowledge what is not working in our lives. If I have taken responsibility as regards my Intent and connected it with the Function, these transits involve a consistent strengthening of power and major achievements. On the contrary, when I have not dealt with this, the consequences can be rather painful and entail loss, blocking or suffering around what I have avoided facing and dealing with. A typical feature of these transits is that they can bring about times of loneliness, inner pain, struggle, effort and frustration. These are all part of Saturn's testing ground.

Basic Practices

a. Using the guidelines (given in Book One, Chapter 7, 'Connection with the Totem Spirit' or Book Two, 'Introduction, Basic Practices, Exploring the Sectors') meet the Totem Spirit of Sector 10.

b. Activate the piece for Sector 10 of your Sacred Circle Pieces (see Book One, Chapter 4, 'The Sacred Circle Pieces' or Book Two, 'Introduction, Basic Practices, The Sacred Circle Pieces').

c. Choose one of the following practices ('Healing Tools') and do it daily, every other day or three times per week, for at least 21 days.

Healing Tools

1. **Facing Your Fears:** Every night for 30 minutes enter totally into your fears. For this purpose you can employ the structure

of Facing the Demon (see Book One, Chapter 7, 'Facing the Demon'). Turn the light off, create as much darkness as possible and sit. Then start becoming afraid. Think of all kinds of dreadful things, grievances, demons, spectres, murderers, sexual maniacs, etc. Create them and become really shaken up by your imagination. Exaggerate the fear. See yourself surrounded by killers and dangerous psychopaths. Experience whatever you are afraid of. Go into the fear as deeply as possible. Be total. Cry, shake, shiver. Allow yourself to be scared. During the day, whenever fear arises, let it flow, accept it. Don't judge it as wrong. Do not think that you have to overcome it and be brave. Accept fear. Let it move through you and allow it to be released.

2. **Using Clay or Stones:** As a regular practice this is another way of activating and balancing the energy of Sector 10, especially during the transits of Saturn. When there are blocks and your system seems paralysed with fear, depression or uncertainty, employing clay and stones triggers the energy of flexibility and the capacity to transform and create new structures. It also allows scattered energies to be focused and grounded. You can make simple sculptures or constructions representing your Intent or the foundations that you are willing to establish in your life.

3. **Defining the Spirit Father:** Each one of us incorporates parts inherited from our parents that often continue to survive as constrictions in our lives. These parts have been received from the parents of our parents, and so on, in a huge hallucinatory interchange of fear and separation. To get to know where all this started from, in the context of aeons, is a waste of time. What I can do is to take my responsibility for those inherited parts that characterise my life and release them This is the best way of honouring my parents and ancestors. In Sector 10, I face the father role, that representing authority, the one who establishes the behavioural patterns and the structure of reference, a role which is not necessarily related to a specific sex gender. With the following technique I define my *Spirit Father*. Take a comfortable position and establish your Intent: that of meeting your Spirit Father. Visualise him. Create his eyes, hair, mouth, face, expressions, voice, and general attitude. Make him exactly as you want him to be. Define him in the best possible way. Create the ideal figure of father and allow him to interact with you. Feel

totally supported by him. Then take this father into yourself. Feel his qualities as a part of yourself. Remember, this is your creation which is within you. All his positive qualities are there for you to draw upon. Acknowledge, treasure and use these attributes within you.

4. **Portraying Problems:** Draw a picture of your biggest current problem. If you work with clay, you can also make a sculpture of it. Take your time to express the problem in all its details. You can also draw an abstract image. Once you have done it, expose the drawing or sculpture somewhere in your room or take it with you and look at it whenever you experience problems or grievances. Allow the drawing and sculpture to teach you. Through your Spirit Guide, regularly send love and light towards it.

5. **Staff of Power:** Shamans and medicine men of different traditions often carry with them a staff of power. It is a reminder to be firm in their truth, not in an arrogant or pompous way, but with confidence and security as regards their own nature. The staff also represents the vertical axis, the conduit between Heaven and Earth, the above and the below. It reminds me that, like the staff, I have the same function. The beginning of the winter season is ideal for constructing a staff. Find or collect a piece of wood that you resonate with. You can also decorate it with natural objects like shells, feathers and small stones. Make sure that you collect everything in an honouring way (asking permission, giving information about your Intent, leaving an offering, etc.). Then start the construction or the activation of the staff. Take all the time you need to work on it.

6. **Being in the Darkness**: 'The escape from darkness involves two stages: First, the recognition that darkness cannot hide. This step usually entails fear. Second, the recognition that there is nothing you want to hide even if you could. This step brings escape from fear. When you have become willing to hide nothing, you will not only be willing to enter into communion but will also understand peace and joy.'[1] Set aside some time for being in the darkness. Go into a place which is totally dark or just sit in your room and obscure it completely. Stay there for at least a quarter of an hour. Open up to all your feelings and thoughts. See your fears or whatever comes up and write about them or draw them.

7. **Using the Energy of Sector 9:** Grievances related to Sector 10 tend to create limits and block possibilities of developments. They sustain an attitude that sees the worst and most negative aspects of life in everything. As Saturn is related to the process of crystallisation it can degenerate through chronic states of depression, inactivity, misery and apathy. A way to release such states is that of shifting into the energy of Sector 9 and living and acting from the Jupiter perspective. In this case it involves making a conscious effort to acknowledge what is good, harmonious, beautiful and funny in life. For this purpose you can use any of the practices given in Sector 9. Also do your best to find sources of Jupiter energies around you (whatever makes you laugh, gives you a sense of adventure and excitement, stirs you up, etc.). Be with people and situations that provide this energy and stay away from those that are chronically negative. Use affirmations like 'Every day, in every way, I am growing better and better' as a mantra and say it again and again during the day. When you are tired, exhausted or overwhelmed by all kind of obligations, taking a break and resting over your situation can also allow you to gain strength and clarity. In these circumstances, you can purposefully switch off your consciousness and allow your shamanic body, or unconscious, to come into play. Simply stop and take a break. You can lie down or sit comfortably, giving yourself a time of rest and sleep.

8. **Using the Energy of Sector 5:** Sector 10 is related to the structure of the physical body and it is often at that level that the most dramatic grievances seem to occur. To allow the flow and release of energy, connect with the Guide and ask the Totem Spirit of Sector 5 to radiate energy to those specific areas of the body corresponding to Saturn (the sign and house where Saturn is, the house whose cusp is in Capricorn). For example, if Saturn is in Gemini and in the sixth house, while the cusp of the first house is in Capricorn, you need to ask the Sun to send energy towards the related physical parts of Gemini (hands, arms, lungs), sixth house (intestine) and first house (head). In this case your body could block energy in those specific areas that also reflect into correspondences these parts have with related people and situations. Giving these parts awareness and conscious attention releases not only physical grievances, but also those caused by Sector 10 in other areas. For details about physical parts and their

correspondence to zodiacal signs see the *Anatomy/Physiology* category given for each sector.

9. **The Paheka Sadohe Korah** (Chant of the Totem Spirits and Guides): For Sector 10 the chant is *Sauter Kitayah Sadoh*. Please use this practice only if you intend to establish or support a regular relationship with the Totem Spirit of Sector 10. If you intend to use this chant, you can either sing it from time to time to accompany a cycle of twelve shamanic journeys in Sector 10 or as a practice on its own to be done preferably once or twice a day for at least seven minutes during a period of 21 days.[2]

10. **The Chant and Scale of Saturn:** When you feel sad, alone, blocked, depressed, fearful, confronted with authority problems or you simply wish to either activate or balance the energy of Sector 10, you can employ the Scale of Saturn and its chant:

Dah Ti Kah, Dah Ti Kah, Dah Ti Kah, Dah Ti Kah, Oh Ay

Upon singing it, you can visualise the image of the planet Saturn spinning with its rings. If you use the Sacred Circle, you can sit or stand in Sector 10 or the sector where Saturn is positioned in your natal chart. You can also stay in the sector where Saturn is transiting at the moment. After calling your Guide, according to your habitual procedures, connect with your Intent and Function. Ask your Guide to draw the energy of Saturn and the Totem Spirit of Sector 10. Then sing the chant (*Dah Ti Kah,* four times, followed by *Oh Ay* at the end). It does not matter how you chant it, how many times and with what quality of voice. The Scale of Saturn creates strong emissions of energy all over the body and releases beliefs based on fear and separation. Witness what happens during the practice and, if you notice grievances, find your way to acknowledge or express them, without identifying yourself with their content. In the first stage open yourself to the lower expression of Saturn. Feel anxiety, apprehension and all kinds of fright. Your heart is heavy and blocked. You would run away, but you are paralysed. Invest as much energy as you can to express this stage and when you reach its peak, begin to gather the energy. Then let it go and give it away as an offering. Sing the chant and move into the second stage. Imagine a sphere of blue light rotating in the first chakra. Continue to feel yourself blocked. At the same time you are attentive and vigilant. You are getting ready to meet your biggest fear. Meet your demon. Look at it straight and directly. Allow yourself to experience its energy. Reach a peak and then gather that energy and lift it to the next stage. In the third stage, after the chant, see the sphere of blue fire rotating around the first chakra and expanding throughout the spine, as a river of light, until it reaches the brain. Your mind becomes clearer and you start receiving ideas on how to change your situation. You gradually identify the steps to take. You take full responsibility for the limits you have created in your life and release them once and for all. Meet the Spirit of Sector 10. Invest a maximum amount of energy in this phase and lift it to the higher level. In the fourth stage the light blue energy starts to pulsate in the sixth chakra and mobilises self-discipline, integrity and determination. You feel that you begin to manifest your plans and that they become real. In the final stages, allow the blue light to pulsate in your solar plexus, heart and throat. Focus on your Intent and see how it develops as you allow the energy of Saturn to reach its peak.[3]

Astroshamanic Reports

With the Guide I enter into a dense and obscure sky. The air is so heavy that I can almost touch it. It is not easy to breathe. Far away I can spot the dim light of a planet. After a while we land there. The ground is luminous and covered by thick sand. The Guide changes into an ostrich which I get on to reach a dilapidated house on a hillock. I am aware that it is the dwelling place of the Totem Spirit of Sector 10. I enter the house and I notice the Spirit sitting in the half-light. It looks very coarse and serious. The whole house is in a state of total decay. The Spirit is dressed in tattered clothes. I ask him timidly, 'What can I do to heal the blocks in the relationship with you?' He answers first in a way which is totally incomprehensible to me. I am surprised by the fact that although he looks rough and cold, he seems to emanate a lot of love. Then his words become more accessible. I can get some understanding through his coarse accent. I get something like: 'Go down to the depth of your roots and return to the source. You created all these blocks. Don't be misled by their fruits. Look at their roots. They emanate from your being. Take back your responsibility and perceive the passion of this process. This does not mean that you have to feel guilty and be suffocated by the burden of your duties. This is the usual way in which my image is disfigured and besmirched. It means employing the physical world for what it really is. Lead whatever disturbs and blocks you toward your original responsibility. Do it with joy and remember that in this joy true authority abides.' The Spirit then gives me a precious Medicine. 'As you firmly hold it,' he says, 'you solemnly proclaim that all your perceptions are your responsibility. In this way you allow the release of Graha to be operative and reconduct all separated components to their original source. Go directly into the cause and roots. Take care of this Medicine and use it to heal you and everyone. By holding it firmly you are carried to your current responsibility.'

The Intent for journeys in Sector 10 is often that of establishing a *pact*, that is, an agreement aimed at manifesting a specific result. This pact is an actual contract where two parties commit themselves to provide services and achieve results. The features of Sector 10 facilitate such an approach and constitute a way out for most issues involving manifestation.

In a preceding meeting with the Guide, I had set the basis for a pact. Now the Guide takes me to Sector 10 to examine the conditions of the contract. I approach the summit of a high mountain that dominates the entire landscape. It is the Rock of Haxar, *the mount of grounding, of giving form, of realisation, of the building process. There I see various characters. They have a serious air and seem to be much involved in what they do. They look at me heedlessly as if to say 'Aha, you would like to establish a pact with us? We are the* Kiteri. *Be aware that we mean business. If you want to fool about, go somewhere else!' I reply that I am ready to commit and be reliable. They underline the fact that my Guide has to be present and give authorisation. 'As for the pact, all you have to do is to respect the conditions of the agreement. The realisation of the desired outcome will be dealt with by us. [...]' I examine the conditions of the contract in all its details with my Guide. Then I call the Kiteri. Their austere and stern appearance hides the vigour of their loving vibrations. I perceive their total commitment to serve me. Their way of surrendering is full of dignity and respect. They really mean what they say and I feel the strong responsibility of making an agreement with them. They look at me as if they were saying: 'Do you really mean it? Are you serious? Do you really want to work with us?' That's what they communicate with their gaze. Now my Intent is being boosted and as I confirm it I renew my contract and pact. I am ready to use them; my Intent is there. I am serious about it. I am not going to wander in other directions. My Intent is crystal clear: this is my way. We are going to build it: we have that project in operation which emanates from my Centre and no compromise is allowed. Then I meet the Totem*

Spirit. 'My dear, I was waiting for you,' it says. 'You know how well you feel whenever you come here. This is your place; here you find your roots. This is what is to be done, the first priority. So, whenever you find yourself wondering what to do, remember: the first thing is coming here to your source and getting your real nourishment that you can then take out into the world. Your connection with us will then ground everywhere and expand. Manipulate whatever is necessary to achieve this. The pact is at work: insist on it and let your aim flourish. Be careful, grounded, determined to achieve, crystal clear and solid. Whenever you find situations of confusion, be a rock, the Rock of Haxar, *which is the highest and most solid. You transform into it whenever there is confusion and weakness. You become rigid with your Intent, indestructible, like a fierce guardian of the temple, determined, no compromise. Be like that. In Sector 10 we are serious about our work. There is responsibility and commitment; this is our way and you made the pact with us. Be committed and responsible. Do not give space to shallow behaviour. Do not care about what others feel when you are like that: it is not your concern. Be expectant. Work is very easy. Have no other things in mind but your Intent. And by doing that, whatever comes into contact with you is going to be transformed by your Intent. Whatever you touch becomes Intent. Continue to climb; go on, climb in your dreams and waking times. Find joy and ecstasy in climbing. Celebrate that and enjoy the present moment. Do not care about the goal as the Intent is dwelling within you. Remember: stay* petrified *when there is confusion; be a solid monument of the Intent when something is not working. Do that! Remember to use your Spirit Medicine. Remember it! This is the great secret of Saturn which makes it powerful. If you attend to your responsibility you can go on, otherwise you see only my fearful image.'*

1   *A Course in Miracles, Text,* p. 11.
2   See Sector One, note 4.
3   See Sector One, note 5.

SECTOR ELEVEN

~ Sɪɢɴ: Aquarius ~ House: Eleventh ~
~ Pʟᴀɴᴇᴛ: 1) Uranus, Saturn 2) Jupiter ~
~ Rᴀʏ: 5th (Concrete Knowledge/Science) ~
~ Eʟᴇᴍᴇɴᴛ: Air ~ Quᴀʟɪᴛʏ: Fixed ~ Dɪʀᴇᴄᴛɪᴏɴ: North ~
~ Sᴇᴀsᴏɴ: Winter ~ Tᴏᴛᴇᴍ Sᴘɪʀɪᴛ: Uriah Tapeh ~
~ Eᴘɪᴄ Sᴛᴀᴛᴇs: Ukar, Raku ~

Aɴɪᴍᴀʟs:	Mythic, alien and non-ordinary animals (dragon, phoenix, griffin, etc.). Otter, seagull, stork, swan.
Pʟᴀɴᴛs:	Include all phenomena of aberration, mutation or alteration in the vegetal realm (for example, plants subject to radioactivity, artificial vegetables, grafting). Traditional associations with Aquarius are: almond, anise, ash, bean, caraway, citron, endive, fern, hazelnut, ivy, mace, marjoram, parsley, pecan, pistachio, poppy, sage, willow, rare and unusual plants, flowers with petals very close to each other.
Mɪɴᴇʀᴀʟs:	Aluminium, amber, aquamarine, black pearl, blue sapphire, electrum, garnet, jacinth, labradorite, lapis lazuli, larimar, obsidian, opal, platinum, radioactive elements, radium, uranium.
Sᴘɪʀɪᴛs:	Uriel (*Angels*); Taddheus, St. Francis of Assisi, St. John Baptist (*Christian*); Horus, Nut (*Egyptian*); Uranus, Deucalion, Hebe, Ganymede, Hephaestus (*Greek*); Varuna (*Hindu*); Itzamma (*Maya*); Dyonisus, Juno (*Roman*); Fool, Star (*Tarot*).
Aɴᴀᴛᴏᴍʏ:	Ankle, lower leg, tibia, fibula, blood circulation, cellular oxidation.
Assᴏᴄɪᴀᴛɪᴏɴs:	The unusual and unconventional, science, electronics, radio, television, aeronautics, inventions, genius,

novelty, eccentricity, deformities, freaks, abnormality, unexpected or disruptive happenings, changes, anarchism, revolution, upheaval, surprises, shocks, explosions, catastrophes, earthquakes, accidents, divorce, separation, exiles, strikes, freedom, independence, emancipation, occultism, societies, communities, eco-villages, associations.

COLOURS: Violet, electric blue, tartans, shocking colours.

DETECTORS: 4th son/daughter, partner of 1st son/daughter, 5th brother/sister, partner of 1st son/daughter. 10-2, 9-3, 8-4, 7-5, 6-6, 5-7, 4-8, 3-9, 2-10, 1-11, 12-12.

GRIEVANCES: *Excess:* addiction to change, aggressiveness, autocracy, brusqueness, eccentricity, explosiveness, fanaticism, intolerance, irresponsibility, licentiousness, perversity, ruthlessness, unreliability, urge to shock, wilfulness. *Deficit:* conformism, dependence, fear of change, rigidity. *Physical:* accidents, afflictions of circulatory system, diabetes, fractures, varicose veins.

QUALITIES: Breakthrough, change, community, detachment, freedom, friendship, intuition, inventiveness, originality, progress, revelation, surprise, synchronicity, uniqueness.

In Sector 11, I move beyond the feeble barricades that keep together my perception of consensus reality and personal reality. I follow the stream of intuitive sparks drawing me to wider and higher realms. Here my perception shifts abruptly, as dimensional gaps shed light on exciting and surprising environments. Consciousness expands beyond the illusory veils of my shallow identification, finding new assimilation: social groups, movements, communities, tribes, esoteric orders, galaxies. The pressure of Sector 11 is not an easy one to manage in the context of conventional life. It mercilessly bares all mirages and inconsistencies in my conditioning, fomenting a state of dismay in the ordinary mind. Sector 11 is always available to provide unexpected and revitalising perspectives, allowing me to claim freedom from blocks and stagnation caused by the identification with physical, emotional, mental and spiritual vehicles. It is the alternative organ which springs up as a last resource when the traditional anatomy of Sector 10 gets stuck and is unable to proceed further. This stimulates breakthrough initiatives and revolutionary changes that can hardly be conceived from the perspective of previously existing systems. Such patterns, if not accepted or integrated, can manifest through extreme acts of rebellion projected on events of everyday life: accidents, aggression, shock, loss, theft, damage, separation. Although these episodes could appear accidental, they are the evident fruit of elaborate strategies on the various fronts of the plan of separation (ego) and the Plan of Salvation (Spirit Guide).

In certain moments of life, the pressure for change is inevitable. At times radical changes or spectacular mutations become subtle tactics employed by the ego to cheat itself or other egos of the attainment of inner changes that indeed have never occurred. This reminds me of the French saying *Le plus ça change, le plus c'est la même chose*, that is, 'The more things change, the more they are the same'. What urges me to create radical changes in life? What forces me to leave my home, job, partner, parents, friends? The true change in Sector 11 has nothing to do with what occurs outside, although this could at times work as the echo of a veritable change. The latter operates from the inner. It is a sort of a reawakening to something that is always there and therefore does not actually imply any real change. It is an act of remembrance that determines a radical shift in the perception of what is apparently outside. 'Projection makes perception. The world you see is what you gave it, nothing more than that. But though it is no more than that, it is no less. Therefore, to you it is important. It is the witness to your state of mind, the outside picture of an inward condition. As a man thinketh, so does he perceive. Therefore, seek not to change the world, but choose to change your mind about the world.'[1] The rebellious surge and genius of Sector 11, shooting into the world with the sincere Intent to serve and change it, inevitably reaches this conclusion and becomes the heroic protagonist of the only possible revolution: the multidimensional one.

Aquarius: The seasonal period of Aquarius is often characterised by abundant snow, rain and weather of general purification. In this part of the year floods took place in ancient Babylon and the name of the sign seems to be associated to such events. For the Celts this time corresponds to the end of winter and coincides with the festivity of *Imbolc*. It was a very significant period for past agricultural societies: fields began to wake up and it was necessary to purify them. For this purpose rituals were celebrated with bonfires, sacrifices and also general cleaning of houses and fields.

Whereas the sign of Leo represents the apex of individuality and self-awareness, Aquarius marks the shift from individual to collective consciousness. Here the major concern is the wider world, humanity as a whole and even what lies beyond: Earth, solar system, galaxy, universe, other dimensions, and more. It is the sign that distinguishes an evolved level of awareness which, like that of Pisces, is not easily understood by ordinary perception. The nature of Aquarius hardly adapts itself to conventional life and is often involved in extreme and unusual deeds. The urge for emancipation and change can also degenerate into automatic behaviour causing constant rebellion and the refusal of any rules or structure. When the energy of Aquarius is lived harmoniously, it brings lucidity, lightness, union with others, altruism, devotion to communitarian ideals and unconditional service.

Eleventh House: It is traditionally related to friendship, social groups, communities, associations, intellectual relationships, ideals, humanitarian enterprises and all the great goals of life. In this context, the ambitions of the tenth house and the flowering of the medium coeli connect with the social environment and give rise to situations of alliance or conflict, collective identification, community and synergy. 'A social system high in synergy is one in which the conflict between selfishness and altruism does not arise, one whose language may lack these very concepts, one in which it is very difficult to hurt others because it is very obvious that such behaviour would be injurious to oneself.'[2] Synergy is the simultaneous action of various energies aimed at achieving a specific intent. It is that property of systems whereby the whole is greater than the sum of its parts. Such circumstances can produce an unpredictable and miraculous power of realisation that moves far beyond the apparent consistency of the forces involved.

⛢ ***Uranus:*** Uranus is the first planet met after Saturn: the herald of a new dimension. It is considered the higher octave of Mercury: the transpersonal mental energy carrying intelligence a stage further into the realm of the primeval thought of separation. Uranus is associated with the subtle energy of the seventh chakra and with the transpersonal area existing above. People under a strong influence of Uranus can experience the urge to go their own way and stand against consensus reality. They are often solitary or regarded as weird and a danger to the status quo.

The position of Uranus indicates the areas where the soul can pierce the illusion of ordinary reality to access the pure awareness of its authentic nature. Through Uranus I can employ extreme states of crisis and shock as catalysing agents to bring true perception and stimulate new developments in my life. Here radical changes, sudden awakenings, quantum leaps and miracles are possible. All this can happen with extreme speed, at times traumatically. Out of nothing events unfold and contribute to accelerate an integral change in the flow of life. Those with this planet dominant in their charts have an unconventional mind that allows them to anticipate future events and trends. They usually have non-ordinary talents that develop only when the individual manages to emancipate from the consensus reality and follow his authentic path.

The transits of Uranus predispose to major changes and often determine a desire for freedom that, when the individual is connected with his Guide, can allow major breakthroughs. On the contrary, when the person is not ready or opposes his process of transformation, change can occur in abrupt, violent and chaotic ways. Uranus may determine a state of mental and nervous hyperactivity, providing abundant energies and precious intuitions, but also crisis and erratic behaviour. According to Barbara Hand Clow,[3] Uranus rules the *kundalini,* and its transit of opposition (around the age of 40) corresponds to the time of maximum natural arousal of this energy. For some subjects, prone to the influence of the planet or training themselves with special techniques, awakening of this energy is possible also at earlier stages. It is often said that the premature opening of kundalini, when accurate preparation is lacking, can easily cause psychic and mental damage. During the opposition of Uranus the energetic potential is usually ideal for this experience to develop effectively. In the first stages of the transit kundalini energy erupts from the root chakra and ascends bumping into areas clogged by grievances. This can block the flow of the whole system and create major disturbances that will continue until root causes are dealt with. During this stage it is common to experience frequent strong physical sensations such as trembling, itching, bursts of heat, palpitations, or other non-ordinary perceptions.

Basic Practices

a. Using the guidelines (given in Book One, Chapter 7, 'Connection with the Totem Spirit' or Book Two, 'Introduction, Basic Practices, Exploring the Sectors') meet the Totem Spirit of Sector 11.

b. Activate the piece for Sector 11 of your Sacred Circle Pieces (see Book One, Chapter 4, 'The Sacred Circle Pieces' or Book Two, 'Introduction, Basic Practices, The Sacred Circle Pieces').

c. Choose one of the following practices ('Healing Tools') and do it daily, every other day or three times per week, for at least 21 days.

Healing Tools

1. **Shaking:** Using techniques for shaking the body, besides realigning the vertebrae and releasing tensions held in the body's joints, is an effective way of promoting the energy of Sector 11. This sort of practice can be employed, preferably accompanied by a drumming or rattling tape. Feel the vertical axis running from the above, the Higher World, all the way down through your spine into the below, the Lower World. Open yourself to the sound of the drum and feel the vertical axis vibrating throughout your body. Let its pulse take over and allow it to tune in to the right frequency. As you shake, let all energies that need to be released flow. Empty your mind. Shake out your anxiety, criticisms, worries, plans. Continue until there is nothing else but the awareness of this connection between the above and the below. Allow the form of your body and all possible forms around you to dissolve and melt. Breathe and surrender to the shaking. Feel the gaps within you and allow them to be filled by the music. Keep your shaking easy and energetic at the same time. No effort. Continue for 15 minutes. Then stop abruptly. Remain still, as though you were frozen. Do not move. Stay in this immobility for at least 5 minutes. Allow the energy to move freely and do its healing work. Then sit or lie down. Breathe and enter into the silence. Connect with your Guide. Allow him to direct the energy and create the necessary balance and changes.

2. **Kundalini:** This is one of Osho's most popular meditations. It is practised in the evening and with specific music available

in most record shops. It consists of four stages of 15 minutes each. The first stage is about shaking (and can work as in the preceding practice). The second is dance. The third is stillness and the fourth involves lying down and continuing being still.

3. **Dealing with Saturn:** Sector 10 brings order, discipline and structure; Sector 11 often thrives on chaos, rebellion and formlessness. When Uranus is dominant, either by transit or natal position, dealing with Saturn (Aquarius' old ruler) and making a conscious effort to apply its qualities can help bring balance in life. Avoid taking impulsive decisions. Take your time when considering radical changes. Use grounding techniques and find ways to create order around you. When you have a Uranus transit which is about to hit, write a list identifying all that you find restrictive, blocking and limiting in your life. Reflect carefully on the content of the list. It describes the areas where some changes are needed. Work with your Guide on that; ask in which way you can bring real change and not just impulsive shifts. Begin to work in your inner world first. See how you experience radical changes there, then allow them to take place gently in the outer world. Let the Guide and your inner allies work for you in this respect.

4. **Activities Connecting with Sector 11:** When Uranus is unbalanced it can easily bring feelings and thoughts of alienation or separation from the world which prevent the potent energy activated by the planet from finding outlets in the environment. In these circumstances it could be very useful to direct your energy to areas related to Sector 11. A typical example is that of activities involving groups and communities. Join a circle or sharing group, attend workshops, take part in group projects, spend some time in a community, do voluntary shifts in a centre, connect with old friends, etc. Also devoting time to learning new skills, expressing original talents, visiting a planetarium, exploring the night sky, connecting with the Higher World, working with computers, doing unusual and non-ordinary things are further ways to express the energy of Sector 11.

5. **Looking Differently**: Every day for ten minutes, try looking at the environment and people around you in as many different ways as possible. Observe people sideways; put your head down between your knees, and watch things

upside down; jump several times and look at people that way; concentrate on other people's nostrils when they speak. Be creative and find as many original ways of looking as you can. Also employ other senses: for example, listen only to the vowels when people talk; withdraw all the attention that you invest in looking and spend ten minutes considering only what you get from your smell or touch. Watch what happens as you do all this. What do you notice of the world around you as you see it from different perspectives? Does your perception change? Do your thoughts and views also change?

6. **Experiential Astrology or Astroshamanism:** Being aware of the energies available in the present and focusing on your basic Intent allows effective employment of the energy activated by Uranus. An individual session of experiential astrology or astroshamanism could be useful at this stage, as well as an analytical look at your astrological chart and transits aimed at defining the astrological potential of the current time. Astrology is ruled by Uranus and provides a helpful sense of structure when the energy of Uranus is hitting. Have a look at your astrological chart and identify the position of all planets in sign and house. You can also check a *Table of Fixed Stars* and see if you have a fixed star close to any of your planets or angles with an orb of 1°. Then go into your Spirit Circle and meet all the energies involved one by one. Connect with your Guide; then open up to receive a keyword, image or sound for each planet, fixed star and sector.

7. **Accidents:** These are revealing elements of the action of Uranus. When an accident occurs, it does not matter whether big or small (like breaking a dish or bumping into something), try and reconstruct attentively what were you thinking or doing at that moment. Sometimes an accident works as a decoy to distract you from something relevant that is happening. When it is a serious accident, it can even lead to states of amnesia and incapacity to remember what was going on before. These events could be subtle tricks of the ego. From a spiritual perspective accidents are not accidental events. Behind them there is a precise motivation of which we can be aware or not. At times accidents have an important function in the process of transformation: although their immediate consequences seem unpleasant, they can lead to new visions of reality and determine the condition of major changes.

When you have an accident, no matter its degree of seriousness, this is often a signal from a part of your being that invites you to break from a situation of block and grievance. Stop for a while and examine what is going on. Do you feel anger, rebellion, grievance? Are you denying or projecting anything? During the course of this month be aware of all situations involving accidents no matter how small. Also include accidents occurring to other people and all the world around you. See how you react to them.

8. **Breathing:** Besides being an indispensable activity for surviving on Earth, breathing is also one of the main practices in many spiritual traditions. Leonard Orr, pioneer of Rebirthing, teaches a simple technique that can be practised under all circumstances. First inhale and exhale in an ordinary way with your nose for two or three times. Gradually allow your breathing to be longer and fuller. Then, with the exhalation, let go completely of all the air in your lungs, relaxing your body. Repeat this model of three ordinary breaths and a longer one for at least four times.

9. **Council or Ceremonial Sharing:** (see Book One, Chapter 4, 'Moving and Staying in the Circle'): This typical practice of Sector 11 is also one of the major tools for decision making, healing and energy connection in many spiritual communities. Attend some form of council or sharing available in your environment or create one with your friends.

10. **Connecting with a Star:** This is a powerful ritual to activate the relationship with the Higher World. It is preferable to see the star you work with or the portion of the sky where it is located. (The energy of the stars can be tapped also without physically sighting them. For this latter purpose use a map of the sky.) You can decide in advance with what star to work or allow that choice to occur spontaneously as you look at the sky. After using the customary practices to connect with your Intent and Guide, address yourself toward the point of the sky where your star is located. Ask your Guide to act as mediator during the connection. Look up and face the star or constellation of your choice. Focus the attention on your breath. Allow it to move deeply and slowly in all parts of your body and let it also spread throughout the land where you are and the whole Earth. As you inhale, allow the energy of the star to fill your system, receiving energy and

channelling it within yourself, the land, its people, the planet. As you exhale, release whatever you have in excess in that moment, let go of any grievance and also allow yourself to be a channel of grievances existing in your environment and planet. Once this process is concluded, be still and let the energies be absorbed by your system. Ask your Guide to balance what you have received. Then thank the star and finish the ceremony. Make sure that you do not expose yourself to the energy of the star for more than 15 minutes. Also eat moderately and refrain from the use of drugs, alcohol, sugar, coffee, red meat and any other stimulant for at least twelve hours before and after this ritual.

11. **Chi Kung:** The Chinese art of *Chi Kung* (literally meaning 'internal energy exercise') and in particular the *Zhan Zhuang* ('standing like a tree') lineage is a powerful and healing shamanic tool. Employing some of the basic practices, besides enhancing Sector 11, can be an additional outstanding aid to energetically connecting with the Spirit Guide and Circle.[4]

12. **The Paheka Sadohe Korah** (Chant of the Totem Spirits and Guides): For Sector 11 the chant is *Uriah Tapeh Sadoh.* Please use this practice only if you intend to establish or support a regular relationship with the Totem Spirit of Sector 11. If you intend to use this chant, you can either sing it from time to time to accompany a cycle of twelve shamanic journeys in Sector 11 or as a practice on its own to be done preferably once or twice a day for at least seven minutes during a period of 21 days.[5]

13. **The Chant and Scale of Uranus:** When you feel unstable, aggressive, erratic, extremely rebellious, or simply wish either to activate or balance the energy of Sector 11, you can employ the Scale of Uranus and its chant:

Nah Mitriah, Nah Mitriah, Nah Mitriah,
Nah Mitriah, Nah Simitri

If you use the Sacred Circle, sit or stand in Sector 11 or the sector where Uranus is positioned in your natal chart. You can also stay in the sector where Uranus is transiting at the moment. Call your Guide, according to your habitual procedures. Then sing the chant of the Sun (*Oh Hay Yah,* four times, followed by *Oh*) and that of Earth/Moon (*Si Idriah,* four times, followed by *Neh Ah Mah Set*). The use of these chants, repeated also at the end of the scale, is suggested in order to keep focus (Sun) and grounding (Earth) and avoid the destabilising effects from Uranus. Ask your Guide to draw the energy of Uranus and the Totem Spirit of Sector 11. Then sing the chant of Uranus (NAH MITRIAH, four times, followed by NAH SIMITRI at the end). Continue the practice moving gradually from lower to higher expressions of Uranus.[6]

Astroshamanic Reports

I was born in Bologna (Italy) in an old house in via Santa Margherita, very close to Piazza Maggiore, the main square of the town. I don't have vivid memories of my natal home as my parents moved to a new place when I was just two years old. I can only recall the new home. As for the old one, I rely on the descriptions provided by my parents. They didn't like to talk much about that house. This was probably because it reminded them of when they were very poor and had to work hard to make a living. Maybe there were also other obscure reasons, at least that is what I often perceived out of my Scorpio Moon and ascendant. My natal home was enveloped by a deep sense of mystery. It is now a gloomy, deserted and cumbersome relic, disfiguring the decorum and sumptuousness of the buildings that proudly stand in the exclusive city centre. Nobody has lived in that house for decades and most inhabitants of the area would like it to be demolished. Yet, the house is still there. It was just a few minutes walk from the new house. Therefore, whenever I went out, I would often pass in front of it. As a matter of fact, the earliest memory I can recollect of my childhood is about an episode that took place as I was walking by that house. That occurrence also marks my first acknowledged non-ordinary experience, and frankly the most powerful of all. I will attempt to describe a part of it. One day, Nonno Sandrino, that is, my grandfather, took me for a stroll. He lived in San Venanzio, a small rural village in the countryside, and used to come from time to time to visit me and my parents. As he was not accustomed to town life, he always looked forward to spending some time roaming around with me. His character was different from that of most adults. When I went out with him, although he would try and make some timid attempts to behave like an adult, he could not help betraying some typical traits common in most children. That made me feel very at ease. On that day, as I was holding his hand, I passed by the door of the house in via Santa Margherita. The door was big and very old. It was shut, but in some way I could vividly sense what was beyond it. As my grandfather was chatting with the newsvendor, who had his kiosk nearby, I began to stare at the door. I was magnetically drawn by something emanating from there. After a while it was as if I were both outside and inside the door. Outside there was the street with all its life and noises: motorcycles, people talking, cars. Inside there was a totally different environment: enchanting, sweet, warm, silent, mysterious and yet very familiar. What amazed me most was the fact that this place did not look at all new to me. As I was standing between these two realities existing inside and outside the door, I felt so full of excitement and wonder. I decided to move a step further towards the door so as to tune in to a feeble voice that seemed to come from there. As I approached the door's threshold, I began to hear it distinctively. It was speaking an unusual idiom – neither Italian, nor the Bologna's dialect, which my grandfather and mother spoke, nor the Sicilian dialect employed by my father when we went to Sicily to visit his relatives. It was a completely different language and again, at once, it had the most familiar forms of expression I had ever heard. At that time I had problems in learning Italian. My vocabulary was very limited and I could hardly understand most of the words contained in a phrase. Moreover I had paramount difficulties in correctly pronouncing certain consonants. The language coming from the door, on the contrary, was so easy. The voice said something that could be translated as follows: 'O beautiful Son of the Sky, come to *Handor*, your original Home of Light. We're waiting for you.' Although this sounded rather strange, I was not at all surprised by the voice. It was not the first time I heard it, although I could not remember when the other time had been. I realised that the voice had already called me on many other occasions. However, the first time I acknowledged it with clarity was on that day. 'Enter the door,' the voice said and continued with insistence, as if waiting for some action or answer of mine. I looked carefully at the door. I noticed that there was a strange form vaguely emerging as a halo around the door. It looked like a big conic ice-cream. That cone was also immediately familiar to me. I had seen it many other times. It was similar to the hat used by the *Bhi Jinah* (see Direction West, *Bhi Jinah*), the beings that populated most of my *fantasies*. Actually *cornetti*, that is conic ice-creams, were also some of the most celebrated delicacies among children of my age. Yet there was something beyond the ice-cream that fascinated me. 'Yes, I know this door and I do realise it is my home,' I finally answered with a self-assurance that surprised me. My confidence, compared with my customary shyness, was astonishing. At that the voice replied: 'Why don't you enter then?' The invitation was tempting. Also it seemed to be too easy and impulsive. I decided to pause and ponder: 'As a matter of fact there are not so many interesting things outside. Most of the time I get bored. I could well return to this place called *Handor*. It is just a question of moving a few meters up to the door and opening it. Very easy. My grandfather won't even notice me.' I was almost about to rush to the door, when another call came. 'What about your parents who are waiting for you at the other home?' I halted in sheer amazement. I had completely forgotten about them. But even more astonishing and embarrassing was the fact that after recovering my memory about my parents, the attraction toward the door continued to be as strong as before. 'This door must be really powerful,' I reflected; 'I can't even go to bed or to the bathroom without my mum or dad. And now I could not care less! What's happening to me? Perhaps I could go home and tell this story to my parents." As soon as I thought that, I remembered that I had already made the attempt to relate similar stories, like that of the Bhi Jinah and their conic hats. On those occasions either my parents would pretend not to hear me or change the topic of conversation. In the beginning they would also buy me an ice-cream. The first time they did it, it was such a disappointment. There I was with that sugarish sticky and slushy thing. I got into such a bad mood. I told them that I wanted something else. My parents immediately tried to meet my request by purchasing another brand of ice-cream. This one at first sight appeared quite exciting. It was a cone wrapped with golden-coloured paper. When I opened it and found another version of the previous ice-cream I got very cross. My parents were also annoyed and accused me of teasing them. Well, let's go back to the door... After a while Nonno Sandrino looked at me and asked what was the matter with me. 'I'd better invent an excuse and continue to walk,' I thought. I did and we went on walking. In the meantime I brooded over what to do. 'After going to the park I would pass by the door again. I have some time to make up my mind.' When I arrived at the park, I went straight to the most prominent tree which I used to call *Albero Grande* (Great Tree). I asked for advice. 'You know where that door is,' said the Tree, 'and you can go there whenever you want. First reflect upon it. Are you really sure that you want to pass the door alone? It took you so much time to get down and play the Game in this area.' 'What Game?' I asked. 'The Game of the Cone,' replied the Tree. 'What does it mean?' I inquired. 'It is about bringing people together,' explained the Tree. I got very curious about this story, yet I also felt it very familiar and again this was amazing. I asked for more details. 'Look around,' added the Tree. I did that and saw the sky, the grass, the other trees, some boys playing with a ball, their mothers sitting and talking, a man with a bicycle, a group of birds, a cat, my grandfather and other things whose name I did not know. Then I thought of other people or things that I could not see in the park, like my parents, cousins, friends and toys. 'Shall I move through the door with all these people and things?' I asked. 'Yes, and even more,' answered the Tree. 'Where?' I inquired. 'Look again at what you *see* around you in case you have forgotten something.' As soon as the Tree suggested that, I immediately realised that he was referring to the Bhi Jinah; I contemplated the environment and I could not help seeing various groups of them filling the spaces that existed among the things and beings that I had seen before. 'Shall I take them as well?' I asked with some hesitation [...] 'Of course,' replied the Tree, 'It is with the Bhi Jinah that you are going to bring all the people together.' [...] 'It seems a great game,' I commented. 'In this way we are all going to move through the door of the cone and be together and have fun. That's great! Now that I have understood how things are, I'm going to tell my grandfather, then my mum and my dad.' At this point the Tree stressed the fact that perhaps it would be difficult for them to understand. Upon reflecting I realised that my parents and all the humans I had met so far used to talk only among themselves. 'They do not have any conversation with trees, animals, doors, toys, not to mention the Bhi Jinah. They call the Bhi Jinah *nothing* and they say that adult people do not waste time with nothing. [...] How can I manage to explain that?' 'As in all good games, patience and time is required,' answered the Tree. 'The first part of the Game consists of pretending to become a human being. You are to get acquainted with human manners and customs. When you have managed that, the second part is to find the way to the door.' 'But what is the point? I already know very well where that door is?' I objected. 'Yes of course, you do now.' answered the Tree. 'But once you get involved in behaving like a human being, you are likely to forget. As you are aware, human beings only talk with other humans and don't see the Bhi Jinah... The second part of the Game is exhilarating, as it involves a lot of tricks. I won't go into it now. I'll just mention that the second part of the Game will allow you to find the door again. Well, now, once you find the door, the third part of the Game starts. It is about actually moving through the door and letting other people move through too. It is the best part of the Game and also the most intricate. Often it is so easy to be carried away by the desire to find others to help that in the end you could forget again where the door is, and then are forced to go back to the second part and search for the door again. This is the Game of the Cone. It is an old game and is a lot of fun. Also it always ends well. This does not mean that it is easy. Sometimes it doesn't seem a game at all. And it is just this fact that it does not look like a game, that makes it so beautiful and stimulating. That's the excitement and the challenge of it. Another strange thing here is that the more you make errors, the more you learn, and you are always given another chance. There is no other game like it!" I was conquered by the words of the Tree who, being an ancient aged oak, was an expert about the Game. One thing worried me however: 'If humans only communicate among themselves,' I enquired, 'then it means that when I become a man, you are not going to talk with me any more, and neither the animals, the stones, the toys and the Bhi Jinah. And then what will I do?' The Tree clarified, 'This is not really the case. As far as I am concerned, as a representative of the trees, I am ready to continue talking with you, and so perhaps will the Bhi Jinah. The point is that one of the most frequent developments of the Game involves losing the connection with us. Remember this is part of the Game and won't last for long. In this way you get to know the universe you are in. You are also going to contribute to the retrieval of something which is very much needed on the other side of the door. Be confident, you will receive all the instructions. They will come to you when the time is due. Besides a Bhi Jinah contingent is going to be next to you all the time and accompany you throughout your ventures.' [...] Well, frankly, what the Tree said was not truly put exactly like that. There was something more and also something less. And, as a matter of fact, the language employed was neither English nor Italian. Yet, I feel that, as far as my current understanding of the experience is concerned, what I have provided here is the best translation I can think of, for the time being.

The following is a message received during an exploration of Sector 11.

Sing your song of devotion daily, make it a prayer and a give-away. You give expression to whatever is there and accept your responsibility as you are now. You take on your role as an active force and keep constant contact with us. Answers will reach you as you satisfy this condition. Give what you can give: devotion, constant attention, commitment, active force. In Sector 11 you find your original potential. You act undisturbed, you are one with your work and abide by it. You are here in this planet and at the same time you connect with us through the subtle breath. Keep the connection all the time and trust that it will provide all answers. Communicate with us and let everything go through the channel. Do not judge what you are sending; this is not your responsibility. You are a channel and are just to let go. It is not your business to judge what is a grievance and a blessing. That is the reason for your being where you are. You knew it was not going to be that easy. You accept your condition and receive help from your Guides. You are not the one to judge. You perform your letting go and remain crystal clear. Nothing belongs to you and you share whatever. Keep connected to the breath and let it lead your life. Your adherence to the higher Intent connected with the Function is all that matters and everything will come with no effort on your part. This requires great determination, being a spiritual warrior, fulfilling your original mission. Go along, great Son of Handor!

[1] *A Course in Miracles, Text,* p. 445.

[2] Bruce Nevin, *Astrology Inside Out: A New Approach to Astrology,* Para Research, p. 34.

[3] Barbara Hand Clow, *Liquid Light of Sex: Understanding Your Key Life Passages,* Bear & Company, 1991.

[4] For further information: Master Lam Kam Chuen, *Chi Kung: The Way of Healing,* Broadway Books, New York, 1999 and *Stand Still, Be Fit: The Way of Energy,* Gaia Books, London, 1995.

[5] See Sector One, note 4.

[6] See Sector One, note 5.

SECTOR TWELVE

~ **SIGN:** Pisces ~ **HOUSE:** Twelfth ~
~ **PLANET:** 1) Neptune, Jupiter 2) Pluto ~
~ **RAY:** 2nd (Love/Wisdom), 6th (Devotion/Idealism) ~
~ **ELEMENT:** Water ~ **QUALITY:** Mutable ~
~ **DIRECTION:** North ~ **SEASON:** Winter ~
~ **TOTEM SPIRIT:** Taepeh ~
~ **EPIC STATES:** Vuolly, Yllouv. ~

ANIMALS:	All fish and sea creatures in general, bull, butterfly, dolphin, fabulous sea animals (siren, triton, hydra, etc.), heron, horse, lizard, puma, swan, whale, wild boar, wolf.
PLANTS:	All plants growing in water, coffee, fern, moss, myrrh, narcotic and anaesthetic herbs, mushrooms, opiates, orchid, parasitic plants, peyote, poppy, tobacco, seaweed, water lily.
MINERALS:	All mysterious or unseen minerals, amethyst, aquamarine, beryl, coral, diamond, fluorite, green tourmaline, jade, labradorite, moonstone, neptunium, opal, platinum.
ANATOMY/ PHYSIOLOGY:	Appendix, feet, pineal gland, right-brain functions, thalamus.
SPIRITS:	Asariel (*Angels*); Bridget, Rhiannon (*Celtic*); Kwan Yin, Nu Kwa (*China*); Matthias, Jonah, St. Brendan the Navigator, St. Joseph of Copertino (*Christian*); Isis, Bes (*Egyptian*); Nethuns (*Etruscan);* Poseidon, Atagartis, Cassiope (*Greek*); Varuna (*Hindu*); Susanowo (*Japanese*); Aegir, Njord (*Nordic*); Neptune, Cosus, Dyonisus (*Roman*); Ea (*Sumerian*); Hanged Man, Moon (*Tarot*).

ASSOCIATIONS:	Aestheticism, inspiration, mysticism, spiritualism, devotion, transcendence, trance, visions, magicians, sea and marine life, fishing industry, alcohol, drugs, anaesthetics, poisons, inflation, chaos, confusion, mysteries, disappearances, illegal activities, charitable institutions, dance, music, theatre, cinema, actors, glamour, deceit, disguises, intrigue, perversion, plots, seduction, daydreaming, dreams, coma, nebulousness, madness, hospitals, prisons.
COLOURS:	Red-violet.
DETECTORS:	1st and 7th brother/sister of father, partner of 1st brother/sister of mother, 4th brother/sister of mother, 1st brother/sister of mother of partner. 11-2, 10-3, 9-4, 8-5, 7-6, 6-7, 5-8, 4-9, 3-10, 2-11, 1-12.
GRIEVANCES:	*Excess:* addiction, escapism, dishonesty, dramatisation, fraudulency, gullibility, hallucination, hysteria, hypersensitivity, impracticality, instability, irrationality, perversion, seduction, self-deception, self-indulgence, shyness, suicidal tendencies, vagueness, victimisation. *Deficit:* coldness, disconnection with spiritual dimension and alternative states of consciousness, inability to fantasise or dream, lack of imagination. *Physical:* alcoholism, cysts, digestive and nervous diseases, drug-addiction, epilepsy, feet trouble, glandular disorders, infections, insomnia, mysterious ailments, poisoning, sleepiness, tumours.
QUALITIES:	Compassion, empathy, imagination, inspiration, openness, surrender, unity, vision.

With Sector 12, I sink into transcendental spheres of cosmic conscience, melting down the outworn armour of my spurious identity and amalgamating exponentially with all that converges on the path. My awareness dilates to include everything and everyone, stretching up to highest dreams and plunging down into dreadful nightmares. Here I experience a jubilant blending with ordinary and non-ordinary beings, sensing their consciousness as mine, while systematically uncovering the veils of infinite paradisiacal realms. I leave aside all concerns for that dressed ape standing on a remote boulder of this universe, whom I supposed to be me, and extend into my multidimensional nature, dissolving into each being, becoming them and the universe. I am ebullient at the opportunity to reach the utmost peaks of ecstatic achievement available in this horizontal dimension. When I manage to attain them, I meet my existential apex. When I cling to those pinnacles, refusing to return and fully apply my Function, I find myself wretched and beguiled.

The voyage in Sector 12 can be extremely intricate, as grievances tend to proliferate in most unobtrusive and sophisticated forms. This area includes the highest and lowest aspects of human experience. The task of mastering Sector 12 and the energy of its planet, Neptune, is extremely challenging. If one succeeds in such an enterprise, then there is probably no need to *incarnate* into this world any more. Here the ego plays its last cards, which are also those that were used at the start of the Game. Out of the foremost place of unconditional love and fusion with the whole, looms up an ego which has astutely learned to survive through the tactical negation of its own existence. As a consequence, the attentive exploration of Sector 12 sheds light on the enigmas of life and reveals, to those who employ their veritable sight, the true nature of all appearances. In the border zone between Sector 12 and Sector 1 dwells the mighty gap, the crucial point of the Sacred Circle, that place where separation achieves its supreme standards of performance. Trapped in the illusory perception of ordinary consciousness, energy reaches its apex, comes to an end and then starts again, back from Sector 1 and, unaware of its previous experiences, pretends to be born and set off for a new journey. In Sector 12, I ultimately wish to cruise away from such tedious routines and dissolve into the ecstatic sense of oneness with creation, a total state of melting devoid of any limits both in time and space, an infinite ocean of bliss, unceasingly undulating and flowing. This type of experience is the true basic characteristic of life and, as such, is accessible at any moment. Yet, in order to reach it and make it part of my constant awareness, I need to employ tools capable of piercing the dominant perception of separation which is common in the human dimension. For this purpose various disciplines have been developed by mystics, shamans and spiritual researchers throughout the ages. Those who, with the aid of such tools, move into the ecstatic realm of Sector 12, can gently proceed toward their ultimate goal. They are likely to be exempted from moping around the veils of illusion which find here their most fertile land. Shamans and Guides are bridges between the realm of unity and that of separation. A strenuous training and commitment opens up the gates to their activity. The typical qualities of Sector 10 and Saturn – like self-discipline, determination and maturity – needs first to be mastered in order to truly access what lies beyond the territory of Sector 12.

)(***Pisces:*** The seasonal time of Pisces is a period of atmospheric turbulence and copious rain. The snow melts and swells the rivers from which the Earth absorbs water necessary for the imminent explosion of Spring.

Among the different typologies of signs, Pisces is the one that is closest to the experience of unity. Here the longing for the end of the journey is effervescent. Yes! Reaching my true home, having a peaceful time at last. Located in the final stage of the zodiacal path, Pisces represents the maximum point of potential transformation of human consciousness. Here the circle buds into a new cycle and, according to the quality of my perception, decides upon its next developments: circular and repetitive or spiralling and transforming. The access to the essence of this sign allows me to unseal dimensional passages and stargates. This safely occurs when grievances have been properly released throughout the path of the previous sectors. If that is not the case, Pisces can easily tumble down into a chaotic unconscious whirlpool and succumb to the devouring anguish of its hallucination.

Twelfth House: It is traditionally related to selfless service, devotion, inner life, isolation, places of retreat or evasion, sacrifice, secret enemies and fears, hospitals and prisons, spiritual teachers and centres, ecstasy and transcendence. In this house all events of life are confronted so as to set up a new cycle. It is the final release of experiences accumulated during the whole life, a disruptive, yet shrouded time, of transmutation signified by the covert presence of Pluto, Pisces' esoteric ruler. This house is the burial ground of the ego which, confronted with the crumbling of its previous devices, is urged to invent an ultimate contraption to preserve its hallucinatory existence. In karmic astrology it is often termed as the *house of unfinished business*, indicating the incomplete affairs arising from other dimensions or preceding incarnations.

The presence of planets in this house can identify arcane energies which often overpower us, as they are carried out from so-called *past lives* or, as I see them, realities that exist beyond the limits of our current identification. When their causes are not recognised, they appear as fatalistic or conflicting events of which we seem to be the victims. These energies are transformed productively when they are forwarded to our highest Intent connected with the Function. Their undoing is often enhanced by unconditional service to others or specific causes that inspire us. When I operate to release sufferings and illusions in somebody or something else, I am simply working on myself from another perspective. In order to help a situation or person in relinquishing his grievances, I need to have in myself something corresponding to those grievances, as well as the medicine that can heal him and me and us. 'Teacher and pupil, therapist and patient, are all insane or they would not be here. Together they can find a pathway out, for no one will find sanity alone.'[1]

Ψ *Neptune:* Neptune represents the transpersonal expression, or higher octave, of Venus, the embodiment of cosmic and mystic love. This energy expresses in every direction. In all that exists it recognises the Whole. The position of Neptune in the natal chart indicates where our desire of ecstatic melting with the Whole is projected or can find satisfaction. Here we are likely to experience the most idealistic traits and values of our soul, its potentials of vision and transcendence, actually lived in our life or confined in the dimension of fantasies and dreams. These values are at times projected in the strong idealisation of specific areas of life (relationships, work, family, art, etc.) or blocked and confused by evasive states, whose aim is to elude the responsibilities for these areas in the forlorn hope that sooner or later things will adjust by themselves.

The relationship with Neptune is essential for those who operate as spiritual teachers. In particular it is necessary to work as channel, bridge or activator and to be careful not to identify the ego with the source of power. Also it is important to remember that the flow of energy is never one way. I can truly give when my Intent is that of enabling whoever receives to be also in a condition to give. If I am not willing to receive from those to whom I give, no matter how heroic or sacred my efforts appear, my attitude is bound to be manipulated by the ego.

The transits of Neptune determine a strong desire for transcendence and ecstatic melting. If the individual is well grounded in his relationship with the spiritual dimension, he can easily experience powerful mystical events and creative insights, vivid connections with non-ordinary realities, lucid dreams and visions. On the contrary, for more rigid ego minds, Neptune transits may become rather uncomfortable, as all major certainties in life tend to be extremely nebulous. Weird feelings of depression and confusion may arise. What appears to be sure at a given moment, suddenly dissolves or reveals itself in a different form later on. These shifts, although not always comfortable, are true blessings in the process of transformation as they signal that I am ready to move to another level. During Neptune's transits I can also discover the visions that are useful for my path and discard those which are decoys and cause delays. In particular, the time around the age of forty or forty-one, when Neptune reaches its square to itself, right after the Uranus opposition, brings major opportunities to direct the energies activated by Uranus in accordance with the wider plans of our multidimensional nature.

Basic Practices

a. Using the guidelines (given in Book One, Chapter 7, 'Connection with the Totem Spirit' or Book Two, 'Introduction, Basic Practices, Exploring the Sectors') meet the Totem Spirit of Sector 12.

b. Activate the piece for Sector 12 of your Sacred Circle Pieces (see Book One, Chapter 4, 'The Sacred Circle Pieces' or Book Two, 'Introduction, Basic Practices, The Sacred Circle Pieces').

c. Choose one of the following practices ('Healing Tools') and do it daily, every other day or three times per week, for at least 21 days.

Healing Tools

1. **Dances Associated with Sector 12:** Dance and music in general are an integral part of Sector 12 and easily align to its frequencies. Certain dances are particularly associated with this sector. They usually involve flowing, unstructured, receptive and flexible movements, yet they also range over the whole spectrum of dancing possibilities, encompassing them all in a melting and unifying continuum. Before starting the dance, focus on your Intent and use your customary procedures for creating a sacred space. At the end, stay still and silent for at least five minutes, then release the sacred space and make brief notes about your experience. Here follow some examples of dances that can be employed. a) *Neptune Dance:* If possible use a tape with the sound of waves

or maritime creatures (whales or dolphins). Visualise and feel this dance as if it took place in the waters of an ocean or lake. You can imagine yourself as a fish or siren, moving freely, riding currents up and down, flowing with the waves and at times gently resisting them. Sense your spine as extremely flexible and supple. Allow each movement to join with the next, without interruption, in a constant fluctuation of all parts of your body and being. b) *Ecstatic Dance:* Move in a dreamy and blissful manner, as if you were eternally united with your sacred partner, your beloved perennially at one with you. Feel your heart inundated with ecstatic rapture and let it vibrate in unison with your lover. Allow such glowing shivering to expand in all directions, reaching all the possible lovers of the world and universe, embracing your friends, relatives and the people you know and do not know, every single being that exists or has ever existed, with no exception. You can also move as if you were a great mystic or enlightened master. Feel yourself as you lift up slightly from the earth, levitating in bliss and sanctity. Spread blessings and light out to everyone you meet. Imagine devoted crowds of pilgrims gathering at your feet. Melt with each person or thing you find around or in your thoughts. Be elegant, delicate and feel subtle vibrations moving in all parts of your body. Pretend to be Buddha, Jesus, Krishna, etc. If you are total in your dance and motion, you can literally and truly become what you act in the dance. Sector 12 is the realm of theatre, cinema, great actors and all forms of illusion (or reality?). c) *Osho Nataraj Meditation:* This is a practice devised by Osho and accompanied by a specific tape. It consists of 40 minutes of total dance with eyes closed, followed by 20 minutes of stillness and silence, then 5 final minutes of celebration. The purpose here is that of forgetting the dancer (and all the related self-awareness) and becoming the dance itself. Here the division between dancer and dance must disappear as only in this way dance can be a meditation. d) *Sufi Whirling:* This is a most ancient technique based on whirling with open eyes on the spot. The practice may be divided into two stages. The first stage is the whirling itself. It goes in anticlockwise direction, usually with the right arm held high with palm upwards, and the left arm low with palm downwards. For the first minutes the whirling is slow, then gradually the rotation speeds up until the dancer becomes a lively whirlpool of energy. The movement continues for

30 minutes or more, then the body is allowed to fall down on the floor and the second stage starts. This consists of lying down, placing the belly in contact with the earth and resting in silence for at least 15 minutes. e) *Kirtan:* This is a devotional and mystical Hindu dance which generally consists of three stages. The first is based on dancing, singing, jumping, clapping the hands with total involvement. The second stage is silent and still while lying down. The third is dancing and singing again. f) *Tarantella:* A traditional fast rotating dance of Southern Italy and other Mediterranean countries used as a cure for Tarantism (a mania for dancing caused by the bite of a tarantula spider) and which was indeed an excuse to justify the public performance of shamanic trance dance. This ancient shamanic healing practice takes place at the centre of a circle of people who move around like planets or rays of the Sun.[2] g) *Five Rhythms:* This is a dance in five stages devised by Gabrielle Roth. It is accompanied by specific music and instructions. h) *Trance Dance:* This is a powerful practice that can be effectively used as a method for astroshamanic voyages. Eyes are kept closed or covered with a blindfold. You can employ a shamanic drumming or rattling recording or specific music. When the music starts, gently align your body to the rhythm and gradually let it go freely. Allow your shamanic journey to resonate through the movements of your body. At the end of the dance (that could last from 20 to 45 minutes), be still for at least 5 minutes and take time to silently integrate your experience. Then, as usual, write down or draw your observations and insights in your Journal. (See Book One, Chapter 9, 'Astroshamanic Dance'.)

2. **Balancing Neptune**: When under the influence of Neptune things can appear rather uncertain. If you have based your life on conventional security and perception, these can reveal themselves as sheer illusions or dissolve into nothingness. In order not to get stranded or lost when the energy of Neptune is activated, it is essential to keep a connection with Sector 10. It can be helpful to commit to a form of structure or planning that provides a safe container for the transpersonal experiences of Neptune. It is also preferable to ponder carefully before taking any important decision. Here follow some methods useful to balance Neptune: take frequent showers or baths; have periodic physical privacy; eat grounding organic foods: particularly grains, legumes, fish

and, in extreme cases, meat; stay away from all types of drugs; avoid confused, addicted and spaced out people; spend time with practical, down-to-earth friends; write down your dreams; dance and sing; take regular breaks and walks in nature; work in the garden or tend to the plants in your flat; massage your body, and your feet in particular; offer your services as volunteer in a spiritual community or charity organisation. To stand and walk barefoot on the earth or to bring your attention to your feet and feel the weight of your body on them is one of the most effective methods to come back from moments of absent-mindedness or spaced-out states. Those who have Neptune prominent in their chart tend to be extremely light sensitive and often need to protect their eyes or to operate in an environment of semi-obscurity. For certain individuals the difficulties caused by grievances related to Sector 12 can be overwhelming and reach extremes. When it is impossible to find any way out, Neptune offers its remedy par excellence: *surrender*. The most powerful form of healing occurs when I admit my impotence as an isolated ego mind and learn to surrender myself to the will of God. This attitude is the key to the programme of Alcoholics Anonymous. Their slogan is 'Let go and let God', while the prayer that they repeat at every meeting is 'God grant me the serenity to accept the things I cannot change, the courage to change the things I can, and the wisdom to know the difference. Amen'. When I truly experience such words, going beyond fighting with the outer reality and meeting the true vibration of my visions, then the energy of Sector 12 opens up and begins to flow.

3. **Protection**: The high sensitivity of those who are strongly exposed to the influence of Sector 12 can benefit from the use of techniques of protection. These are useful to avoid contamination and attacks from external agents which apparently exist in the astral spheres. In this respect what is essential to remember is that the best protection against being affected by *psychic attacks* or *negative influences* is to guard against any temptation to *psychically attack* or *negatively influence* others. To speak or think badly about someone; imagine gloomy and fearful scenes; repeat negative phrases and thoughts; complain about, label, judge and curse people are all examples of *psychic attacks*. The basic assumption of astroshamanic techniques of protection is the acknowledgement that *each person or situation that I meet in my*

life is a mirror that reflects the content of my mind. In this way I accept each type of grievance as a product of mine and I become available for its release. When I feel exhausted and drained, restless, angry, overwhelmed by thoughts and emotions of all kinds, it is because my energy is going out and losing touch with its source, or I am receiving a lot of energy which I am not giving away. Tiredness and strain mainly come from the enervating effects of being involved in constant judgements. To draw back the energy which has been lost during the day, you can imagine a magnet in the shape of a cone dwelling in the solar plexus. Allow it to pull energy back from the situations and places of your daily routine. If a certain episode or person was particularly draining, imagine them in front of you and start pulling energy back. Retrieve your grievances and all types of projections, totally cleansing what is in front of you. Imagine that they too have a magnetic cone and are involved in the same operation: pulling back all muddled energy from your system. If you encounter difficulties in releasing grievances, do not hesitate to ask your Guide to operate directly on that situation or person. Instead of feeling guilty for what you sense, and therefore strengthening the grievance, surrender to your Guide and give him consent to operate. We are not those worthless non-entities that we often believe ourselves to be: *our consent is essential.* Without that Guides cannot move a single finger. When you give permission to the Guide and Spirits to work, miracles inevitably happen You can say something like: 'O beloved Guide! I perceive grievances now and find it difficult to move away from this situation. I take responsibility for that. I realise I cannot make it alone. I choose to ask for your help! I release this grievance to you so that you can transform it according to our true common will.' (For further details on protection, see Book One, Chapter 4, 'Protection'.)

4. **Sleeping as the Universe** is an Osho's technique which involves sitting silently for a while before going to bed. If possible, look at the night sky with all its stars. Meditate on the fact that you are boundless or that the universe itself marks your boundaries. Include everything and everyone in this perception. See the Sun rising and setting within you, the planets and all the galaxies moving through you, all the beings of the Earth and the universe are you. Feel immensely blissful in this expanded state of consciousness. Make it your

identification and reality. For 21 days, every night when you go to sleep, enter into this expanded consciousness. Fall asleep as though you were the universe, allowing stars to move within you. Upon waking up in the morning, again remember your expanded state. Get up as the universe. Do this even if you find it hard to believe it. Simply act and take this practice as a game. Also during the day, as many times as you can, remember. Whenever you have time or do not know what to do, enter into this universal consciousness. Drop your limited identifications. Feel this oceanic expansion as many times as possible and soon you will begin to attune to it very easily. Then you will start to pick up signals from the universe, retrieving your true inheritance and memory, uncovering most arcane secrets.

5. **Cinema as a Tool:** The realm of cinema belongs to Sector 12 and, although it is generally a source of proliferation of addictions and grievances, it can at times be transformed in a meditative and healing tool. As you watch a movie, try to remember that what you see is unreal. The screen is just a big blank white sheet. The images that move there are the result of a projection coming from a machine on the opposite side of the hall. Notice how you tend to forget about it, how you take the movie for the reality. Whenever this occurs, just shake yourself and remember again that what you see is not real. Be careful in your selection of movies or television programmes. The information that reaches you through those media is very invasive and can clog your system, preventing it from processing properly and polluting your true visions. During this month be alert about your exposure to cinema and television. Make it a point to watch only what comes out of a conscious choice and, if possible, abstain from television, movies and videos for some time.

6. **The Cosmic Soup:** Prepare a hot soup with vegetables, cereals, legumes, seeds and herbs. Use at least one ingredient from each sector and make sure that you also include a large variety of colours. Serve the soup very hot in a bowl. Contemplate its steam moving upwards. Smudge yourself with that steam, connect with your Intent and sing a chant of power. Watch the soup and its various ingredients. Find here all the experiences and people, past, present and future of your life. Observe attentively each component of the soup. Feel that what you now see outside of you will soon become

part of your body. Then begin to eat your soup, slowly, sipping and absorbing its taste. Take whatever you see and think and feel back to you. At the end of the meal, stay in silence for some minutes. Allow the energetic essence of the soup to spread throughout your system.

7. **Dreams (Looking at Your Hands):** The more you connect with your inner world through shamanic experiences, the more you are going to appreciate darkness, night and the time you spend sleeping and dreaming. During dreaming the soul goes on a journey. It travels through various layers and reaches dimensions of wisdom emanating from ancient or future times. This wisdom reveals itself through dreaming experiences where the basic myths of the universe directly express themselves. Among many tribal cultures these dreams were very frequent and were given much attention. Dreaming was not regarded as something personal or private. It was a tribal and sacred activity that could provide guidance for the whole community. Also the ancient Egyptians and Greeks highly valued dreams and would connect with their gods by sleeping in special temples and receiving guidance. Dreaming was also one of the major arts of sorcerers in ancient Mexico. Don Juan, in the works of Carlos Castaneda, defines this art as a way of dreaming in which you do not become totally unconscious and remain aware that you are dreaming. One of the most typical practices when working with dreams is that of *looking at your hands*. This technique consists in remembering, before sleeping, to execute the order to look at your hands during the dream.[3] By doing this, the dreamer becomes aware that this order comes from the *non-dreaming* dimension and therefore creates a connection with that. This is a great achievement as it builds a bridge between different realities. Here the hands are not important as such. They are simply a strategic expedient. Any other parts of the body or tool will do, as what matters is simply to remember the order to do something during the dream. For this purpose, in astroshamanism, Spirit Medicines and Sacred Tools (see Book One, Chapter 8) are also used. Once you learn this trick, it is a question of holding the image of one of these Spirit Medicines or Tools in the dream, that is, to focus on them and to avoid them disappearing. If they begin to fade away, you can pronounce their names or turn your eyes to other objects and then return again to the gift when the other objects tend to disappear. The purpose is that of managing to hold the

vision of more things and then of the whole scene. In this way I can be able to easily explore specific locations in the non-ordinary realities of the dream and operate healing. The message here is that of remembering my Intent and my whole self when I am dreaming or find myself in any possible altered state of consciousness, including the most prominent of all, i.e. ordinary reality.

8. **Nightmares and Unpleasant Dreams:** At times I have nightmares or dreams that stir up pain or weird feelings. An unpleasant dream is frequently the crucial part of a process of release and forgiveness. In these instances I usually run a brief ritual. After opening up the Sacred Circle, I allow the grievances that have emerged to be released. I also express my gratitude for the work which has been carried on during the night. When a dream is particularly mysterious or distressful, the Guide can work as major source of support. Guides are experts in interpreting the deeper significance of dreams. Simply ask your Guide for direct explanations about the dream. You can also enter into your Spirit Circle and set up a screen to replay the dream. Then you can watch the dream in a videotape format, repeating the intriguing scenes, playing them in slow motion and pausing when necessary.

9. **Working with Dreams:** This is a very effective practice as it allows you to employ for spiritual purposes an ample part of your time that you are going to use anyway. What follows is a process that can help you in retrieving and mastering the subtle dimensions of dreams. Each night, before going to bed, open your sacred space. Call the directions and, if possible, smudge your bed and yourself. Then make an invocation, enter your Spirit Circle and connect with your Guide. Give thanks for the experiences of the day and confirm the adherence to your Intent and Function. As you sit or lie on your bed, review the day back from the last events to the beginning. In the course of this process, if you become aware that there were moments in which you did not act in accordance with your Intent, replay that time as if you had a videotape. Delete what went wrong and substitute the undesirable sequence with a right course of action. For example, if you were rude to your partner, see yourself being gentle and giving attention to her. Then strongly affirm that the next time you are presented with a similar scene, you will conform to your highest Intent and Function. As you

continue to review the day you can also notice if you have collected unpleasant emotions and ideas. Release them and allow them to be transformed, and reaffirm your commitment to your sacred path. When you have completed the whole process, give yourself the command to see and use, at a certain stage of your dream, one of the Spirit Medicines, or corresponding Sacred Tools, that you have received during your astroshamanic journeys. You can also give yourself the task of simply looking at your hands. It does not matter whether this is going to happen that same night, just repeat this practice every time you go to sleep. Then count back from twelve to one, affirming that you will remember all that occurs during your dreams. Upon waking up, stretch yourself like a cat, give thanks for what happened throughout the night, and note it down in your journal. If you have difficulties in recalling the dreams, try and wake up gently, lying in a relaxed state for some moments. Then make an effort to remember the first feelings or thoughts that came to your mind upon waking. These will help bring back the content of your dream and also give indications about its deeper essence. If you still feel unclear about your dream, make sure to identify any image or detail that you recollect. Write it down or draw it, no matter how incoherent it may seem. These fragmented pieces usually act as catalysts and spontaneously draw significant information at a later stage during the day. By employing this process you have the chance to clear and release from your system any grievance that may have caused harm to you and others. Be constant and patient in your practice. Take note of what happens to you every day and operate with simplicity.

10. **The Paheka Sadohe Korah** (Chant of the Totem Spirits and Guides): For Sector 12 the chant is *Taepeh Sadoh*. Please use this practice only if you intend to establish or support a regular relationship with the Totem Spirit of Sector 12. If you intend to use this chant, you can either sing it from time to time to accompany a cycle of twelve shamanic journeys in Sector 12 or as a practice on its own to be done preferably once or twice a day for at least seven minutes during a period of twenty-one days.[4]

11. **The Chant and Scale of Neptune:** This chant operates on the sixth and seventh chakra, and is particularly useful to release grievances associated with Sector 12. The chant is a

source of inspiration and helps to bring clarity in moments of uncertainty and confusion. It contributes to the development of serenity, expectancy or acceptance of what cannot be changed, and can provide spiritual guidance on how to be of best service in this world and universe. It is also the only chant that can properly be done for other people, as it stimulates the energy of their Guides rather than interfering with their path. In the sphere of relationship, the scale focuses on unconditional love and unity, releasing the subtle grievances of romantic and special relationships. The words of the chant are as follows:

Oh Myss, Oh Myss, Oh Myss, Oh Myss, Oh

Please be aware that the final *s* of *Myss* is very long and hissing. After calling your Guide, according to your habitual procedures, connect with your Intent and Function. Then sing the chant of the Sun (*Oh Hay Yah*, four times, followed by *Oh*) and that of Earth/Moon (*Si Idriah*, four times, followed by *Neh Ah Mah Set*). The use of these chants, repeated also at the end of the scale, is recommended for centering (Sun) and grounding or creating proper boundaries (Earth). They also avoid the destabilising effects of Neptune's transpersonal perception. Visualise the planet Neptune in orbit very far out in the solar system, inscrutable and surrounded by a foggy aura of gases. Then sing the chant of Neptune (*Oh Myss*, four times, followed by *Oh* at the end). Continue the scale, moving gradually from lower to higher expressions of Neptune.[5]

Astroshamanic Reports

The following is an excerpt from a letter sent to a friend during the time of Pisces and describing some of my early experiences in Findhorn.

In the illusory sphere of time, days, hours and minutes alternate in a steady and tender migration toward the original land, Handor, *the Peak of Light. The path is glowing and well marked for those who can see beyond their body's eyes. No more weary wandering along barren territories in search of forlorn goals. The road radiates here and now, so candid and genuine. I have constantly encountered it in my millennial roaming, yet I always managed to keep away from it, deflected by the spurs of intoxicating enterprises and morbid temptations, or baffled by the complicated technology of my space suit. The time has come to return home, to that dwelling place which has always been there for me.*

It is the hour of the calm and glorious reawakening. All proceeds with implacable candour. From the obscure insanity of a lethargic nightmare, the eyes blink and gently delve into the immensity of an ecstatic world. The power of that realm is so permanent that the eyelids lower in the twilight of the ultimate frontier: the half-asleep time of Spirit, where decrepit dreams vanish and the recall of reality gently takes over. Still the eyes open up to such light, and gently drop and close again. This is the state in which I often find myself in these final days of Winter and that, in my perception, depicts all I view in my outer environment.

Here the landscape is sublime. Stars and planets expose their lights through these long nights. It is incredible with how much care the fiction of the outer world has been programmed: a detailed imitation of the bliss which constantly reigns in the inner world. It is as well extraordinary to notice how this imitation so easily crumbles in all its parts, just like ice thawing in the presence of heat. Beyond the statuary fiction of daily insanity, there exists a world of unspeakable beauty that, although it is still an ingredient of such a fiction, it represents its ultimate frontier. The point where fiction gradually begins to smell as real, the thin and timid reflection of what exists elsewhere. In that site I have always lived and continue to live. For what I have seen of life around and within me, I have never seen anything that does not truly belong to that place.

A few days ago, as I was involved in my homecare work, I had a glance out of one of the eastern windows of Cluny Hill College. There I was dazzled by the sight of my image. There I was, walking along the nearby road on the day I first arrived in the area. It was the eve of the Spring Equinox, one day before the start of my Experience Week. I wanted to see the place where I would spend my time the day after. How shaky and chagrined was my heart at that time! As I was contemplating the impressive facades of the building, I noticed the shape of a person standing by a window in the eastern side. I could not see him properly. His features were unfocused. Yet I could sense the love and light that emanated from his being. Now I have discovered that it was me who was standing by that window. From the height of that window, I warmly greeted myself, directing a glowing ray to what was once myself. For some instants I managed to trespass the dimension of time. I dared to observe the puppet of myself. Also now I can repeat the same enterprise for, although I am still a naive amateur on this path of undoing, I have grasped some basic clues about the fiction of time. And now, as I swing my fingers on the computer keyboard, I can sense the presence of another part of myself. He watches over me with tender compassion and relentless support. I greet him and rejoice at the imminence of another encounter. And after each shift of observation the goal approaches closer and closer.

A similar experience also happened to me in 1989 during one of my nights in the hotel where I used to work. As I was passing by the mirror of the bathroom, I saw the reflection of an unusual figure. It was radiant with beauty and potency. It looked a bit like my physical body, yet it moved differently and stared at me with a wide and jubilant smile which I didn't have on my face at that moment. This being has always been close to me. His ardent glee burns away all grievances. I do not have to do anything to deserve his love and support. There is neither a price to pay, nor a condition to fulfil. I need only to remember. Merely remember that this love has always existed and always will be there for me. Well, as you can guess, this is the Guide. There is neither growth nor a process of becoming. The world of the Guide, that is the world of God, exists in an eternal present that was there and will be there and is here and now, yes right now!

My only function is that of keeping the connection with the Guide and holding and implementing the vision of the Sacred Cone. *This is the only choice that counts. As a matter of fact my daily activities consist of cruising through myriads of unfathomable decisions and illusory possibilities that attempt to distract me from such a choice. And at the end of the day, once I reach my Spirit Circle, at times exhausted and downcast, I let out a deep breath of relief and tell my Guide: 'I have managed again today!' And when I do not manage? Well, this is indeed the crucial part of the Game. When I forget and allow myself to be confused by the ego's insanity, then I have the chance of being reminded and of forgiving myself for* not having managed. *And as I do that, a chorus of sublime voices sing in unison: 'Again today you have managed!'*

Here are some of my early explorations of Sector 12.

After a long chant and drumming in honour of Neptune, I find myself on a wide beach streaming along a mint-green sea. Suddenly I am pervaded by a shivering warm euphoria. Looking at the horizon, I can't make out the difference between the sea and the sky. They melt so beautifully. I am drawn to enter into the water. It is warm. Fish and jellyfish creatures are all around. My Intent is that of contacting the Spirit of Sector 12. I notice an underwater road leading to a central point. As I move toward that area, I meet a clump of seaweed. The seaweed begins to caress my body and helps it release thick layers of fear which are making it difficult for me to swim. I relinquish my fears and offer them to the seaweed. In exchange it gives me a soothing and penetrating massage. It heals the wounds created by the expulsion of fear. Then a sea horse appears. It starts to laugh, saying that all is a joke. With my Spirit Guide I move on and approach a white coral castle.

I enter its sumptuous garden-pool. It is populated by alluring Sirens. They have big breasts through which I begin to flow. As I do this, they literally disintegrate a loop of ancient grievances which I have dragged around on my back. This is very pleasant and sensual. I experience feelings of sheer ecstasy which become more adamant when I sense the reassurance that they will last forever. I ask the Sirens who they are. They reply: 'We are the Keepers of Bliss and Ecstasy. In any situation you may find yourself in, this place is always open for you to receive bliss. Here this beauty and love is perpetually available. Your body is one with everything and you float in the universe, allowing your cells to dance and enjoy the ultimate communion. That is our medicine: you realise we are part of the same body and dwell here forever. Then I enter the coral castle. The hall is full of aquatic beings. As I meet them, we hug. It is a peculiar hug in which my cells mix with theirs and create infinite combinations of shapes. With such a way of hugging, all concepts of mine and theirs disintegrate as sheer nonsense. In the centre of the hall I notice the prominence of a huge jelly shape. It is the Totem Spirit of Sector 12. It has many forms. One is strong and holds a trident. It moves with aggressive and disciplined gestures, stirring lofty waves and typhoons. Another form has the quality of the Sirens. I address the Spirit as follows: 'I'm happy to be here and pleased with the gifts I have received from your people. Please let me know how I can use your power in a productive way for myself and the environment I live in. What is your medicine?' Mixed with the sounds of waves and winds, the Spirit replies: 'We're happy that you have come at last. The way of developing our power is that of visiting us as often as you can. It is about creating a relationship with us, that relationship you have forgotten about. There is a taboo in your programme about coming here and it prevents you from experiencing an ecstasy which is always available to you. The first requisite is that you feel worthy to meet us. As far as I am concerned, we are totally available to be in your company at all times. This means that what truly matters is whether you are available to meet us. The first step is about coming here and seeing us. Once you are here, you get to know how things are and realise, out of your own direct experience, that we are all part of the same ocean of love. What you see here as me is just the point of emanation. Sirens are my body-parts, as well as seaweed and fish and you. Everything is part of me here. The way to use my power is by getting to know it. In the environment you come from, this power is manipulated and entangled, hence when you are here you get the real picture. Here, take this gift and receive it as my medicine.'

On this journey I ask the Spirit of Sector 12 how to deal with the feelings of separation that I sometimes sense with certain people. 'In those instances,' the Spirit answers, 'you place the separated form in front of you, either physically or in your visualisation, and then go within it, mixing cells until you realise there is nothing but you there. This is about loving yourself. If you can promise that this love is available, that you are willing to take care of it, problems are going to dissolve. Here you get in touch with sheer reality and find no strategies. Your dreams become a reality and you gather everything and acknowledge it as part of you. Such an encounter is like the one you had with the aquatic beings in the hall of the coral castle. If problems continue, it means that you have lost sight of the focus point. Therefore, although cells apparently mix, they are so frightened that they go nuts. If this is the case, you need to face my disciplined and aggressive side. Find this focus point and from there expand further, returning to it at regular intervals. By holding the gift I have given you, you can reach that focus point.'

[1]   *Psychotherapy: Purpose, Process and Practice: An Extension of the Principles of A Course in Miracles,* Foundation for Inner Peace, p. 7.

[2]   For further information: Ernesto De Martino, *La terra del rimorso,* Il Saggiatore, Milano, 1961. Henry E. Sigerist, *The Story of Tarantism* in Dorothy M. Schullian and Max Schoen, *Music and Medicine,* New York, 1948. Marius Schneider, *La danza de espadas y la tarantela. Ensayo musicológico etnográfico y arquelógico sobre los ritos medicinales,* Barcelona, 1948; (reprint in Italian) Argo, Lecce, 1999.

[3]   Carlos Castaneda, *Journey to Ixtlan,* Pocket Books, p. 98.

[4]   See Sector One, note 4.

[5]   See Sector One, note 5.

BIBLIOGRAPHY

Achterberg, Jeanne, *Imagery in Healing: Shamanism and Modern Medicine*, New Science Library, Boston, MA, 1985.

Allen, Marcus, *Astrology for the New Age: An Intuitive Approach*, CRCS Publications, Sebastopol, CA, 1979.

Andrews, Ted, *Magickal Dance: Your Body as an Instrument of Power*, Llewellyn, St. Paul, MN, 1993. *Animal-Speak*, Llewellyn, St. Paul, MN, 1995.

Arrien, Angeles, *The Four-Fold Way: Walking the Paths of the Warrior, Teacher, Healer and Visionary*, Harper, San Francisco, CA, 1993.

Arroyo, Stephen, *Astrology, Karma and Transformation: The Inner Dimensions of the Birth Chart*, CRCS, Sebastopol, CA, 1992; *Astrology, Psychology and the Four Elements: An Energy Approach to Astrology and Its Use in the Counselling Arts*, CRCS, Sebastopol, CA, 1975.

Ashcroft-Novicki, Dolores, *The Ritual Magic Workbook: A Practical Course of Self-Initiation*, The Aquarian Press, Wellingborough, 1986.

Baldwin, Christina. *Calling the Circle: The First and Future Culture*, Bantam Books, New York, NY, 1998.

Boncompagni, Solas, *Il mondo dei simboli: numeri, lettere e figure geometriche*, Edizioni Mediterranee, Roma, 1984.

Bragdon, Emma, *A Sourcebook for Helping People in Spiritual Emergency*, Lightening Up Press, Los Altos, CA, 1988.

Bryant, Page, *Starwalking: Shamanic Practices for Traveling into the Night Sky*, Bear & Company, Santa Fe, NM, 1997.

Caddy, Eileen, *God Spoke to Me*, Findhorn Press, Findhorn, 1971; *Flight Into Freedom and Beyond*, Findhorn Press, Findhorn, 2002; *The Spirit of Findhorn*, Findhorn Press, Findhorn, 1977.

Cahill, Sedona and Joshua Halpern, *The Ceremonial Circle: Practice, Ritual, and Renewal for Personal and Community Healing*, Harper, San Francisco, CA, 1992.

Castaneda, Carlos, *Magical Passes: The Practical Wisdom of the Shamans of Ancient Mexico*, HarperCollins, London, 1998; *A Separate Reality*, Simon and Schuster, New York, NY, 1971; *Tales of Power*, Simon and Schuster, New York, NY, 1974; *The Teachings of Don Juan: A Yaqui Way of Knowledge*, University of California Press, Berkeley, CA, 1968.

Cavendish, Richard, *The Black Arts*, Routledge & Kegan Paul, London, 1967.

Cerchio, Bruno, *Simbologia astrologica*, Edizioni Mediterranee, Roma, 1981.

Clifton, Chas S., *Witchcraft Today: Book Three, Witchcraft and Shamanism*, Llewellyn, St. Paul, MN, 1994.

Clow, Barbara Hand, *Liquid Light of Sex: Understanding Your Key Life Passages*, Bear & Company, Santa Fe, NM, 1991.

Cook, Angelique S. and G. A. Hawk, *Shamanism and the Esoteric Tradition*, Llewellyn, St. Paul, MN, 1992.

Cornelius, Geoffrey, *The Starlore Handbook*, Duncan Baird Publishers, London, 1997.

Cunningham, Donna, *An Astrological Guide to Self-Awareness*, CRCS Publications, Sebastopol, CA, 1978; *Astrology and Spiritual Development*, Cassandra Press, San Rafael, CA, 1989; *Astrology and Vibrational Healing*, Cassandra Press, San Rafeal, CA, 1988; *Being a Lunar Type in a Solar World*, Samuel Weiser, York Beach, ME, 1982; *Healing Pluto Problems*, Samuel Weiser, York Beach, ME, 1986; *Moon Signs: The Key to Your Life*, Ballantine, New York, NY, 1988.

Davis, Martin, *Astrolocality Astrology*, The Wessex Astrologer, Bournemouth, 1999.

Davis-Wolfe, Mattie and David Thomson, *Walking the Sacred Wheel: A Year's Journey of Initiation around the Sacred Wheel*, Sacred Circles Institute, Mukilteo, WA, 1995.

De Solange, Mailly Nesle, *Astrology: History, Symbols and Signs*, Inner Traditions International, New York, NY, 1985.

Dobyns, Zipporah Pottenger, *Expanding Astrology's Universe*, ACS Publications, San Diego, CA, 1983; *Finding the Person in the Horoscope*, TIA Publications, Los Angeles, CA, 1973.

Drake, Michael, *The Shamanic Drum: A Guide to Sacred Drumming*, Talking Drum Publications, Goldendale, WA, 1991.

Drury, Nevill, *The Elements of Shamanism*, Longmead, Shaftesbury, 1982; *The Shaman and the Magician*, Routledge & Kegan Paul, London, 1978.

Eliade, Mircea, *Shamanism: Archaic Techniques of Ecstasy*, Princeton University Press, Princeton, NJ, 1972; *Yoga: Immortality and Freedom*, Princeton University Press, Princeton, NJ, 1970.

Farioli, Marcella, *Le religioni misteriche*, Xenia, Milano, 1998.

Foundation for Inner Peace, *A Course in Miracles*, Foundation for Inner Peace, Glen Ellen, CA, 1992; *Psychotherapy; Purpose, Process, and Practice: An Extension of the Principles of A Course in Miracles*, Foundation for Inner Peace, Mill Valley, CA, 1976.

Frances, Lynn and Richard Bryant-Jefferies, *The Sevenfold Circle: Selfawareness in Dance*, Findhorn Press, Findhorn, 1998.

Giamario, Daniel and Carolyn Brent, *The Shamanic Astrology Handbook*, JCAU Publications, Tucson, AZ, 2002.

Gilchrist, Cherry, *Planetary Symbolism in Astrology*, Saros Fundation, 1980.

Ginzburg, Carlo, *The Night Battles: Witchcraft and Agrarian Cults in the Sixteenth and Seventeenth Centuries*, John Hopkins University Press, Baltimore, 1983.

Goodman, Felicitas D., *Speaking in Tongues: A Cross-Cultural Study of Glossolalia*, University of Chicago Press, Chicago, IL, 1972; *Where the Spirits Ride the Wind: Trance Journeys and Other Ecstatic Experiences*, Indiana University Press, Bloomington, IN, 1990.

Gore, Belinda, *Ecstatic Body Postures: An Alternate Reality Workbook*, Bear & Company, Santa Fe, NM, 1995.

Grof, Christina and Stanislav Grof, *The Stormy Search for the Self: A Guide to Personal Growth through Transformational Crisis*, Jeremy Tracher, New York, NY, 1990.

Guttman, Ariel and Kenneth Johnson, *Mythic Astrology: Archetypal Powers in the Horoscope*, Llewellyn, St. Paul, MN, 1996.

Halifax, Joan, *Shamanic Voices: A Survey of Visionary Narratives*, E.P. Dutton, New York, NY, 1979.

Hand, Robert, *Planets in Transits,* Para Research, Rockport, MA, 1976.

Haram, *Manuale laico di astrologia*, Savelli, Milano, 1979.

Harding, M. Esther, *Women's Mysteries: Ancient and Modern*, Rider & Co., London, 1935.

Harner, Michael, *The Way of the Shaman*, Harper, San Francisco, CA,1990.

Hess, Helene, *The Zodiac Explorer's Handbook: A Unique Guide to Using Your Birth Chart for Inner Exploration*, The Aquarian Press, Wellingborough, 1986.

Hoffman, Kay, *The Trance Workbook: Understanding and Using the Power of Altered States*, Sterling Publishing, New York, NY, 1998.

Hoeller, Stephan A., *Gnosticism: New Light on the Ancient Tradition of Inner Knowing*, Theosophical Publishing House, Wheaton, IL, 2002.

Horn, Arthur David, (with Lynette Anne Mallory-Horn), *Humanity's Extraterrestrial Origins: ET Influences on Humankind's Biological and Culural Evolution*, Silberschnur, Lake Montezuma, AZ, 1994.

Ingerman, Sandra, *Soul Retrieval: Mending the Fragmented Self,* Harper, San Francisco, CA, 1991.

Jenkins, Palden, *Living in Time: Learning to Experience Astrology in Your Life,* Gateway Books, Bath, 1987.

Jones, Prudence (ed.), *Creative Astrology: Experiential Understanding of the Horoscope,* The Aquarian Press, London, 1991.

Jordan, Michael, *Encyclopedia of Gods: Over 2500 Deities of the World*, Kyle Cathie Ltd, London, 1992.

Judith, Anodea, *Wheels of Life: A User's Guide to the Chakra System,* Llewellyn, St. Paul, MN, 1987.

Jung, Carl Gustav, *Collected Works of C.G. Jung: Vol. 13, Alchemical Studies,* Princeton University Press, Princeton, NJ, 1967; *Memories, Dreams, Reflections,* Fontana Press, London, 1995.

Kaku, Michio, *Hyperspace: A Scientific Odyessy Through the 10th Dimension,* Oxford University Press, Oxford, 1994.

Lam Kam Chuen, Master, *Chi Kung: The Way of Healing*, Broadway Books, New York, 1999; *Stand Still, Be Fit: The Way of Energy*, Gaia Books, London, 1995.

Lamparelli, Claudio, *Tecniche della meditazione orientale*, Mondadori, Milano, 1985.

Lapassade, Georges, *Dallo sciamano al raver: saggio sulla transe*, Urra, Milano, 1997.

Lemesurier, Peter, *The Healing of the Gods: The Magic of Symbols and the Practice of Theotherapy*, Element Books, Longmead, 1988.

Marciniak, Barbara, *Bringers of the Dawn: Teachings from the Pleiadans*, Bear & Company, Santa Fe, 1992; *Family of Light*, Bear & Company, Santa Fe, NM, 1998.

Matthews, John, *The Celtic Shaman: A Handbook*, Element, Rockport, MA, 1992.

Matthews, Caitlin and John Matthews, *The Western Way: A Practical Guide to the Western Mystery Tradition*, Arkana, London, 1985.

Mayo, Jeff, *The Planets and Human Behavior*, CRCS Publications, Sebastopol, CA, 1985.

McKenna, Terence, *Food of the Gods: The Search for the Original Tree of Knowledge*, Rider, London, 1992.

McEvers, Joan (ed.), *Spiritual, Metaphysical and New Trends in Modern Astrology*, Llewellyn, St. Paul, MN, 1988.

Meadows, Kenneth, *Earth Medicine: A Shamanic Way to Self Discovery*, Element, Shaftesbury, Dorset, 1991.

Merriman, Raymond, *Evolutionary Astrology: The Journey of the Soul Through States of Consciousness*, Seek-It Publications, Bloomfield, MI, 1991.

Mindell, Arnold, *The Shaman's Body: A New Shamanism for Transforming Health, Relationships, and the Community*, Harper, San Francisco, CA, 1993.

Mundy, John, *Listening to Your Inner Guide*, Crossroad, New York, NY, 1995.

Myers, Robert 'Buz', *The Moon as a Trigger for Transformation*, RKM (audiocassette).

Nevin, Bruce, *Astrology Inside Out: A New Approach to Astrology*, Para Research, Rockport, MA, 1982.

Nicholson, Shirley (ed.), *Shamanism: an Expanded View of Reality*, Theosophical Publishing House, Wheaton, IL, 1987.

Osho, *Hidden Mysteries*, Rebel Publishing House, Cologne, 1997; *Meditation: The First and Last Freedom*, St. Martin's Press, New York, NY, 1996; *Tantra, Spirituality and Sex*, Rebel Publishing House, Cologne, 1994; *Vigyan Bhairav Tantra, The Book of Secrets: A New Commentary*, Rebel Publishing House, Cologne, 1991.

Picard, Eudes, *Astrologie Judiciare*, Leymarié, Paris, 1936.

Pierpaoli, Paola, *Iniziazione al contatto con lo spirito guida*, Edizioni Mediterranee, Roma, 2003.

Pottenger, Maritha, *Astro Essentials: Planets in Signs, Houses & Aspects*, ACS Publications, San Diego, CA, 1991; *Encounter Astrology*, TIA Publications, Los Angeles, CA, 1978; *Healing with the Horoscope: A Guide to Counselling*, ACS Publications, San Diego, CA, 1982.

Pratesi, Aniela, *Iniziazione all'astrologia evolutiva: il cammino dell'anima attraverso la carta natale*, Edizioni Mediterranee, Roma, 2002.

Reinhart, Melanie, *Chiron and the Healing Journey: An Astrological and Psychological Perspective*, Penguin, London, 1989.

Ridall, Kathryin, *Channeling: How To Reach Out To Your Spirit Guide*, Bantam, New York, NY, 1990.

River, Lindsay and Sally Gillespie, *The Knot of Time: Astrology and Female Experience*, The Women's Press, London, 1987.

Rose, Christina, *Astrological Counselling: A Basic Guide to Astrological Themes in Person to Person Relationships*, The Aquarian Press, Wellingborough, 1982.

Roth, Gabrielle, *Maps to Ecstasy: Teachings of an Urban Shaman*, Mandala, London, 1990.

Rudhyar, Dane, *Astrology and the Modern Psyche: An Astrologer looks at Depth-Psychology*, CRCS, Sebastopol, CA, 1976.

Rutherford, Leo, *The Book of Games and Warm Ups for Group Leaders*, Gale Centre, Loughton, 1994; *Principles of Shamanism*, Thorsons, London, 1996.

Sanchez, Victor, *The Teachings of Don Carlos: Practical Applications of the Works of Carlos Castaneda*, Bear and Co., Santa Fe, NM, 1995.

Sargent, Denny, *Global Ritualism: Myth & Magic Around The World*, Llewellyn, St. Paul, MN, 1994.

Santoro, Franco, *Iniziazione all'astrosciamanesimo: la via zodiacale alla Guida Interiore*, Edizioni Mediterranee, Roma, 2000; *Introduzione agli aforismi provvisori della rete binaria del Sacro Cono*, Sacred Cone Press, Forres, 2000; *Provisoria*, Forlorn Press, Bologna, 1984, (ed.); *A Provisional Guide Book to the First Level of the Operative Training in Astroshamanism*, Sacred Cone Press, Forres, 2001; *ProvOrdo Etnai Sagdhanatabe*, Anaghaseva, Bologna, 1988.

Schermer, Barbara, *Astrology Alive!; Experiential Astrology, Astrodrama and the Healing Arts*, The Aquarian Press, Wellingborough, 1989.

Schneider, Marius, *La danza delle spade e la tarantella*, Argo, Lecce, 1999.

Sicuteri, Roberto, *Astrologia e mito: simboli e miti dello Zodiaco nella Psicologia del Profondo*, Astrolabio, Roma, 1978.

Somé, Malidoma Patrice, *Of Water and the Spirit: Ritual, Magic, and Initiation in the Life of an African Shaman*, Penguin, New York, NY, 1994.

Starhawk, *The Spiral Dance: A Rebirth of the Ancient Religion of the Great Goddess*, Harper, San Francisco, CA, 1989.

Steinbrecher, Edwin C., *The Inner Guide Meditation: A Spiritual Technology for the 21st Century*, Samuel Weiser, York Beach, ME, 1988.

Sun Bear, Wabun Wind and Crysalis Mulligan, *Dancing With The Wheel: The Medicine Wheel Workbook*, Simon & Schuster, London, 1991.

Szanto, Gregory, *Astrotherapy: Astrology and the Realization of the Self*, Arkana, London, 1987.

Vitebsky, Piers, *The Shaman: Voyages of the Soul, Trance, Ecstasy and Healing from Siberia to the Amazon*, DBP, London, 1995,

Volguine, Alexandre, *L'esoterismo dell'astrologia*, Xenia, Milano, 1996.

Wapnick, Gloria and Kenneth Wapnich, *The Most Commonly Asked Questions About A Course in Miracles*, Foundation for A Course in Miracles, Roscoe, New York, NY, 1995.

Wapnick, Kenneth, *Forgiveness and Jesus: The Meeting Place of A Course in Miracles and Christianity*, Foundation for A Course in Miracles, Roscoe, New York, NY, 1983. *Glossary-Index for A Course in Miracles*, Foundation for A Course in Miracles, Roscoe, New York, NY, 1982.

Williamson, Marianne, *A Return to Love: Reflections on the Principles of A Course in Miracles*, HarperCollins, New York, NY, 1996.

Zimmerman, Jack; in collaboration with Virginia Coyle, *The Way of Council*, Bramble Books, Las Vegas, NV, 1996.

Please see *Astroshamanism, Book One* for a complete bibliography.

Index

I denotes book 1; II denotes book 2

ABOUT THE AUTHOR

Franco Santoro is an established shamanic facilitator, healer, author, experiential astrologer and the developer of astroshamanism. In 1964 he started regular connections with non-ordinary dimensions that led him to live a parallel life which was often the cause of conflict in his relationship with conventional reality. In 1976, during a vision quest in Scotland, he had a transformational experience which, after years of practice with shamans and medicine people, allowed him to find clarity about his connections and acknowledge his function as bridge between dimensions. His path of apprenticeship encompassed both the archaic traditions of his Italian natal descent and those of other adopted lineages. From 1996 he has run the *Operative Training in Astroshamanism,* an intensive programme for shamanic practitioners and healers. He is the author of *A Guide Book to Astroshamanism,* Sacred Cone Press, 2001; *Astroshamanism Book One: A Journey Into the Inner Universe,* Findhorn Press, 2003; *Astroshamanism Book Two: The Voyage Through the Zodiac,* Findhorn Press, 2003, *Iniziazione all'astrosciamanesimo: la via zodiacale alla Guida Interiore,* Edizioni Mediterranee, 2000 (in Italian) and other works on related topics. He has also composed and produced a series of recordings, such as *Drumming for the Astroshamanic Voyage,* specially recorded as a companion to the journeys described in his books. Franco lives in Northern Scotland, where he serves as resident member and educator of the Findhorn Foundation, regularly running workshops on astroshamanism, shamanic healing, trance dance and core educational programmes. He also lectures and conducts seminars and consultations worldwide, employing his unique and innovative approach to support individuals or groups in connecting with their authentic nature.

The author appreciates receiving your comments and learning about your experiences with the book.

If you wish to contact the author or would like to receive information about his programmes and work, the address is:

Franco Santoro,
Cluny Hill College,
Forres IV36 2RD,
Scotland, United Kingdom.

Tel. +44 (0)1309 672288.

E-mail: info@astroshamanism.org

Website: www.astroshamanism.org

Resources and Training

Information about resources developed by the author and the Sacred Cone Circle in the areas of astroshamanism, spiritual healing, shamanic trance dance and the exploration of consciousness, can be obtained through the above address or website. The author has available drumming tapes or compact discs especially created to go with *Astroshamanism Book One* and *Book Two,* as well as special recordings to accompany workshops and astroshamanic healing sessions. If you intend to receive first-hand training and tuition in astroshamanism, a schedule of short and long term programmes given by Franco Santoro and his associates is also available from the above address.

FINDHORN *Press*

Findhorn Press is the publishing business of the Findhorn Community which has grown around the Findhorn Foundation in northern Scotland.

For further information about the Findhorn Foundation and the Findhorn Community, please contact:

Findhorn Foundation
The Visitors Centre
The Park, Findhorn IV36 3TY, Scotland, UK
tel 01309 690311• fax 01309 691301
email vcentre@findhorn.org
www.findhorn.org

For a complete Findhorn Press catalogue, please contact:

Findhorn Press

305a The Park, Findhorn

Forres IV36 3TE
Scotland, UK
Tel 01309 690582
freephone 0800-389-9395
Fax 01309 690036

If you live in the USA or Canada, please send your request to:

Findhorn Press

c/o Lantern Books
One Union Square West, Suite 201
New York, NY 10003-3303

Wherever you live, you can consult our catalogue online at

findhornpress.com

and email us at

info@findhornpress.com